FROM
Glencoe
TO
Stirling

3

⊷Tales of a Scottish Grandfather⊷

FROM
Glencoe
TO
Stirling

Rob Roy, the Highlanders &
Scotland's Chivalric Age

Sir Walter Scott

Introduction by
GEORGE GRANT

CUMBERLAND HOUSE
NASHVILLE, TENNESSEE

Introduction copyright © 2001 by George Grant

Published by
    CUMBERLAND HOUSE PUBLISHING, INC.
    431 Harding Industrial Drive
    Nashville, Tennessee 37211
    www.cumberlandhouse.com

Cover design by Unlikely Suburban Design, Nashville, Tennessee

Library of Congress Cataloging-in-Publication Data

Scott, Walter, Sir, 1771–1832.
   [Tales of a grandfather]
  Tales of a Scottish grandfather / Sir Walter Scott ; introduction by George Grant.
     p. cm.
  Includes index.
   Originally published: London : Routledge, 1828.
   Contents: v. 3. From Glencoe to Stirling : Rob Roy, the Highlanders & Scotland's chivalric age.
   ISBN 1-58182-129-8 (v. 3 : pbk. : alk. paper)
   1. Scotland—History. I. Title.
DA761.S55 2001
941.1—dc21   00-065775

Printed in the United States of America

1 2 3 4 5 6 7 8—05 04 03 02 01

CONTENTS

INTRODUCTION

S IR Walter Scott's life was a monument to the vitality of heritage. His writing captured the essence of the heroism, romanticism, and dynamism of the past. His character was a testimony to the vibrant virtues of days gone by. His habits recalled the rites and rituals of a hoary yore. Even his home was a saga in stone, a ballad of yesteryear in pitch and gable and crenellation, and a reliquary of legend, fable, and custom. Everything about Scott (1771–1832) bespoke tradition.

He was born into a respectable, middle-class Edinburgh family, but much of his childhood was spent at his grandfather's farm in the beautiful Border country. It was there that he first became acquainted with the rituals, songs, ballads, folklore, and legends of Scotland that captivated him for the rest of his life. He demonstrated early genius and followed in his father's footsteps, becoming a barrister after completing his university training at the extraordinary age of seventeen. But the practice of law was not able to satisfy his precocious mind, and so he began composing verse and collecting the great ballads of his beloved Border lands. He wrote a great narrative poem, *The Lay of the Last Minstrel,* which proved to be a tremendous commercial and critical success—and that convinced him that literature should be the main business of his life.

Happily married and with a growing family to support, he determined to pursue the literary life away from the constant and pressing demands of the city. He bought a large farm along the Tweed valley in the Border countryside. He called it Abbotsford, and for the rest of his life he made the estate a living demonstration of his highest ideals. Over the years he transformed the humble farmhouse into a magnificent castle estate chock-a-block with remnants, relics, and reminders of the rich history of the region. It was there in his museum-like environs that he created a series of historical novels that made Scott the most popular author in the world. Beginning with *Waverly* in 1814 and continuing through an astonishing thirty-two volumes over the next eighteen years—and including such classics as *Ivanhoe, Rob Roy, Tales of a Scottish Grandfather, Old Mortality, The Antiquarian,* and *Red Gauntlet*—Scott reinvented an entire genre of literature.

He added immeasurably to the Scottish sense of identity. Indeed, he almost single-handedly revived interest in kilts, tartans, Gaelic, bagpipes, Highland dancing, haggis, Celtic music, and all the other distinctive elements of Scottish culture. Tales of the Covenanters, Wallace and Bruce, the Jacobites, Bonnie Price Charlie, and Rob Roy were all brought into the light of day by his intrepid commitment to honoring the past.

All of his books were stamped with his overarching conviction about the importance of tradition. On the cusp of the magnificent flowering of industrial advance, it seemed to Scott that men were sadly afflicted with a kind of malignant contemporaniety. He was alarmed that their morbid preoccupation with self—and thus their ambivalence about and ignorance of the past—had trapped them in a recalcitrant present. As a result, all of Scott's work essentially argued stridently that stable societies must be eternally vigilant in the task of handing on their great legacy—to remember and then to inculcate that remembrance in the hearts and minds of their children.

That is precisely the task the great man undertook with the writing of his beloved *Tales of a Scottish Grandfather* beginning in 1828. The four volumes, written primarily for his grandson, reveled in the great Scottish legacy of freedom. It is not surprising that they quickly became among Scott's most highly regarded books. This third volume in particular, with its emphasis on the great chivalric age between the Reformation and the Jacobite rising, demonstrates the power of heritage to shape the present and steer the future. It is a treasure—no less than all the artifacts Scott assembled at Abbotsford.

George Grant

FROM
Glencoe
TO
Stirling

XLVIII

The End of the Commonwealth

1658-1660

OLIVER CROMWELL, who, in the extraordinary manner I have told you, raised himself to the supreme sovereignty of England, Scotland, and Ireland, was a man of great talents, and, as has been already said, not naturally of a severe or revengeful disposition. He made the kingdoms which he ruled formidable to foreign powers; and perhaps no government was ever more respected abroad than that of the Lord Protector.

At home Cromwell had a very difficult task to perform, in order to maintain his usurped authority. He was obliged on several occasions, as has been successfully done in other countries by usurpers of his class, to convoke some kind of senate or parliament, consisting of his own creatures, who might appear to divide with him the power, and save him, in appearance at least, the odium of governing by his sole authority. But such was the spirit of the English nation, that whenever Cromwell convoked a Parliament, though in a great measure consisting of his own partisans, and though the rest were studiously chosen as mean and ignorant persons, the instant that they met they began to inquire into the ground of the Protector's authority, and proposed measures which interfered with his assumption of supreme power.

In addition to this, the various factions into which the country was divided, all agreed in hating the usurped power of the Protector, and were frequently engaged in conspiracies against him, which were conceived and carried on not only by Cavaliers and Presbyterians, but by Republicans, and even by his own soldiers.

Thus hard pressed on every side, the Protector displayed the utmost sagacity in his mode of defending himself. On two or three occasions, indeed, he held what he called High Courts of Justice, by whose doom both Cavaliers and Presbyterians suffered capital punishment for plots against his government. But it was with reluctance Cromwell resorted to such severe measures. His general policy was to balance parties against each other, and make each of them desirous of the subsistence of his authority rather than run the risk of seeing it changed for some other than their own. At great expense, and by constant assiduity, he maintained spies in the councils of every faction of the state; and often the least suspected, and apparently most vehement, among the hostile parties, were, in private, the mercenary tools of Cromwell.

In the wandering court of Charles II., in particular, one of the most noted cavaliers was Sir Richard Willis, who had fought bravely, and suffered much, in the cause both of the late King and of his son. There was no man among the Royalists who attended on Charles's person so much trusted and honoured as this gentleman, who, nevertheless, enjoyed a large pension from Cromwell, and betrayed to him whatever schemes were proposed for the restoration of the exiled monarch. By this and similar intercourse, the Protector had the means of preventing the numerous conspiracies against him from coming to a head, and also of opposing the machinations of one discontented party by means of the others.

It is believed, however, that, with all his art, the Protector would not have been able to maintain his power for many years. A people long accustomed to a free government were generally incensed at being subjected to the unlimited authority of one man, and the discontent became universal. It seemed that, towards the conclusion of his life, Cromwell was nearly at the end of his expedients; and it is certain that his own conduct then displayed an apprehension of danger which he had never before exhibited. He became morose and melancholy, always wore secret armour under his ordinary dress, never stirred abroad unless surrounded with guards, never returned by the same road, nor slept above thrice in the same apartment, from the dread of assassination. His health broke down under these gloomy apprehensions, and on the 3d of September 1658 he died at the age of sixty. His death was accompanied by a general and fearful tempest; and by another circumstance equally striking in those superstitious times, namely, that he died on the day and month in which he had gained his decisive victories at Dunbar and Worcester.

The sceptre, which Oliver had held with so firm a grasp, was transferred to that of his son, Richard Cromwell; while the funeral of the deceased Protector was solemnised at an expense superior far to what England had bestowed on the obsequies of any of her kings. But this apparent transmission of Oliver's authority to his son was only nominal. A Parliament, which Richard assembled that they might vote him supplies, commenced an inquiry into the nature of the new Lord Protector's title; and a council of officers whom he convoked became refractory, and assumed an authority which he dared not dispute with them. These military despots compelled Richard to dissolve the Parliament, and subsequently obliged him to resign the office of Protector. He descended quietly into humble life, burdened not only by many personal debts but also by the demands of those who had supplied the exorbitant expenses of his father's funeral, which the State unworthily and meanly suffered to descend upon him.

Richard Cromwell, removed from the dangers and the guilt of power, lived a long and peaceable life, and died in 1712, at the age of eighty-six. Two anecdotes respecting him are worth mentioning. When he was obliged to retire abroad on account of his debts, Richard Cromwell, travelling under a borrowed name, was led, from curiosity, to visit Pezenas, a pleasant town and castle in Languedoc. The proprietor was the Prince of Conti, a French prince of the blood royal, who, hearing an English traveller was in the palace, had the curiosity to receive him, that he might learn the latest news from England, which at this time astonished Europe by its frequent changes of government. The French prince spoke to the stranger of Oliver Cromwell as a wicked man and a lawless usurper of the government: but then he acknowledged his deep sagacity, high talents, and courage in danger, and admired the art and force with which he had subjected three kingdoms to his own individual authority. "He knew how to command," continued the prince, "and deserved to be obeyed. But what has become of the poor poltroon, Richard—the coward, the dastard, who gave up, without a blow or struggle, all that his father had gained? Have you any idea how the man could be such a fool, and mean-spirited caitiff?" Poor Richard, glad to remain unknown where he was so little esteemed, only replied, "That the abdicated Protector had been deceived by those in whom he most trusted, and to whom his father had shown most kindness." He then took leave of the prince, who did not learn till two days afterwards that he had addressed so unpleasing a discourse to the person whom it principally regarded.

The other anecdote is of a later date, being subsequent to 1705. Some lawsuit of importance required that Richard Cromwell should appear in the King's Bench Court. The judge who presided showed a generous deference to fallen greatness, and to the mutability of human affairs. He received with respect the man who had been once Sovereign of England, caused a chair to be placed for him within the bar, and requested him to be covered. When the counsel on the opposite side began his speech, as if about to allude to Richard's descent from the obnoxious Oliver, the judge checked him with generous independence. "I will hear nothing on that topic, sir," he said; "speak to the merits of the cause before us." After his appearance in court, Richard Cromwell's curiosity carried him to the House of Peers, where he stood below the bar, looking around him, and making observations on the alterations which he saw. A person, who heard a decent-looking old man speaking in this way, said to him civilly, "It is probably a long while, sir, since you have been in this house?"—"Not since I sat in that chair," answered the old gentleman, pointing to the throne, on which he had been, indeed, seated as sovereign, when, more than fifty years before, he received the addresses of both Houses of Parliament, on his succeeding to his father in the supreme power.

To return to public affairs in London, where, after the abdication of Richard, changes succeeded with as little permanence as the reflection of faces presented to a mirror,—the attempt of the officers of the army to establish a purely military government was combated by the return to Parliament of those republican members whom Oliver Cromwell had expelled, and whom the common people, by a vulgar but expressive nickname, now called the Rump Parliament. This assembly, so called because it was the sitting part of that which commenced the civil war, was again subjected to military violence, and dissolved by General Lambert, who unquestionably designed in his own person to act the part of Oliver Cromwell, though without either the talents or high reputation of the original performer. But a general change had taken place in the sentiments of the nation.

The public had been to a certain degree patient under the government of Oliver, to whom it was impossible to deny all the praise which belongs to firmness and energy; but they saw with disgust these feeble usurpers, by whom his vigorous government was succeeded, bustle amongst themselves, and push each other from the rudder of the state, without consulting the people at large. Remembering the quiet and peaceful condition of the kingdom before the civil wars, when its kings succeeded by hereditary right to a limited power, and when the popular and monarchical branches of the constitution so judiciously balanced each other, that the whole British nation looked back to the period as one of liberty, peace, and lawful order; and comparing this happy and settled state of public affairs with the recent manner in which every successive faction seized upon power when they could snatch it, and again yielded it up to the grasp of another and stronger party, all men were filled with dissatisfaction.

Upon the whole, the thoughts of all the judicious part of the nation were turned towards the exiled prince, and there was a general desire to call him back to the exercise of the government, an inclination which was only suppressed by the strong hand of the armed fanatics. It was absolutely necessary that some military force should be on foot in order to cope with these warlike saints, as they called themselves, before the general disposition of the kingdom could have room or freedom to express itself.

As it was the disturbances in Scotland which first shook the throne of Charles the First, so it was from the same country that the movement took place which eventually replaced on the throne his son and heir. We have already noticed that the kingdom of Scotland had been finally subdued by the efforts of General Monk, who afterwards governed it during the protectorate of Cromwell, and in obedience to his authority.

Monk was a man of a grave, reserved, and sagacious character, who had gained general esteem by the manner in which he managed Scottish affairs. He had taken care to model the veteran troops under his command in that kingdom, so as to subject them to his own separate control, and to remove such officers as were either violent enthusiasts, or peculiarly attached to Lambert, and his council of officers. Thus having under his immediate orders a movable force of between seven and eight thousand men, besides those necessary to garrison Scotland, Monk eagerly watched the contest of the factions in London, in order to perceive and seize on the fit opportunity for action.

This seemed to arrive when the army under Lambert again thrust the Rump Parliament out of doors, and commenced a new military government, by means of a committee of officers, called the Council of Safety. Monk then threw aside the mask of indifference which he had long worn, assembled his forces on the Borders, and declared for the freedom of Parliament, and against the military faction by which they had been suppressed. The persuasion was universal throughout Britain that Monk, by these general expressions, meant something more effectual than merely restoring the authority of the Rump, which had fallen into the common contempt of all men, by the repeated acts of violence to which they had tamely submitted. But General Monk, allowing all parties to suppose what they thought most probable, proceeded deliberately to make his preparations for marching into England, without suffering even a whisper to escape concerning the ultimate objects of the expedition. He assembled the Scottish Convention of Estates, and asked and received from it a supply of six months' pay, for the maintenance of his troops. The confidence entertained of his intentions was such, that the Convention offered him the support of a Scottish army of twenty-four thousand men; but Monk declined assistance which would have been unpopular in England. He then proceeded in his plan of new-modelling his army, with more boldness than before, dismissing many of the Independent officers whom he had not before ventured to cashier, and supplying their places with Presbyterians, and even with secret Royalists.

The news of these proceedings spread through England, and were generally received with joy. Universal resistance was made to the payment of taxes; for the Rump Parliament had, on the eve of its expulsion by Lambert, declared it high treason to levy money without consent of Parliament, and the provinces, where Lambert and his military council had no power of enforcing their illegal exactions, refused to obey them. The Council of Safety wanted money therefore, even for the payment of their troops, and were reduced to extreme perplexity.

Lambert himself, a brave man, and a good officer, saw the necessity of acting with promptitude; and placing himself at the head of a considerable force of veteran soldiers, marched towards Scotland. His numbers were exaggerated by the report of the various spies and agents whom he sent into Monk's army under the guise of envoys. "What will you do?" said one of these persons, addressing a party of Monk's soldiers; "Lambert is coming down against you with such numerous forces that your army will not be a breakfast for him."

"The north must have given Lambert a good appetite," answered one of Monk's veterans, "if he be willing to chew bullets, and feed upon pikes and musket barrels."

In this tone of defiance the two armies moved against each other. Lambert took up his headquarters at Newcastle. Monk, on the other hand, placed his at Coldstream, on the Tweed, a place which commanded the second best passage over that river, Berwick being already in his hands. Coldstream, now a thriving town, was then so miserable that Monk could get no supper, even for his own table, but was fain to have recourse to chewing tobacco to appease his hunger. Next day provisions were sent from Berwick; and the camp at Coldstream is still kept in memory in the English army by the second regiment of guards, which was one of those that composed Monk's vanguard, being called to this day the Coldstream Guards.

The rival generals at first engaged in a treaty, which Monk, perceiving Lambert's forces to be more numerous than his own, for some time encouraged, aware that want of pay, and of the luxuries to which they were accustomed in London, would soon induce his rival's troops to desert him.

Disaffection and weariness accordingly began to diminish Lambert's forces, when at length they heard news from the capital by which they were totally dispirited. During Lambert's absence, the presidency in the Military Committee, and the command of such of the army as remained to overawe London, devolved on General Fleetwood, a weak man, who really was overcome by the feelings of fanaticism which others only affected. Incapable of any exertion, this person suffered the troops under his command to be seduced from his interest to that of the Rump Parliament, which thus came again, and for the last time, into power. With these tidings came to Newcastle others of a nature scarce less alarming. The celebrated General Fairfax had taken arms in Yorkshire, and was at the head of considerable forces, both Cavaliers and Presbyterians, who declared for calling a free Parliament, that the national will might be consulted in the most constitutional manner for once more regaining the blessing of a settled government. The soldiers of Lambert, disconcerted by these events, and receiving no pay, began to break up; and when Lambert himself attempted to lead them back to London, they left him in such numbers that his army seemed actually to melt away, and leave the road to the capital open to Monk and the forces from Scotland.

That general moved on accordingly, without opposition, carefully concealing his own intentions, receiving favourably all the numerous applications which were made to him for calling a new and free Parliament, in order to regenerate the national constitution, but returning no reply which could give the slightest intimation of his ultimate purpose. Monk observed this mystery in order, perhaps, that he might reserve to himself the power of being guided by circumstances—at all events, knowing well, that if he were to declare in favour of any one party, or set of principals, among the various factious opinions which divided the state, the others would at once unite against him, a course which they would be loath to adopt while each as yet entertained hopes that he might turn to their side.

With the eyes of all the nation fixed upon him and his forces, Monk advanced to Barnet, within ten miles of London, and from thence caused the Parliament to understand that they would do well to send from the city the remains of the army of Fleetwood, in case of discord between his troops and those which at present occupied the capital. The Rump Parliament had no alternative but to take the hint, unless they had resolved to try the fate of battle at the head of those insubordinate troops against the steady veterans of the Scottish wars. The late army of Fleetwood, excepting two regiments commanded by men whom Monk could perfectly trust, were ordered to leave the city, and the general of the army of Scotland entered at the head of his troops, who, rough from a toilsome march and bearing other marks of severe service, made a far more hardy and serviceable, though a less showy appearance than those who had so long bridled the people of London.

General Monk, and the remnant of the Parliament met each other with external civility, but with great distrust on both sides. They propounded to him the oath of abjuration, as it was called, by which he was to renounce and abjure all allegiance to the House of Stewart, and all attempts to restore Charles II. But the general declined taking the oath; too many oaths, he said, had been already imposed on the public, unless they had been better kept. This circumstance seemed to throw light on Monk's intentions, and the citizens of London, now as anxious for the King's restoration as ever they had been for the expulsion of his father, passed a vote in Common Council, by which they declared they would pay no taxes or contributions to this shadow of a Parliament until the vacant seats in it should be filled up to the full extent of a genuine House of Commons.

The Rump Parliament had now, they conceived, an opportunity of ascertaining Monk's real purpose, and forcing him to a decisive measure. They laid their express commands on him to march into the city, seize upon the gates, break down the portcullises, destroy the ports, chains, and other means of defending the streets, and take from the contumacious citizens all means of protecting in future the entrance into the capital.

Monk, to the astonishment of most of his own officers, obeyed the commands thus imposed on him. He was probably desirous of ascertaining whether the disposition of his troops would induce them to consider the task as a harsh and unworthy one. Accordingly, he no sooner heard his soldiers exclaiming at the disgrace of becoming the tools of the vengeance of the Rump members against the city of London than he seemed to adopt their feelings and passions as his own, and like them complained, and complained aloud, of having been employed in an unjust and unpopular task for the express purpose of rendering him odious to the citizens.

At this crisis the rashness of the ruling junto, for it would be absurd to term them a Parliament, gave the general, whom it was their business to propitiate if possible, a new subject of complaint. They encouraged a body of the most fanatical sectaries, headed by a ridiculous personage called Praise-God Barebone, to present a violent petition to the House, demanding that no one should be admitted to any office of public trust, or so much as to teach a school, without his having taken the abjuration oath; and proposing that any motion made in Parliament for the restoration of the King should be visited with the pains of high treason.

The tenor of this petition, and the honour and favour which it received when presented, gave Monk the further cause of complaint against the Rump, or Remnant of the Parliament, which perhaps was what he chiefly desired. He refused to return to Whitehall, where he had formerly lodged, and took up his abode in the city, where he found it easy to excuse his late violence upon their defences, and to atone for it by declaring himself the protector and ally of the magistrates and community. From his quarters in the heart of London the general wrote to the Parliament an angry expostulation, charging them with a design to arm the more violent fanatics, and call in the assistance of Fleetwood and Lambert against the army he had marched from Scotland; and recommending to them, in a tone of authority, forthwith to dissolve themselves and call a new Parliament, which should be open to all parties. The Parliament, greatly alarmed at this intimation, sent two of their members to communicate with the general; but they could only extract from him that if writs went instantly forth for the new elections it would be very well, otherwise he and they were likely to disagree.

The assurance that General Monk had openly quarrelled with the present rulers, and was disposed to insist for a free and full Parliament, was made public by the printing and dispersing of the general's letter, and the tidings filled the city with most extravagant rejoicings. The Royalists and Presbyterians, forgetting past animosities, mingled in common joy, and vowed never more to gratify the ambition of factious tyrants by their calamitous divisions. The rabble rung all the bells, lighted immense bonfires in every street, and danced around them, while they drank healths to the general, the secluded members, and even to the King. But the principal part of their amusement was roasting rumps of poultry, or fragments of butcher meat cut into that form, in ridicule of their late rulers, whose power they foresaw would cease whenever a full Parliament should be convened. The revelry lasted the whole night, which was that of 11th February 1660.

Monk, supported at once by military strength and the consciousness of general popularity, did not wait until the new Parliament should be assembled, or the present dissolved, to take measures for destroying the influence of the junto now sitting at Westminster. He compelled them to open their doors, and admit to their deliberations and votes all the secluded members of their body, who had been expelled from their seats by military violence, since it was first practised on the occasion called Colonel Pride's Purge. These members, returning to Parliament accordingly, made by their numbers such a predominant majority in the House that the fifty or sixty persons who had lately been at the head of the Government were instantly reduced to the insignificance, as a party, from which they had only emerged by dint of the force which had been exercised to exclude the large body who were now restored to their seats.

The first acts of the House thus renovated were to disband the refractory part of the army, to dispossess the disaffected officers, of whom there were very many, and to reduce the country to a state of tranquillity; after which they dissolved themselves, 16th March, having first issued writs to summon a new Parliament, to meet on the 25th of April. Thus then finally ended the Long Parliament, as it is called, which had sat for nearly twenty years; the most eventful period, perhaps, in British History.

While this important revolution was on the eve of taking place, Charles the Second's affairs seemed to be at a lower ebb than they had almost ever been before. A general insurrection of the Cavaliers had been defeated by Lambert a few months before, and the severe measures which followed had, for the time, totally subdued the spirit, and almost crushed the party of the Royalists. It was in vain that Charles had made advances to Monk while in Scotland, both through the general's own brother, and by means of Sir John Grenville, one of his nearest and most valued relatives and friends. If Monk's mind was then made up concerning the part which he designed to perform, he at least was determined to keep his purpose secret in his own bosom, and declined, therefore, though civilly, to hear any proposition on the part of the banished family. The accounts which the little exiled court received concerning Monk's advance into England were equally disconsolate. All intercourse with the Cavaliers had been carefully avoided by the cloudy and mysterious soldier, in whose hands Fortune seemed to place the fate of the British kingdoms. The general belief was, that Monk would renew, in his own person, the attempt in which Cromwell had succeeded and Lambert had failed, and again place a military commander at the head of the government; and this opinion seemed confirmed by his harsh treatment of the City.

While Charles and his attendants were in this state of despondence, they were suddenly astonished by the arrival from England of a partisan, named Baillie, an Irish Royalist, who had travelled with extreme rapidity to bring the exiled Prince the news of Monk's decided breach with the remnant of the Long Parliament, and the temper which had been displayed by the City of London when his letter became public. The King and his small Council listened to the messenger as they would have done to one speaking in a dream. Over-wearied and fatigued by the journey, and strongly excited by the importance of the intelligence which he brought them, the officer seemed rather like one under the influence of temporary derangement or intoxication than the deliberate bearer of great tidings. His character was, however, known as a gentleman of fidelity and firmness, and they heard him with wonder again and again affirm, that London was blazing with bonfires, that the universal wish of the people of all sorts, boldly and freely expressed, demanded the restoration of the King to his authority, and that Monk had insisted upon the summoning of a free Parliament, which the junto called the Rump had no longer the power of opposing. He produced also a copy of Monk's letter to the Parliament, to show that the general had completely broken with that body.

Other messengers soon confirmed the joyful tidings, and Sir John Grenville was dispatched to London in all haste, with full powers to offer the general everything which could gratify ambition or love of wealth, on condition of his proving the friend of Charles at this crisis.

This faithful and active Royalist reached the metropolis, and cautiously refusing to open his commission to any one, obtained a private interview with the mysterious and reserved general. He boldly communicated his credentials, and remained unappalled when Monk, stepping back in surprise, asked him, with some emotion, how he dared become the bearer of such proposals. Sir John replied firmly, that all danger which might be incurred in obedience to his sovereign's command had become familiar to him from frequent practice, and that the King, from the course which Monk had hitherto pursued, entertained the most confident hope of his loyal service. On this General Monk either laid aside the mask which he had always worn, or only now formed his determination upon a line of conduct that had hitherto been undecided in his own mind. He accepted of the high offers tendered to him by the young Prince; and, from that moment, if not earlier, made the interest of Charles the principal object of his thoughts. It has been indeed stated, that he had expressed his ultimate purpose of serving Charles before leaving Scotland; but, whatever may have been his secret intentions, it seems improbable that he made any one his confidant.

At the meeting of the new Parliament, the House of Peers, which regained under this new aspect of things the privileges which Cromwell had suspended, again assumed their rank as a branch of the legislature. As the Royalists and Presbyterians concurred in the same purpose of restoring the King, and possessed the most triumphant majority, if not the whole votes, in the new House of Commons, the Parliament had only to be informed that Grenville awaited without, bearing letters from King Charles, when he was welcomed into the

House with shouts and rejoicings; and the British Constitution, by King, Lords, and Commons, after having been suspended for twenty years, was restored at once and by acclamation.

Charles Stewart, instead of being a banished pretender, whose name it was dangerous to pronounce and whose cause it was death to espouse, became at once a lawful, beloved, almost adored prince, whose absence was mourned by the people, as they might have bemoaned that of the sun itself; and numbers of the great or ambitious hurried to Holland, where Charles now was, some to plead former services, some to excuse ancient delinquencies, some to allege the merit of having staked their lives in the King's cause, others to enrich the monarch by sharing with him the spoils which they had gained by fighting against him.

It has been said by historians that this precipitate and general haste in restoring Charles to the throne, without any conditions for the future, was throwing away all the advantage which the nation might have derived from the Civil Wars, and that it would have been much better to have readmitted the King, upon a solemn treaty, which should have adjusted the prerogative of the crown, and the rights of the subject, and settled for ever those great national questions which had been disputed between Charles the First and his Parliament.

This sounds all well in theory; but in practice there are many things, and perhaps the Restoration is one of them, which may be executed easily and safely if the work is commenced and carried through in the enthusiasm of a favourable moment, but which is likely enough to miscarry if protracted beyond that happy conjuncture. The ardour in favour of monarchy with which the mass of the English nation was at this time agitated, might probably have abated during such a lengthened treaty, providing for all the delicate questions respecting the settlement of the Church and State, and necessarily involving a renewal of all the discussions which had occasioned the Civil War. And supposing that the old discord was not rekindled by raking among its ashes, still it should be remembered that great part of Cromwell's army was not yet dissolved, and that even Monk's troops were not altogether to be confided in. So that the least appearance of disunion, such as the discussions of the proposed treaty were certain to give rise to, might have afforded these warlike enthusiasts a pretext for again assembling together, and reinstating the military despotism which they were pleased to term the Reign of the Saints.

A circumstance occurred which showed how very pressing this danger was, and how little wisdom there would have been in postponing the restoration of a legal government to the event of a treaty. Lambert, who had been lodged in the Tower as a dangerous person, made his escape from that state prison, fled to Daventry, and began to assemble forces. The activity of Colonel Ingoldsby, who had been, like Lambert himself, an officer under Cromwell, but who was now firmly attached to Monk, stifled a spark which might have raised a mighty conflagration. He succeeded in gaining over and dispersing the troops who had assembled under Lambert, and, making his former commander prisoner with his own hand, brought him back in safety to his old quarters in the Tower of London. But as the roads were filled with soldiers of the old Cromwellian army, hastening to join Lambert, it was clear that only the immediate suppression of his force, and the capture of his person, prevented the renewal of general hostilities.

In so delicate a state of affairs, it was of importance that the Restoration, being the measure to which all wise men looked as the only radical cure for the distresses and disorders of the kingdom, should be executed hastily, leaving it in future to the mutual prudence of the King and his subjects to avoid the renewal of those points of quarrel which had given rise to the Civil War of 1641, since which time both Royalists and Parliamentarians had suffered such extreme misery as was likely to make them very cautious how the one made unjust attempts to extend the power of the crown, or the other to resist it while within its constitutional limits.

The King landed at Dover on 26th May 1660, and was received by General Monk, now gratified and honoured with the dukedom of Albemarle, the Order of the Garter, and the command of the army. He entered London on the 29th, which was also his birthday; and with him came his two brothers, James, Duke of York, of whom we shall have much to say, and the Duke of Gloucester, who died early. They were received with such extravagant shouts of welcome that the King said to those around him, "It must surely have been our own fault that we have been so long absent from a country where every one seems so glad to see us."

Of Charles the Second, who thus unexpectedly, and as it were by miracle, was replaced on his father's throne, in spite of so many obstacles as within even a week or two of the event seemed to render it incredible, I have not much that is advantageous to tell you. He was a prince of an excellent understanding, of which he made less use than he ought to have done; a graceful address, much ready wit, and no deficiency of courage. Unfortunately, he was very fond of pleasure, and, in his zeal to pursue it, habitually neglected the interests of his kingdom. He was very selfish too, like all whose own gratification is their sole pursuit; and he seems to have cared little what became of friends or enemies, provided he could maintain himself on the throne, get money to supply the expenses of a luxurious and dissolute court, and enjoy a life of easy and dishonourable pleasure. He was good-natured in general; but any apprehension of his own safety easily induced him to be severe and even cruel, for his love of self predominated above both his sense of justice and his natural clemency of temper. He was always willing to sacrifice sincerity to convenience, and perhaps the satirical epitaph, written upon him at his own request, by his witty favourite, the Earl of Rochester, is not more severe than just—

> "Here lies our Sovereign Lord the King,
>   Whose word no man relies on;
> Who never said a foolish thing,
>   And never did a wise one."

After this sketch of the King's character, we shall return to Scotland, from which we have been absent since Monk's march from Coldstream, to accomplish the Restoration.

XLIX

The Restoration

1660-1665

THE Restoration was celebrated with the same general and joyful assent in Scotland which had hailed it in the sister country. Indeed the Scots, during the whole war, can hardly be said to have quitted their sentiments of loyalty to the monarchy. They had fought against Charles I., first to establish Presbytery in their own country, and then to extend it into England; but then even the most rigid of the Presbyterians had united in the resistance to the English invasion, had owned the right of Charles the Second, and asserted it to their severe national loss at the battle of Dunbar. Since that eventful overthrow, the influence of the Church of Scotland over the people at large had been considerably diminished, by disputes among the ministers themselves, as they espoused more rigid or more moderate doctrines, and by the various modes in which it had been Cromwell's policy to injure their respectability, and curb their power. But the Presbyterian interest was still very strong in Scotland. It entirely engrossed the western counties, had a large share of influence in the south and midland provinces, and was only less predominant in the northern shires, where the Episcopal interest prevailed.

The Presbyterian Church was sufficiently alive to their own interest and that of their body, for they had sent to Monk's army, ere it had reached London, an agent or commissioner to take care of the affairs of the Scottish Church in any revolution which should take place in consequence of the general's expedition.

This agent was James Sharp, famous during his life, and still more in his deplorable death. At this time he was a man competently learned, bold, active, and ambitious, displaying much zeal for the interest of the Church, and certainly by no means negligent of his own. This Master James Sharp quickly found, while in London, that there was little purpose of establishing the Presbyterian religion in Scotland. It is true, that King Charles had, on his former expedition into Scotland, deliberately accepted and sworn to the Solemn League and Covenant, the principal object of which was the establishment of Presbytery of the most rigid kind. It was also true that the Earl of Lauderdale, who, both from his high talents and from the long imprisonment which he had sustained ever since the battle of Worcester, had a peculiar title to be consulted on Scottish affairs, strongly advised the King to suffer his northern subjects to retain possession of their darling form of worship; and though he endeavoured to give this advice in the manner most agreeable to the King, ridiculing bitterly the pedantry of the Scottish ministers, and reprobating the uses made of the Covenant, and in so far gratifying and amusing the King, still he returned to the point, that the Covenant and Presbyterian discipline ought not to be removed from Scotland, while the people continued so partial to them. They should be treated, he argued, like froward children, whom their keepers do not vex by struggling to wrest from them an unfitting plaything, but quietly wait to withdraw it when sleep or satiety makes it indifferent to them.

But the respect due to the King's personal engagement, as well as the opinion thus delivered by this worldly-wise nobleman, were strongly contested by those Cavaliers who professed absolute loyalty and devotion to the King, and affected to form their political opinions on those of Montrose. They laid upon the Presbyterian Church the whole blame of the late rebellion, and contended that the infamous transaction of delivering up Charles the First to the Parliamentary forces was the act of an army guided by Presbyterian counsels. In short, they imputed to the Church of Scotland the whole original guilt of the war; and though it was allowed that they at length joined the Royal cause, it was immediately added that their accession only took place when they were afraid of being deprived of their power over men's consciences by Cromwell and his independent schismatics. The King was then reminded, that be had been received by the Presbyterians less as their prince than as a passive tool and engine, whom they determined to indulge in nothing save the name of a sovereign; and that his taking the Covenant had been under a degree of moral restraint, which rendered it as little binding as if imposed by personal violence. Lastly, the King was assured that the whole people of Scotland were now so much delighted with his happy restoration, that the moment was highly favourable for any innovation, either in church or state, which might place the crown firmer on his head; that no change could be so important as the substitution of Episcopacy for Presbytery; and that the opportunity, if lost, might never return.

The King himself had personal reasons, though they ought not to have entered into such a discussion, for recollecting with disgust the affronts and rigorous treatment which he had received from the Presbyterian leaders, before the battle of Dunbar had diminished their power. He had then adopted a notion that Presbytery was not a religion "for a gentleman," and he now committed to Lord Middleton, who was to be his High Commissioner and representative in the Scottish Parliament, full powers to act in the matter of altering the national religious establishment to the Episcopal model as soon as he should think proper.

This determination was signing the doom of Presbytery as far as Charles could do so; for Middleton, though once in the service of the Covenanting Parliament, and as such opposed to Montrose, by whom he was beaten at the bridge of Dee, had afterwards been Major-General of the Duke of Hamilton's ill-fated army, which was destroyed at Uttoxeter in 1648, and ever since that period had fought bravely, though unsuccessfully, in the cause of Charles, maintaining at the same time the tenets of the most extravagant Royalism. He was a good soldier, but in other respects a man of inferior talents, who had lived the life of an adventurer, and who, in enjoying the height of fortune which he had attained, was determined to indulge without control all his favourite propensities. These were, unhappily, of a coarse and scandalous nature. The Covenanters had assumed an exterior of strict demeanour and precise morality; and the Cavaliers, in order to show themselves their opposites in every respect, gave in to the most excessive indulgences in wine and revelry and conceived that in doing so they showed their loyalty to the King, and their contempt of what they termed the formal hypocrisy of his enemies. When the Scottish Parliament met, the members were, in many instances, under the influence of wine; and they were more than once obliged to adjourn because the Royal Commissioner was too intoxicated to behave properly in the chair.

While the Scottish Parliament was in this jovial humour, it failed not to drive forward the schemes of the Commissioner Middleton, and of the very violent Royalists, with a zeal which was equally imprudent and impolitic. At once, and by a single sweeping resolution, it annulled and rescinded every statute and ordinance which had been made by those holding the supreme authority in Scotland since the commencement of the Civil Wars; although, in doing so, it set aside many laws useful to the subject, many which had received the personal assent of the sovereign, and some that were entered into expressly for his defence, and the acknowledgment and protection of his right. By a statute subsequent to the Act Rescissory, as it was called, the whole Presbyterian church government was destroyed, and the Episcopal institutions, to which the nation had shown themselves so adverse, were rashly and precipitately established. James Sharp, to whom allusion has already been made, who had yielded to the high temptations held out to him, was named Lord Bishop of St. Andrews, and Primate of Scotland,[1] and other persons, either ancient members of the Episcopal Church, or new converts to the doctrines which seemed a sure road to preferment, were appointed prelates, with seats in Parliament, and who afterwards attained great influence in the councils of the nation.

It may seem wonderful that such great changes, and in a matter so essential, should have been made without more violent opposition. But

---

[1] "The great stain will always remain, that Sharp deserted and probably betrayed a cause which his brethren intrusted to him, and abused to his own purposes a mission which he ought not to have undertaken, but with the determination of maintaining its principal object. Kirkton says, that when Sharp returned from Scotland, he himself, affecting no ambition for the prelacy, pressed the acceptance of the See of Saint Andrews upon Mr. Robert Douglas, one of his former colleagues. The stern Presbyterian saw into his secret soul, and when he had given his own positive rejection, demanded of his former friend what he would do himself were the offer made to him? Sharp hesitated; —'I perceive,' said Douglas, 'you are clear—you will engage—you will be Primate of Scotland; take it then,' he added, laying his hand on his shoulder, 'and take the curse of God along with it.' The subject would suit a painter."—*Review of* Kirkton's *History*.

the general joy at finding themselves delivered from the domination of England; the withdrawing the troops, and abandoning the citadels by which Cromwell had ruled them, as a foreign conqueror governs a subdued country; and the pleasure of enjoying once more their own Parliament under the authority of their native prince, had a great effect, amid the first tumult of joy, in reconciling the minds of the Scottish people to the change even of the form of religion, when proposed and carried through as the natural consequences (it was pretended) of the restoration of Royal power.

The Scottish nobility, and many of the gentry, especially the younger men, had long resented the interference of the Presbyterian preachers in searching out scandals and improprieties within the bosoms of families; and this right, which the clergy claimed and exercised, became more and more intolerable to those who were disposed to adopt the gay and dissolute manners which distinguished the Cavaliers of England, and who had for some time regarded with resentment the interference and rebukes with which the Presbyterian clergy claimed the right of checking their career of pleasure.

The populace of the towns were amused with processions, largesses, free distribution of liquor, and such like marks of public rejoicing, by which they are generally attracted. And I cannot help mentioning as remarkable, that on 23d April 1661 Jenny Geddes, the very woman who had given the first signal of civil broil, by throwing her stool at the Dean of Edinburgh's head, when he read the service-book on the memorable 23d July 1637, showed her conversion to loyalty by contributing the materials of her green-stall, her baskets, shelves, forms, and even her own wicker-chair to augment a bonfire kindled in honour of his Majesty's coronation and the proceedings of his Parliament.

There were many, however, in Scotland, who were very differently affected by the hasty proceedings of Middleton and his jovial Parliament, of whose sentiments I shall have much to say hereafter.

The greatest evil to be apprehended from the King's return was the probability that he might be disposed to distinguish the more especial enemies of himself and his father, and perpetuate the memory of former injuries and quarrels by taking vengeance for them. Charles had indeed published a promise of indemnity and of oblivion for all offences during the civil war against his own or his father's person. But this proclamation bore an exception of such persons as Parliament should point out as especially deserving of punishment. Accordingly, those who had been actively concerned in the death, or, as it may well be termed, the murder of Charles I., were, with one or two others who had been peculiarly violent during the late times, excepted from pardon; and although but few were actually executed, yet it had been better perhaps to have spared several even of the most obnoxious class. But that is a question belonging to English history. In order that Scotland might enjoy the benefit of similar examples of severity, it was resolved also to bring to trial some of the most active persons there.

Among these, the Marquis of Argyle, whom we have so often mentioned, was by far the most considerable. He had repaired to London, on the Restoration, hoping to make interest with the King but was instantly arrested, and imprisoned in the Tower, and afterwards sent down to Scotland to undergo a trial, according to the laws of that country. There was a strong desire on the part of the Cavalier party that Argyle should be put to death in revenge for the execution of Montrose, to whom, you must remember, he had been a deadly and persevering enemy. Undoubtedly this powerful nobleman had been guilty of much cruelty in suppressing the Royalist party in the Highlands; and had probably been privately accessary to Montrose's tragical fate, though he seemed to hold aloof from the councils held on the subject. But it was then greatly too late to call him into judgment for these things. The King, when he came to Scotland after Montrose's execution, had acknowledged all that was done against that illustrious loyalist as good service rendered to himself, had entered the gate of Edinburgh, over which the features of his faithful general were blackening in the sun, and had received, in such circumstances, the attendance and assistance of Argyle as of a faithful and deserving subject. Nay, besides all this, which in effect implied a pardon for Argyle's past offences, the Marquis was protected by the general Act of Remission, granted by Charles in 1651, for all state offence committed before that period.

Sensible of the weight of this defence, the crown counsel and judges searched anxiously for some evidence of Argyle's having communicated with the English army subsequently to 1651. The trial was long protracted, and the accused was about to be acquitted for want of testimony to acts of more importance than that compulsory submission which the conquering Englishmen demanded from all, and which no one had the power to refuse. But just when the Marquis was about to be discharged, a knock was heard at the door of the court, and a despatch just arrived from London was handed to the Lord Advocate. As it was discovered that the name of the messenger was Campbell, it was concluded that he bore the pardon, or remission of the Marquis; but the contents were very different, being certain letters which had been written by Argyle to General Monk when the latter was acting under Cromwell, in which he naturally endeavoured to gain the general's good opinion by expressing a zeal for the English interest, then headed and managed by his correspondent. Monk, it seems, had not intended to produce these letters if other matter had occurred to secure Argyle's condemnation, desirous, doubtless, to avoid the ignominy of so treacherous an action; yet he resolved to send them, that they might be produced in evidence, rather than that the accused should be acquitted. This transaction leaves a deep blot on the character of the restorer of the English monarchy.

These letters so faithlessly brought forward, were received as full evidence of the Marquis's ready compliance with the English enemy; and being found guilty, though only of doing that which no man in Scotland dared refuse to do at the time, he received sentence of death by beheading.

As Argyle rose from his knees, on which he had received the sentence, he offered to speak, but the trumpets sounding, he stopped till they ended; then he said, "This reminds me that I had the honour to set the crown upon the King's head" (meaning, at the coronation at Scone), "and now he hastens me to a better crown than his own!" Then turning to the Commissioner and Parliament he added, "You have the indemnity of an earthly king among your hands, and have denied me a share in that, but you cannot hinder me from the indemnity of the King of Kings; and shortly you must be before his tribunal. I pray he mete not out such measure to you as you have done to me, when you are called to account for all your actings, and this among the rest."

He faced death with a courage which other passages of his life had not prepared men to expect, for he was generally esteemed to be of a timorous disposition. On the scaffold, he told a friend that he felt himself capable of braving death like a Roman, but he preferred submitting to it with the patience of a Christian. The rest of his behaviour made his words good; and thus died the celebrated Marquis of Argyle, so important a person during this melancholy time. He was called by the Highlanders Gillespie Grumach, or the Grim, from an obliquity in his eyes, which gave a sinister expression to his countenance. The Marquis's head replaced on the tower of the tolbooth that of Montrose, his formidable enemy, whose scattered limbs were now assembled, and committed with much pomp to an honourable grave.

John Swinton of Swinton, representative of a family which is repeatedly mentioned in the preceding series of these tales, was destined to share Argyle's fate. He had taken the side of Cromwell very early after the battle of Dunbar, and it was by his councils, and those of Lockhart of Lee, that the usurper chiefly managed the affairs of Scotland. He was, therefore, far more deeply engaged in compliances with Cromwell than the Marquis of Argyle, though less obnoxious in other respects. Swinton was a man of acute and penetrating judgment and great activity of mind; yet, finding himself beset with danger, and sent down to Scotland in the same ship with Argyle, he chose, from conviction, or to screen himself from danger, to turn Quaker. As he was determined that his family should embrace the same faith, his eldest son, when about to rise in the morning, was surprised to see that his laced scarlet coat, his rapier, and other parts of a fashionable young gentleman's dress at the time, were removed, and that a plain suit of gray cloth, with a slouched hat, without loop or button, was laid down by his bedside. He could hardly be prevailed on to assume this simple habit.

His father, on the contrary, seemed entirely to have humbled himself to the condition he had assumed; and when he appeared at the bar in the plain attire of his new sect, he declined to use any of the legal pleas afforded by the act of indemnity, or otherwise, but answered, according to his new religious principles of nonresistance, that it was true he had been guilty of the crimes charged against him, and many more, but it was when he was in the gall of wickedness and bond of iniquity; and that now, being called to the light, he acknowledged his past errors, and did not refuse to atone for them with his life. The mode of his delivery was at once so dignified and so modest, and the sight of a person who had enjoyed great power, placed under such altered circumstances, appears to have so much affected the Parliament before whom he stood, that his life was spared, though he was impoverished by forfeiture and confiscation. The people in his own country said that if Swinton had not *trembled* he would not have *quaked;* but notwithstanding this pun, his conversion seems to have been perfectly sincere. It is said that he had a principal share in converting to the opinions of the Friends, the celebrated Robert Barclay, who afterwards so well defended their cause in the "Apology for the people called, in scorn, Quakers." Swinton remained a member of their congregation till his death, and was highly esteemed among them.

The escape of Judge Swinton might be accounted almost miraculous, for those who followed him during the same reign, although persons chiefly of inferior note, experienced no clemency. Johnstone of Warriston, executed for high treason, was indeed a man of rank and a lawyer, who had complied with all the measures of Cromwell and those who succeeded him. But it seemed petty vengeance which selected as subjects for capital punishment, Mr. Guthrie, a clergyman, who had written a book imputing the wrath of Heaven against Scotland to the sins of Charles I. and his house, and a man called Govan, merely because he had been the first to bring to Scotland the news of Charles's death, and had told it in terms of approbation.

An act of oblivion was at length passed, but it contained a fatal clause, that those who might be entitled to plead the benefit of it should be liable to certain fines in proportion to their estates. The imposition of those fines was remitted to a committee of Parliament, who secretly accepted large bribes from those who were the most guilty and inflicted severe penalties on such as were comparatively innocent but who disdained to compound for their trespasses.

A transaction of a description still more daring shows the rapacious and reckless character of the commissioner Middleton in the strongest light.

The Marquis of Argyle, as I have already said, had been executed, and his son succeeded to the title of Earl of Argyle only. He had repaired to London, in order to make some interest at court, and had been persuaded that some of the minions of Lord Clarendon, then at the head of affairs, would, for a thousand pounds, undertake to procure for him that minister's patronage and favour. Argyle upon this wrote a confidential letter to Lord Duffus, in which he told him that provided he could raise a thousand pounds, he would be able to obtain the protection of the English minister; that in such case he trusted the present would prove but a *gowk* storm;[1] and after some other depreciating expressions concerning the prevailing party in the Scottish Parliament, he added that "then the King would see their tricks."

---

[1] A short storm, such as comes in the spring, the season of the cuckoo which the Scotch call the Gowk.

This letter fell into the hands of Middleton, who determined, that for expressions so innocent and simple, being in fact the natural language of a rival courtier, Argyle should be brought to trial for *leasing-making;* a crime, the essence of which consisted in spreading abroad falsehoods, tending to sow dissension between the King and the people. On this tyrannical law, which had been raked up on purpose, but which never could have been intended to apply to a private letter, Argyle was condemned to lose his head and forfeit his estate. But the account of such a trial and sentence for a vague expression of ill-humour, struck Charles and his privy council with astonishment when it reached England, and the Chancellor Clarendon was the first to exclaim in the King's presence, that did he think he lived in a country where such gross oppression could be permitted, he would get out of his Majesty's dominions as fast as the gout would permit him. An order was sent down forbidding the execution of Argyle, who was nevertheless detained prisoner until the end of Middleton's government,—a severe penalty for imputing tricks to the Royal Ministry. He was afterwards restored to his liberty and estates, to become at a later period a victim to similar persecution.

It was by driving on the alteration of church government in Scotland, that Middleton hoped to regain the place in Charles's favour, and Clarendon's good opinion, which he had lost by his excesses and severity. A general act of uniformity was passed for enforcing the observances of the Episcopal Church, and it was followed up by an order of council of the most violent character, framed, it is said, during the heat of a drunken revel at Glasgow. This furious mandate commanded that all ministers who had not received a presentation from their lay patrons, and spiritual induction into their livings from the prelates, should be removed from them by military force, if necessary. All their parishioners were prohibited from attending upon the ministry of such nonconformists, or acknowledging them as clergymen. This was at one stroke displacing all Presbyterian ministers who might scruple at once to become Episcopalians.

It appeared by this rash action that Middleton entertained an opinion that the ministers, however attached to Presbyterianism, would submit to the Episcopal model rather than lose their livings, which were the only means most of them had for the support of themselves and families. But to the great astonishment of the commissioners, about three hundred and fifty ministers resigned their churches without hesitation, and determined to submit to the last extremity of poverty rather than enjoy comfort at the price of renouncing the tenets of their Church. In the north parts of Scotland, in the midland counties, and along the eastern side of the Borders, many or most of the clergy conformed. But the western shires, where Presbytery had been ever most flourishing, were almost entirely deprived of their pastors; and the result was, that a number equal to one-third of the whole parish ministers of Scotland were at once expelled from their livings, and the people deprived of their instructions.

The congregations of the exiled preachers were strongly affected by this sweeping change, and by the fate of their clergymen. Many of the latter had, by birth or marriage, relations and connections in the parishes from which they were summarily banished, and they had all been the zealous instructors of the people in religion and often their advisers in secular matters also. It was not in nature that their congregations should have seen them with indifference suddenly reduced from decent comfort to indigence, and submitting to it with patience rather than sacrifice their conscientious scruples to their interest. Accordingly, they showed, in almost every case, the deepest sympathy with the distresses of their pastors and corresponding indignation against the proceedings of the Government.

The cause also for which the clergy suffered was not indifferent to the laity. It is true, the consequences of the Solemn League and Covenant had been so fatal, that at the time of the Restoration none but a few high-flying and rigid Presbyterians would have desired the re-establishment of that celebrated engagement. It depended only on the temper and moderation of the court to have reduced what was once the idol of all true Presbyterians to the insignificance of an old almanac, as it had been termed by the Independents. But there was great difference between suffering the Covenant to fall into neglect, as containing doctrines too highly pitched and readily susceptible of misrepresentation, and in complying with the Government by ridiculing as absurd, and renouncing as odious, a document which had been once so much respected.

The Parliament, however, commanded the Solemn League and Covenant to be burned at the Cross of Edinburgh, and elsewhere, with every mark of dishonour; while figures, dressed up to resemble Western Whigamores, as they were called, were also committed to the flames, to represent a burning of Presbyterianism in effigy. But as those who witnessed these proceedings could not but recollect, at the same time, that upon its first being formed, the same Covenant had been solemnly sworn to by almost all Scotland,—nobility, gentry, clergy, burgesses, and people, with weeping eyes, and uplifted hands, and had been solemnly taken by the King himself, and a very large proportion of the statesmen, including the present ministers,—it was natural they should feel involuntary respect for that which once appeared so sacred to themselves, or to their fathers, and feel the unnecessary insults directed against it as a species of sacrilege.

The oaths, also, which imposed on every person in public office the duty of renouncing the Covenant as an unlawful engagement, were distressing to the consciences of many, particularly of the lower class; and, in general, the efforts made to render the Covenant odious and contemptible rather revived its decaying interest with the Scottish public.

There was yet another aggravation of the evils consequent on the expulsion of the Presbyterian clergy. So many pulpits became vacant at once, that the prelates had no means of filling them up with suitable persons, whose talents and influence might have supplied the place of the exiled preachers. Numbers of half-educated youths were hastily sent for from the northern districts, in order that they might become *curates,* which was the term used in the Scottish Episcopal Church for a parish priest, although commonly applied in England to signify a clergyman hired to discharge the duty of another. From the unavoidable haste in filling the vacancies in the Church, these raw students, so hastily called into the spiritual vineyard, had, according to the historians of the period, as little morality as learning, and still less devotion than either. A northern country gentleman is said to have cursed the scruples of the Presbyterian clergy, because, he said, ever since they threw up their livings it was impossible to find a boy to herd cows— they had all gone away to be curates in the west.

The natural consequences of all these adverse circumstances were, that the Presbyterian congregations withdrew themselves in numbers from the parish churches, treated the curates with neglect and disrespect, and, seeking out their ancient preachers in the obscurity to which they had retired, begged and received from them the religious instruction which the deprived clergymen still thought it their duty to impart to those who needed and desired it, in despite of the additional severities imposed by the Government upon their doing so.

The Episcopal Church Courts, or Commission Courts, as they were termed, took upon them to find a remedy for the defection occasioned by the scruples of the people. Nine prelates, and thirty-five commissioners from the laity, of whom a bishop, with four assistants, made a quorum, were entrusted with the power of enforcing the acts for the preservation of the newly re-established Episcopal Church. These oppressive ecclesiastical courts were held wherever there was a complaint of nonconformity; and they employed all the rigours of long imprisonment, heavy fines, and corporal punishment, upon those who either abandoned the worship of their own parish church or went to hear the doctrine of the Presbyterian clergy whose private meetings for worship were termed conventicles.

These conventicles were at first held in private houses, barns, or other buildings, as was the case in England, where (though in a much more moderate degree and by milder measures) the general conformity of the Church was also enforced. But as such meetings, especially if numerously attended, were liable to be discovered and intruded upon by peace-officers and soldiers, who dispersed them rudely, sometimes plundering the men of their purses, and the women of their cloaks and plaids, the Scottish Presbyterians had recourse to an expedient of safety, suggested by the wild character of their country, and held these forbidden meetings in the open air, remote alike from observation and interruption, in wild, solitary, and mountainous places, where it was neither easy to find them nor safe to disturb them unless the force which assailed the congregation was considerable.

On the other hand, the Privy Council doubled their exertions to suppress, or rather to destroy, the whole body of nonconformists. But the attention of the English ministers had been attracted by the violence of their proceedings. Middleton began to fall into disfavour with Charles, and was sent as governor to Tangier in a kind of honourable banishment, where he lost the life which he had exposed to so many dangers in battle by a fall down a staircase.

Lauderdale, who succeeded to his power, had much more talent. He was ungainly in his personal appearance, being a big man with shaggy red hair, coarse features, and a tongue which seemed too large for his mouth. But he possessed a great portion of sense, learning, and wit. He was originally zealous for the Covenant, and his enemies at court had pressed forward the oaths by which it was to be renounced with the more eagerness, that they hoped Lauderdale would scruple to take them; but he only laughed at the idea of their supposing themselves capable of forming any oath which could obstruct the progress of his rise to political power.

Being now in full authority, Lauderdale distinctly perceived that the violent courses adopted were more likely to ruin Scotland than to establish Episcopacy. But he also knew that he could not retain the power he had obtained, unless by keeping on terms with Sharpe, the Primate of Scotland, and the other bishops, at whose instigation these wild measures were adopted and carried on; and it is quite consistent with Lauderdale's selfish and crafty character, to suppose that he even urged them on to further excesses, in order that, when the consequences had ruined their reputation, he might succeed to the whole of that power of which, at present, the prelates had a large share. The severities against dissenters, therefore, were continued; and the ruinous pecuniary penalties which were imposed on nonconformists were raised by quartering soldiers upon the delinquents, who were entitled to have lodging, meat, and drink in their houses and forage for their horses, without any payment till the fine was discharged. These men, who knew they were placed for the purpose of a punishment in the families where they were quartered, took care to be so insolent and rapacious that if selling the last article he had of any value could raise money, to rid him of these unwelcome guests, the unfortunate landlord was glad to part with them at whatever sacrifice.

The principal agents in this species of crusade against Calvinism were the soldiers of the King's horse-guards, a body raised since the Restoration upon the plan of the French household troops, the privates of which were accounted gentlemen, being frequently the younger sons of men of some pretension to family; cavaliers by profession, accustomed to practise the debauchery common among the dissolute youth of the period, and likely, from habit and inclination, to be a complete pest and torment to any respectable house in which they might be quartered. Other regiments of horse, upon the ordinary establishment, were raised for the same purpose.

The west of Scotland, and in particular Dumfriesshire, Ayrshire, and Galloway, were peculiarly harassed, as being more averse to the Episcopalian establishment, or, as the Council termed it, more refractory and obstinate than any others. For the purpose of punishing those nonconformists, Sir James Turner was sent thither with a considerable party of troops, and full commission from the Privy Council

to impose and levy fines and inflict all the other penalties for enforcing general compliance with the Episcopal system. Sir James was a
soldier of fortune, who had served under David Lesley and afterwards
in the army of Engagers, under the Duke of Hamilton. He was a man
of some literature, having written a treatise on the Art of War, and
some other works, besides his own Memoirs. Nevertheless, he
appears, by the account he gives of himself in his Memoirs, to have
been an unscrupulous plunderer, and other authorities describe him
as a fierce and dissolute character. In such hands the powers assigned
by the Commission were not likely to slumber, although Sir James
assures his readers that he never extorted above one-half of the fine
imposed. But a number of co-operating circumstances had rendered
the exercise of such a commission as was entrusted to him less safe
than it had hitherto been.

L

The Age of the Martyrdom

1665-1678

WHEN the custom of holding field conventicles was adopted, it had the effect of raising the minds of those who frequented them to a higher and more exalted pitch of enthusiasm. The aged and more timid could hardly engage on distant expeditions into the wild mountainous districts and the barren moors, and the greater part of those who attended divine worship on such occasions were robust of body and bold of spirit, or at least men whose deficiency of strength and courage were more than supplied by religious zeal. The view of the rocks and hills around them, while a sight so unusual gave solemnity to their acts of devotion, encouraged them in the natural thought of defending themselves against oppression, amidst the fortresses of nature's own construction, to which they had repaired to worship the God of nature, according to the mode their education dictated and their conscience acknowledged. The recollection that in these fastnesses their fathers had often found a safe retreat from foreign invaders must have encouraged their natural confidence, and it was confirmed by the success with which a stand was sometimes made against small bodies of troops, who were occasionally repulsed by the sturdy Whigs whom they attempted to disperse. In most cases of this kind they behaved with moderation, inflicting no further penalty upon such prisoners as might fall into their hands than detaining them to enjoy the benefit of a long sermon. Fanaticism added marvels to encourage this new-born spirit of resistance. They conceived themselves to be under the immediate protection of the Power whom they worshipped, and in their heated state of mind expected even miraculous interposition. At a conventicle held on one of the Lomond hills in Fife, it was reported and believed that an angelic form appeared in the air, hovering above the assembled congregation, with his foot advanced, as if in the act of keeping watch for their safety.

On the whole, the idea of repelling force by force, and defending themselves against the attacks of the soldiers, and others who assaulted them, when employed in divine worship, began to become more general among the harassed nonconformists. For this purpose many of the congregation assembled in arms, and I received the following description of such a scene from a lady whose mother had repeatedly been present on such occasions.

The meeting was held on the Eildon hills, in the bosom betwixt two of the three conical tops which form the crest of the mountain. Trusty sentinels were placed on advanced posts all around, so as to command a view of the country below, and give the earliest notice of the approach of any unfriendly party. The clergyman occupied an elevated temporary pulpit, with his back to the wind. There were few or no males of any quality or distinction, for such persons could not escape detection, and were liable to ruin from the consequences. But many women of good condition, and holding the rank of ladies, ventured to attend the forbidden meeting, and were allowed to sit in front of the assembly. Their side-saddles were placed on the ground to serve for seats, and their horses were *tethered,* or piqueted, as it is called, in the rear of the congregation. Before the females, and in the interval which divided them from the tent, or temporary pulpit, the arms of the men present, pikes, swords, and muskets, were regularly piled in such order as is used by soldiers, so that each man might in an instant assume his own weapons. When scenes of such a kind were repeatedly to be seen in different parts of the country, and while the Government relaxed none of that rigour which had thrown the nation into such a state, it was clear that a civil war could not be far distant.

It was in the autumn of 1666 that the severities of Sir James Turner, already alluded to, seem to have driven the Presbyterians of the west into a species of despair, which broke out into insurrection. Some accounts say, that a party of peasants having used force to deliver an indigent old man, whom a guard of soldiers, having pinioned and stretched upon the ground, were dragging to prison, in order to compel payment of a church fine, they reflected upon the penalties they had incurred by such an exploit, and resolved to continue in arms, and to set the Government at defiance. Another account affirms, that the poor people were encouraged to take up arms by an unknown person, calling himself Captain Gray, and pretending to have orders to call them out from superior persons, whom he did not name. By what means soever they were first raised, they soon assembled a number of peasants, and marched to Dumfries with such rapidity that they surprised Sir James Turner in his lodgings and seized on his papers and his money. Captain Gray took possession of the money and left the party, never to rejoin them; having, it is probable, discharged his task, when he had hurried these poor ignorant men into such a dangerous mutiny. Whether he was employed by some hot-headed Presbyterian, who thought the time favourable for a rising against the prelates, or whether by Government themselves, desirous of encouraging an insurrection which, when put down, might afford a crop of fines and forfeitures, cannot now be known.

The country gentlemen stood on their guard, and none of them joined the insurgents; but a few of the most violent of the Presbyterian ministers took part with them. Two officers of low rank were chosen to command so great an undertaking; their names were Wallace and Learmont. They held council together, whether they should put Sir James Turner to death or not; but he represented to them that, severe as they might think him, he had been much less so than his commission and instructions required and authorised; and as, upon examining his papers, he was found to have spoken the truth, his life was spared, and he was carried with them as a prisoner or hostage. Being an experienced soldier, he wondered to see the accurate obedience of these poor countrymen, the excellent order in which they marched, and their attention to the duties of outposts and sentinels. But, probably, no peasant of Europe is sooner able to adapt himself to military discipline than a native of Scotland, who is usually prudent enough to consider that it is only mutual co-operation and compliance with orders which can make numbers effectual.

When they had attained their greatest strength, and had assembled at Lanark, after two days' wandering, the insurgents might amount to three thousand men. They there issued a declaration, which bore that they acknowledged the King's authority and that the arms which they had assumed were only to be used in self-defence. But as, at the same time, they renewed the Covenant of which the principal object was, not to obtain for Presbytery a mere toleration, but a triumphant superiority, they would probably, as is usual in such cases, have extended or restricted their objects as success or disaster attended their enterprise.

Meantime, General Dalziel, commonly called Tom Dalziel, a remarkable personage of those times, had marched from Edinburgh at the head of a small body of regular forces, summoning all the lieges to join him, on pain of being accounted traitors. Dalziel had been bred in the Russian wars, after having served under Montrose. He was an enthusiastic Royalist, and would never shave his beard after the King's death. His dress was otherwise so different from what was then the mode, that Charles the Second used to accuse him of a plan to draw crowds of children together, that they might squeeze each other to death while they gazed on his singular countenance and attire.[1] He was a man of a fierce and passionate temper, as appears from his once striking a prisoner on the face, with the hilt of his dagger, till the blood sprung—an unmanly action, though he was provoked by the language of the man, who called the general "a Muscovian beast, who used to roast men."

This ferocious commander was advancing from Glasgow to Lanark, when he suddenly learned that the insurgents had given him the slip, and were in full march towards the capital. The poor men had been

---

[1] "Dalziel was bred up very hardy from his youth, both in diet and clothing. He never wore boots, nor above one coat, which was close to his body, with close sleeves, like those we call jockey-coats. He never wore a peruke, nor did he shave his beard since the murder of K. Charles I. In my time, his head was bald, which he covered only with a beaver hat, the brim of which was not above three inches broad. His beard was white and bushy, and yet reached down almost to his girdle. He usually went to London once or twice a year, and then only to kiss the King's hand, who had a great esteem for his worth and valour. His usual dress and figure when he was in London, never failed to draw after him a great crowd of boys and young people, who constantly attended at his lodgings and followed him with huzzas as he went to and from the Court. As he was a man of humour, he would always thank them for their civilities, when be left them, and let them know exactly at what hour he intended to return. In compliance to his Majesty, he went once to court in the very height of the fashion; but as soon as the King and those about him laughed sufficiently at the strange figure he made, he reassumed his usual habit, to the great joy of the boys, who had not discovered him in his court dress."—CAPT. CREICHTON'S *Memoirs, in Swift's Works.*

deceived into a belief that West Lothian was ready to rise in their favour, and that they had a large party of friends in the metropolis itself. Under these false hopes, they approached as far as Colinton, within four miles of Edinburgh. Here they learned that the city was fortified and cannon placed before the gates; that the College of Justice, which can always furnish a large body of serviceable men, was under arms, and, as their informer expressed it, every advocate in his bandaliers.[1] They learned at the same time that their own depressed party within the town had not the least opportunity or purpose of rising.

Discouraged with these news, and with the defection of many of their army—for their numbers were reduced to eight or nine hundred, dispirited and exhausted by want, disappointment, and fatigue—Learmont and Wallace drew back their diminished forces to the eastern shoulder of the Pentland hills, and encamped on an eminence called Rullion Green. They had reposed themselves for some hours, when, towards evening, they observed a body of horse coming through the mountains by a pass leading from the west. At first the Covenanters entertained the flattering dream that it was the expected reinforcement from West Lothian. But the standards and kettledrums made it soon evident that it was the vanguard of Dalziel's troops, which, having kept the opposite skirts of the Pentland ridge till they passed the village of Currie, had there learned the situation of the insurgents, and moved eastward in quest of them by a road through the hills.

Dalziel instantly led his men to the assault. The insurgents behaved with courage. They twice repulsed the attack of the Royalists. But it was renewed by a large force of cavalry on the insurgents' right wing, which bore down and scattered a handful of wearied horse who were there posted, and broke the ranks of the infantry. The slaughter in the field and in the chase was very small, not exceeding fifty men, and only a hundred and thirty were made prisoners. The King's cavalry, being composed chiefly of gentlemen, pitied their unfortunate countrymen, and made little slaughter; but many were intercepted and slain by the country people in the neighbourhood, who were unfriendly to their cause, and had sustained some pillage from their detached parties.

About twenty of the prisoners were executed at Edinburgh as rebels, many of them being put to the torture. This was practised in

---

[1] "The bandalier was a small wooden case covered with leather, containing a charge of powder for a musket; twelve generally hung on the same shoulder belt."

various ways—sometimes by squeezing the fingers with screws called thumbikins, sometimes by the *boot,* a species of punishment peculiar to Scotland. It consisted in placing the leg of the unfortunate person in a very strong wooden case, called a Boot, and driving down wedges between his knee and the frame, by which the limb was often crushed and broken.

But though these horrid cruelties could tear the flesh and crush the bones of the unfortunate victims, they could not abate their courage. Triumphing in the cause for which they died, they were seen at the place of execution contending which should be the first victim, while he who obtained the sad preference actually shouted for joy. Most of the sufferers, though very ignorant, expressed themselves with such energy on the subject of the principles for which they died, as had a strong effect on the multitude. But a youth named Hugh M'Kail, comely in person, well educated, and of an enthusiastic character, acted the part of a martyr in its fullest extent. He had taken but a small share in the insurrection but was chiefly obnoxious for a sermon in which he had said that the people of God had been persecuted by a Pharaoh or an Ahab on the throne, a Haman in the state, and a Judas in the church; words which were neither forgotten nor forgiven. He was subjected to extreme torture in order to wring from him some information concerning the causes and purposes of the rising; but his leg was crushed most cruelly in the boot without extracting from him a sigh or sound of impatience. Being then condemned to death, he spoke of his future state with a rapturous confidence, and took leave of the numerous spectators in the words of a dying saint, careless of his present suffering, and confident in his hopes of immortality.

"I shall speak no more with earthly creatures," he said, "but shall enjoy the aspect of the ineffable Creator himself.—Farewell, father, mother, and friends—farewell, sun, moon, and stars—farewell, perishable earthly delights—and welcome those which are everlasting—welcome, glory—welcome, eternal life—and welcome, death!"—There was not a dry eye among the spectators of his execution, and it began to be perceived by the authors of these severities, that the last words and firm conduct of this dying man made an impression on the populace the very reverse of what they desired. After this the superintendents of these executions resorted to the cruel expedient which had been practised when the Royalist followers of Montrose suffered, and caused trumpets to be sounded, and drums beaten, to drown the last words of these resolute men.

The vengeance taken for the Pentland rising was not confined to these executions in the capital. The shires of Galloway, Ayr, and Dumfries were subjected to military severities, and all who had the slightest connection with the rebellion were rigorously harassed. A party of Ayrshire gentlemen had gathered together for the purpose of joining the insurgents, but had been prevented from doing so. They fled from the consequences of their rashness; yet they were not only arraigned, and doom of forfeiture passed against them in their absence, but, contrary to all legal usage, the sentence was put in execution without their being heard in their defence; and their estates were conferred upon General Dalziel and General Drummond, or retained by the officers of state to enrich themselves.

But the period was now arrived which Lauderdale aimed at. The violence of the Government in Scotland at length attracted the notice of the English court; and when inquired into, was found much too gross to be tolerated. The Primate Sharpe was ordered to withdraw from administration; Lauderdale, with Tweeddale, Sir Robert Murray, and the Earl of Kincardine, were placed at the head of affairs, and it was determined by affording some relief to the oppressed Presbyterians to try at least the experiment of lenity towards them.

Such of the ejected clergy as had not given any particular offence were permitted to preach in vacant parishes, and even received some pecuniary encouragement from Government. This was termed the Indulgence. Had some such measure of toleration been adopted when Presbytery was first abolished, it might have been the means of preventing the frequency of conventicles; but, when resorted to in despair, as it were, of subduing them by violence, the mass of discontented Presbyterians regarded accession to the measure as a dishonourable accommodation with a government by whom they had been oppressed. It is true the gentry, and those who at once preferred Presbytery, and were unwilling to suffer in their worldly estate by that preference, embraced this opportunity to hear their favourite doctrines without risk of fine and imprisonment. The Indulged clergy were also men, for the most part, of wisdom and learning, who, being unable to vindicate the freedom and sovereignty of their Church, were contented to preach to and instruct their congregations, and discharge their duty as clergymen, if not to the utmost, at least as far as the evil times permitted.

But this modified degree of zeal by no means gratified the more ardent and rigid Covenanters, by whom the stooping to act under the Indulgence was accounted a compromise with the Malignants—a luke-warm and unacceptable species of worship, resembling salt which had lost its savour. Many, therefore, held the Indulged clergy as a species of king's curates; and rather than listen to their doctrines, which they might have heard in safety, followed into the wilderness those bold and daring preachers whose voices thundered forth avowed opposition and defiance against the mighty of the earth. The Indulged were accused of meanly adopting Erastian opinions, and acknowledging the depen-dence and subjection of the Church to the civil magistrate,—a doctrine totally alien from the character of the Presbyterian religion. The elevated wish of following the religion of their choice, in defiance of danger and fear, and their animosity against a government by whom they had been persecuted, induced the more zealous Presbyterians to prefer a conven-ticle to their parish church; and a congregation where the hearers attended in arms to defend themselves to a more peaceful meeting when, if surprised, they might save themselves by submission or flight. Hence these conventicles became frequent, at which the hearers attended with weapons. The romantic and dangerous character of this species of worship recommended it to such as were constitutionally bold and high-spirited; and there were others, who, from the idle spirit belonging to youth, liked better to ramble through the country as the lifeguard to some outlawed preacher, than to spend the six days of the week in ordinary labour, and attend their own parish church on the sev-enth, to listen to the lukewarm doctrine of an Indulged minister.

From all these reasons, the number of armed conventicles increased; and Lauderdale, incensed at the failure of his experiment, increased his severity against them, while the Indulgence was withdrawn as a measure inadequate to the intended purpose, though, perhaps, it chiefly failed for want of perseverance on the part of the Government.

As if Satan himself had suggested means of oppression, Lauderdale raked up out of oblivion the old and barbarous laws which had been adopted in the fiercest times, and directed them against the noncon-formists, especially those who attended the field conventicles. One of those laws inflicted the highest penalties upon persons who were inter-communed, as it was called—that is, outlawed by legal sentence. The nearest relations were prohibited from assisting each other, the wife the husband, the. brother the brother, and the parent the son, if the sufferers had been intercommuned. The Government of this cruel time applied these ancient and barbarous statutes to the outlawed Presbyterians of the period, and thus drove them altogether from human society. In danger, want, and necessity, the inhabitants of the wilderness, and expelled from civil intercourse, it is no wonder that we find many of these wanderers avowing principles and doctrines hostile to the Government which oppressed them, and carrying their resistance beyond the bounds of mere self-defence. There were instances, though less numerous than might have been expected, of their attacking the houses of the curates, or of others by whose information they had been accused of nonconformity; and several deaths ensued in those enterprises as well as in skirmishes with the military.

Superstitious notions, also, the natural consequences of an uncertain, melancholy, and solitary life among the desolate glens and mountains, mingled with the intense enthusiasm of this persecuted sect. Their occasional successes over their oppressors, and their frequent escapes from the pursuit of the soldiery, when the marksmen missed their aim, or when a sudden mist concealed the fugitives, were imputed, not to the operation of those natural causes by means of which the Deity is pleased to govern the world, and which are the engines of his power, but to the direct interposition of a miraculous agency, overruling and suspending the laws of nature, as in the period of Scripture history.

Many of the preachers, led away by the strength of their devotional enthusiasm, conceived themselves to be the vehicles of prophecy, and poured out tremendous denunciations of future wars, and miseries more dreadful than those which they themselves sustained; and, as they imagined themselves to be occasionally under the miraculous protection of the heavenly powers, so they often thought themselves in a peculiar manner exposed to the envy and persecution of the spirits of darkness, who lamed their horses when they were pursued, betrayed their footsteps to the enemy, or terrified them by ghastly apparitions in the dreary caverns and recesses where they were compelled to hide themselves.

But especially the scattered Covenanters believed firmly, that their chief persecutors received from the Evil Spirit a proof against leaden bullets—a charm, that is, to prevent their being pierced or wounded

by them. There were many supposed to be gifted with this necroman-
tic privilege. In the battle of Rullion Green, on the Pentland hills, many
of the Presbyterians were willing to believe that the balls were seen
hopping like hailstones from Tom Dalziel's buff coat and boots. Silver
bullets were not supposed to be neutralised by the same spell; but that
metal being scarce among the persecuted Covenanters, it did not afford
them much relief.

I have heard of an English officer, however, who fell by baser
metal. He was attacking a small house in Ayrshire, which was
defended by some of the Wanderers. They were firing on both sides,
when one of the defenders, in scarcity of ammunition, loaded his piece
with the iron ball which formed the top of the fire-tongs, and taking
aim at the officer with that charge, mortally wounded him whom lead
had been unable to injure. It is also said that the dying man asked to
know the name of the place where he fell; and being told it was
Caldens, or Caldons, he exclaimed against the Evil Spirit, who, he
said, had told him he was to be slain among the Chaldeans, but who
as it now appeared, had deceived him by cutting him off when his
death was totally unexpected.

To John Graham of Claverhouse, a Scottish officer of high rank,
who began to distinguish himself as a severe executor of the orders of
the Privy Council against nonconformists, the Evil Spirit was supposed
to have been still more liberal than to Dalziel, or to the Englishman who
died at Caldons. He not only obtained proof against lead, but the devil
is said to have presented him with a black horse, which had not a single
white hair upon its body. This horse, it was said, had been cut out of the
belly of its dam, instead of being born in the usual manner. On this
animal Claverhouse was supposed to perform the most unwonted feats
of agility, flying almost like a bird along the sides of precipitous hills,
and through pathless morasses, where an ordinary horse must have
been smothered or dashed to pieces. It is even yet believed, that
mounted on this steed, Claverhouse (or Clavers, as he is popularly
called) once turned a hare on the mountain named the Brandlaw, at the
head of Moffatdale, where no other horse could have kept its feet. But
these exertions were usually made whilst he was in pursuit of the Wanderers, which was considered as Satan's own peculiar pleasing work.

These superstitious notions were the natural consequences of the
dreary and precarious existence to which these poor fugitives were
condemned, and which induced them to view as miraculous whatever

was extraordinary. The persons supposed to be proof against bullets were only desperate and bold men who had the good fortune to escape the danger to which they fearlessly exposed themselves; and the equestrian exploits of Claverhouse, when stripped of exaggeration, were merely such as could be executed by any excellent horseman and first-rate horse to the amazement of those who were unaccustomed to witness feats of the kind.

The peculiar character and prejudices of the Covenanters are easily accounted for. Yet when it is considered that so many Scottish subjects were involved in the snares of these cruel laws, and liable to be prosecuted under them (the number is said to have reached eighteen or twenty thousand persons), it may seem wonderful that the Government could find a party in the kingdom to approve of and help forward measures as impolitic as they were cruel. But, besides the great command which the very worst government must always possess over those who look for advancement and employment under it, these things, it must be considered, took place shortly after the Royalists, the prevalent party at that time, had been themselves subjected to proscription, exile, judicial executions, and general massacre. The fate of Montrose and his followers, the massacres of Dunnavertie and Philiphaugh, above all, the murder of King Charles, had taken place during the predominance of the Presbyterians in Scotland, and were imputed, however unjustly, to their religious principles, which were believed by the Cavaliers to be inconsistent with law, loyalty, and good order. Under such mistaken sentiments, many of the late Royalist party lent their arms eagerly to suppress the adherents of a sect, to the pre-eminence of which they traced the general misery of the civil wars, and their own peculiar misfortunes.

Thus we find the Lady Methven of the day (a daughter of the house of Marischal, and wife of Patrick Smythe of Methven) interrupting a conventicle in person. A large meeting of this kind had assembled on the grounds of her husband, then absent in London, when the lady approached them at the head of about sixty followers and allies, she herself leading them on with a light-horseman's carabine ready cocked over her arm, and a drawn sword in the other hand. The congregation sent a party of a hundred armed men to demand her purpose, and the Amazonian lady protested, if they did not leave her husband's estate, it should be a bloody day. They replied that they were determined to preach, whether she would or not; but Dame Ann Keith's unshaken determination overcame their enthusiasm, and at length compelled them to retreat. After this affair, she wrote to her husband that she was providing arms, and even two pieces of cannon, hearing that the Whigs had sworn to be revenged for the insult she had put on them. "If the fanatics," she concludes, "chance to kill me, comfort yourself it shall not be for nought. I was once wounded for our gracious King, and now, in the strength of Heaven, I will hazard my person with the men I can command, before these rebels rest where you have power." No doubt Lady Methven acted against these "vagueing gipsies," as she terms them, with as much honesty and sincerity of purpose as they themselves entertained in resisting her.

But the principal agents of government, in the persecution of these oppressed people, were the soldiery, to whom, contrary to the rule in all civilised countries, unless in actual warfare, power was given to arrest, examine, detain, and imprison such persons as they should find in the wildernesses, which they daily ransacked to discover delinquents, whose persons might afford plunder, or their purses pay fines. One of these booted apostles, as the Presbyterians called the dragoons, Captain Creichton by name, has left his Memoirs in which he rather exults in, than regrets, the scenes of rapine and violence he had witnessed, and the plunder which he collected. The following is one of his stories:—

Being then a Life-guardsman, and quartered at Bathgate, he went out one Sunday on the moors with his comrade Grant, to try if they could discover any of the Wanderers. They were disguised like countrymen, in gray coats and bonnets. After eight or ten miles' walking, they descried three men on the top of a hill, whom they judged to be placed there as sentinels. They were armed with long poles. Taking precautions to come suddenly upon this outpost, Creichton snatched one of the men's poles from him, and asking what he meant by carrying such a pole on the Lord's day, immediately knocked him down. Grant secured another—the third fled to give the alarm, but Creichton overtook and surprised him also, though armed with a pistol at his belt. They were then guided onward to the conventicle by the voice of the preacher, Master John King (afterwards executed), which was so powerful that Creichton professes he heard him distinctly at a quarter of a mile's distance, the wind favouring his force of lungs.

The meeting was very numerously attended; nevertheless, the two troopers had the temerity to approach, and commanded them in the

King's name to disperse. Immediately forty of the congregation arose in defence, and advanced upon the troopers, when Creichton, observing a handsome horse with a lady's pillion on it, grazing near him, seized it, and leaping on its back, spurred through the morasses, allowing the animal to choose its own way. Grant, though on foot, kept up with his comrade for about a mile, and the whole conventicle followed in full hue and cry, in order to recover the palfrey, which belonged to a lady of distinction. When Grant was exhausted, Creichton gave him the horse in turn, and being both armed with sword and pistol, they forced their way through such of the conventiclers as attempted to intercept them, and gained the house of a gentleman whom Creichton calls Laird of Poddishaw. Here they met another gentleman of fortune, the Laird of Polkemmet, who, greatly to his disturbance, recognised, in the horse which the troopers had brought off, his own lady's nag on which without his knowledge, as he affirmed, she had used the freedom to ride to the conventicle. He was now at the mercy of the Life-guardsman, being liable to a heavy fine for his wife's delinquency, besides the forfeiture of the palfrey. In this dilemma, Mr. Baillie of Polkemmet invited the Life-guardsman to dine with him next day, and offered them the horse with its furniture as a lawful prize. But Creichton, perceiving that the lady was weeping, very gallantly gave up his claim to the horse, on condition she would promise never to attend a conventicle again. The military gentlemen were no losers by this liberality; for as the lady mentioned the names of some wealthy persons who were present at the unlawful meeting, her husband gave the parties concerned to understand that they must make up a purse of hush-money for the benefit of Creichton and his comrade, who lived plentifully for a twelvemonth afterwards on the sum thus obtained.

This story, though it shows the power trusted to the soldiers, to beat and plunder the persons assembled for religious worship, is rather of a comic than a serious cast. But far different were the ordinary encounters which took place between the Covenanters and the military. About forty or fifty years ago, melancholy tales of the strange escapes, hard encounters, and cruel exactions of this period, were the usual subject of conversation at every cottage fireside; and the peasants, while they showed the caverns and the dens of the earth in which the Wanderers concealed themselves, recounted how many of them died in resisting, with arms in their hands, how many others were executed by judicial forms, and how many were shot to death without even the least pretence of a trial. The country people retained a strong sense of the injustice with which their ancestors had been treated, which showed itself in a singular prejudice. They expressed great dislike of that beautiful bird the Green-plover, in Scottish called the Peaseweep. The reason alleged was that these birds being, by some instinct, led to attend to and watch any human beings whom they see in their native wilds, the soldiers were often guided in pursuit of the Wanderers, when they might otherwise have escaped observation, by the plover being observed to hover over a particular spot. For this reason the shepherds, within my own remembrance, often destroyed the nests of this bird when they met with them.

A still sadder memorial of those calamitous days was the number of headstones and other simple monuments which, after the Revolution, were erected over the graves of the persons thus destroyed, and which usually bore, along with some lines of rude poetry, an account of the manner in which they had been slain.

These mortal resting-places of the victims of persecution were held so sacred, that about forty years since an aged man dedicated his life to travel through Scotland, for the purpose of repairing and clearing the tombs of the sufferers. He always rode upon a white pony, and from that circumstance, and the peculiarity of his appearance and occupation, acquired the nickname of Old Mortality.[1] In later days, the events of our own time have been of such an engrossing character that this species of traditional history is much forgotten, and moss and weeds are generally suffered to conceal the monuments of the martyrs.

---

[1] See the Introduction (1830) to *Old Mortality*.

LI

On to Bothwell Bridge

1678-1679

WE have said before that Lauderdale, now the Chief Minister for Scotland, had not originally approved of the violent measures taken with the nonconformists, and had even recommended a more lenient mode of proceeding, by granting a toleration, or Indulgence, as it was called, for the free exercise of the Presbyterian religion. But being too impatient to wait the issue of his own experiment, and fearful of being represented as lukewarm in the King's service, he at length imitated and even exceeded Middleton, in his extreme severities against the nonconformists.

The Duke of Lauderdale, for to that rank he was raised when the Government was chiefly entrusted to him, married Lady Dysart, a woman of considerable talent, but of inordinate ambition, boundless expense, and the most unscrupulous rapacity. Her influence over her husband was extreme and, unhappily, was of a kind which encouraged him in his greatest errors. In order to supply her extravagance, he had recourse to the public fines for nonconformity, church penalties, and so forth, prosecutions for which, with other violent proceedings we have noticed, were pushed on to such an extremity as to induce a general opinion that Lauderdale really meant to drive the people of Scotland to a rebellion, in order that he himself might profit by the confiscations which must follow on its being subdued.

The Scottish nobility and gentry were too wise to be caught in this snare; but although they expressed the utmost loyalty to the King, yet many, with the Duke of Hamilton, the premier peer of Scotland, at their head, remonstrated against courses which, while they beggared the tenantry, impoverished the gentry and ruined their estates. By way of answer to their expostulations, the western landholders were required to enter into bonds, under the same penalties which were incurred by those who were actual delinquents, that neither they nor their families, nor their vassals, tenants, or other persons residing on their property, should withdraw from church, attend conventicles, or relieve intercommuned persons. The gentry refused to execute these bonds. They admitted that conventicles were become very frequent, and expressed their willingness to assist the officers of the law in suppressing them; but, as they could exercise no forcible control over their tenants and servants, they declined to render themselves responsible for their conformity. Finally, they recommended a general indulgence, as the only measure which promised the restoration of tranquillity.

Both parties, at that unhappy period (1678), were in the habit of imputing the measures of their enemies to the suggestions of Satan; but that adopted by Lauderdale, upon the western gentlemen's refusing the bond, had really some appearance of being composed under the absolute dictation of an evil spirit. He determined to treat the whole west country as if in a state of actual revolt. He caused not only a body of the guards and militia, with field artillery, to march into the devoted districts, but invited, for the same purpose, from the Highland mountains, the clans by which they were inhabited. These wild mountaineers descended under their different chiefs, speaking an unknown language, and displaying to the inhabitants of the Lowlands their strange attire, obsolete arms, and singular manners. The clans were surprised in their turn. They had come out expecting to fight, when, to their astonishment, they found an innocent, peaceful, and unresisting country in which they were to enjoy free quarters, and full license for plunder. It may be supposed that such an invitation to men to whom marauding habits were natural offered opportunities not to be lost, and accordingly the western counties long had occasion to lament the inroad of the Highland Host. A committee of the Privy Council, most of whom were themselves chiefs of clans, or commanders in the army, attended to secure the submission of the gentry, and enforce the bonds. But the noblemen and gentry continuing obstinate in their refusal to come under obligations which they had no means of fulfilling, the Privy Council issued orders to disarm the whole inhabitants of the country, taking even the gentlemen's swords, riding horses, and furniture, and proceeding with such extreme rigour that the Earl of Cassilis, among others, prayed they would either afford him the protection of soldiers or return him some of his arms to defend his household, since otherwise he must be subject to the insolence and outrages of the most paltry of the rabble.

To supply the place of the bonds, which were subscribed by few or none, this unhappy Privy Council fell upon a plan, by a new decree, of a nature equally oppressive. There was, and is, a writ in Scotland, called *lawburrows,* by which a man who is afraid of violence from his neighbour, upon making oath to the circumstances affording ground for such apprehension, may have the party bound over to keep the peace, under security. Of this useful law, a most oppressive application was now made. The King was made to apply for a lawburrows throughout a certain district of his dominions, against all the gentlemen who had refused to sign the bond; and thus an attempt was made to extort security from every man so situated, as one of whom the King had a natural right to entertain well-founded apprehensions!

These extraordinary provisions of law seem to have driven not the Presbyterians alone, but the whole of the west country, into absolute despair.

No supplication or remonstrance had the least effect on the impenetrable Lauderdale. When he was told that the oppression of the Highlanders and of the soldiery would totally interrupt the produce of agriculture, he replied, "It were better that the west bore nothing but windle-straws and sandy-lave-rocks,[1] than that it should bear rebels to the King." In their despair, the suffering parties determined to lay their complaints against the Minister before the King in person. With this purpose, not less than fourteen peers, and fifteen gentlemen, of whom many were threatened with writs of lawburrows, repaired to London to lay their complaints at the foot of the throne. This journey was taken in spite of an arbitrary order, by which the Scottish nobility had been forbidden, in the King's name, either to approach the King's person or to

---

[1] Dog's grass and sea-larks.

leave their own kingdom; as if it had been the purpose to chain them to the stake, like baited bears, without the power of applying for redress, or escaping from the general misery.

Lauderdale had so much interest at court as to support himself against this accusation by representing to the King that it was his object to maintain a large army in Scotland, to afford assistance when his Majesty should see it time to extend his authority in England. He retained his place, therefore, and the supplicants were sent from court in disgrace.[1] But their mission had produced some beneficial effects; for the measures concerning the lawburrows and the enforced bonds were withdrawn, and orders given for removing the Highlanders from the west counties, and disbanding the militia.

When the Highlanders went back to their hills, which was in February 1678, they appeared as if returning from the sack of some besieged town. They carried with them plate, merchant-goods, webs of linen and of cloth, quantities of wearing apparel, and household furniture, and a good number of horses to bear their plunder. It is, however, remarkable, and to the credit of this people, that they are not charged with any cruelty during three months' residence at free quarters, although they were greedy of spoil and rapacious in extorting money. Indeed, it seems probable that, after all, the wild Highlanders had proved gentler than was expected, or wished, by those who employed them.

An event now occurred, one of the most remarkable of the time, which had a great effect upon public affairs and the general feeling of the nation. This was the murder of James Sharp, Archbishop of St. Andrews and Primate of Scotland. This person, you must remember, having been the agent of the Presbyterians at the time of the Restoration, had, as was generally thought, betrayed his constituents; at least, he had certainly changed his principles, and accepted the highest office in the new Episcopal establishment. It may be well supposed that a person so much hated as he was, from his desertion of the old cause and violence in the new, was the object of general hostility, and that, amongst a sect so enthusiastic as the nonconformists, some one should be found to exercise judgment upon him—in other words, to take his life.

---

[1] "It is reported that Charles, after a full hearing of the debates concerning Scottish affairs, said, 'I perceive that Lauderdale has been guilty of many bad things against the people of Scotland; but I cannot find that he has acted anything contrary to my interest;' a sentiment unworthy of a sovereign."—HUME.

The avenger who first conceived himself called to this task was one Mitchell, a fanatical preacher, of moderate talents and a heated imagination. He fired a pistol, loaded with three bullets, into the coach of the Archbishop, and missing the object of his aim, broke the arm of Honeyman, Bishop of the Orkneys, who sat with Sharp in the carriage, of which wound he never entirely recovered, though he lingered for some years. The assassin escaped during the confusion. This was in 1668, and in 1674 the Archbishop again observed a man who seemed to watch him, and whose face was imprinted upon his mind. The alarm was given, and Mitchell was seized. Being closely examined by the Lords of the Privy Council, he at first absolutely denied the act charged against him. But to the Chancellor he confessed in private—having at first received a solemn promise that his life should be safe—that he had fired the shot which wounded the Bishop of Orkney. After this compromise, the assassin's trial was put off from time to time, from the determined desire to take the life which had been promised to him. In order to find matter against Mitchell, be was examined concerning his accession to the insurrection of Pentland; and as he refused to confess anything which should make against himself, he was appointed to undergo the torture of the boot.

He behaved with great courage when the frightful apparatus was produced, and not knowing, as he said, that he could escape such torture with life, declared that he forgave from his heart those at whose command it was to be inflicted, the men appointed to be the agents of their cruelty, and those who satiated their malevolence by looking on as spectators. When the executioner demanded which leg should be enclosed in the dreadful boot, the prisoner, with the same confidence, stretched out his right leg, saying, "Take the best; I willingly bestow it in this cause." He endured nine blows of the mallet with the utmost firmness, each more severely crushing the limb. At the ninth blow he fainted, and was remanded to prison. After this he was sent to the Bass, a desolate islet, or rather rock, in the Firth of Forth, where was a strong castle then occupied as a state prison.

On the 7th of January 1678, ten years after the deed was committed, and four years after he was made prisoner, Mitchell was finally brought to his trial; and while his own confession was produced against him as evidence, he was not allowed to plead the promise of life upon which he had been induced to make the fatal avowal. It is shameful to be obliged to add that the Duke of Lauderdale would not permit the records of the Privy Council to be produced and that some of the privy councillors swore that no assurance of life had been granted, although it had been accurately entered and is now to be seen on the record. The unfortunate man was therefore condemned. Lauderdale, it is said, would have saved his life; but the Archbishop demanding his execution as necessary to guard the lives of privy councillors from such attempts in future, the Duke gave up the cause with a profane and brutal jest, and the man was executed, with more disgrace to his judges than to himself, the consideration of his guilt being lost in the infamous manœuvres used in bringing him to punishment.

I have already said that, in the commencement of Lauderdale's administration, Archbishop Sharp was removed from public affairs. But this did not last long, as the Duke found that he could not maintain his interest at court without the support of the Episcopal party. The primate's violence of disposition was supposed to have greatly influenced the whole of Lauderdale's latter government. But in Fife, where he had his archiepiscopal residence, it was most severely felt; and as the nonconformists of that county were fierce and enthusiastic in proportion to the extremity of persecution which they underwent, there was soon found a band among them who sent abroad an anonymous placard, threatening that any person who might be accessary to the troubles inflicted upon the Whigs in that county should be suitably punished by a party strong enough to set resistance at defiance.

The chief person among these desperate men was David Hackston of Rathillet, a gentleman of family and fortune. He had been a free liver in his youth, but latterly had adopted strong and enthusiastic views of religion, which led him into the extreme opinions entertained by the fiercest of the Whig party. John Balfour of Kinloch, called Burley, the brother-in-law of Hackston, is described by a covenanting author as a little man of stern aspect, and squint-eyed; none of the most religious, but very willing to engage in any battles or quarrels which his comrades found it necessary to sustain. He was at this time in danger from the law, on account of a late affray, in which he had severely wounded one of the Life-guards. It is alleged that both these persons had private enmity at Archbishop Sharp. Balfour had been his factor in the management of some property, and had failed to give account of the money he had received; and Hackston, being bail for his brother-in-law, was thrown into jail till the debt was made good. The remainder of the band were either small proprietors of land, or portioners, as they are called in Scotland, or mechanics, such as weavers and the like.

These enthusiasts, to the number of nine, were out, and in arms, on 3d May 1679, with the purpose of assaulting (in the terms of their proclamation) one Carmichael, who acted as a commissioner for receiving the fines of the nonconformists. This person had indeed been in the fields hunting that morning, but chancing to hear that there was such a party looking out for him, he left his sport and went home.

When Rathillet and his friends were about to disperse in sullen disappointment, the wife of a farmer at Baldinny sent a lad to tell them that the Archbishop's coach was upon the road returning from Ceres towards St. Andrews. The conspirators were in that mood when our own wishes and thoughts, strongly fostered and cherished, are apt to seem to us like inspiration from above. Balfour, of Burley, affirmed he had felt a preternatural impulse forcing him to return to Fife, when it was his purpose to have gone to the Highlands, and that on going to prayers he had been confirmed by the Scripture text, "Go, have not I sent thee?" Russell, another of the party, also affirmed he had been long impressed with the idea that some great enemy to the Church was to be cut off, and spoke of some text about Nero, which assuredly does not exist in Scripture.

They all agreed, in short, that the opportunity offered was the work of Heaven; that they should not draw back, but go on; and that instead of the inferior agent for whom they had been seeking in vain, it was their duty to cut off the prime source of the persecution, whom Heaven had delivered into their hands. This being determined upon, the band chose Hackston for their leader; but he declined the office, alleging that the known quarrel betwixt him and the Archbishop would mar the glory of the action, and cause it to be imputed to private revenge. But he added, with nice distinction, that he would remain with them, and would not interfere to prevent what they felt themselves called upon to do. Upon this Balfour said, "Gentlemen, follow me."

They then set off at speed in pursuit of the carriage, which was driving along a desolate heath, about three or four miles from St. Andrews, called Magus Moor.[1] Fleming and Russell, two of the assassins, rode into

---

[1] The precise spot of Sharp's death is now enclosed in a plantation about three miles to the west of St. Andrews.

a farmyard, and demanded of the tenant if the equipage on the road before them was the Archbishop's coach. Guessing their purpose, he was too much frightened to answer; but one of the female servants came out and assured them, with much appearance of joy, that they were on the right scent. The whole party then threw away their cloaks, and pursued as fast as they could gallop, firing their carabines on the carriage, and crying out, "Judas, be taken!" The coachman drove rapidly, on seeing they were pursued by armed men; but a heavy coach on a rugged road could not outstrip horsemen. The servants who attended the carriage offered some resistance, but were dismounted and disarmed by the pursuers. Having come up with the carriage, they stopped it by cutting the traces and wounding the postilion, and then fired a volley of balls into the coach, where the Archbishop was seated with his daughter. This proving ineffectual, they commanded the prelate to come forth and prepare for death, judgment, and eternity. The old man came out of the coach, and creeping on his knees towards Hackston, said, "I know you are a gentleman—you will protect me?"

"I will never lay a hand upon you," said Hackston, turning away from the suppliant.

One man of the party, touched with some compassion, said, "Spare his gray hairs."

But the rest of the assassins were unmoved. One or two pistols were discharged at the prostrate Archbishop without effect; when conceiving, according to their superstitious notion, that their victim was possessed of a charm against gun-shot, they drew their swords, and killed him with many wounds, dashing even his skull to pieces, and scooping out his brains. The lady,[1] who made vain attempts to throw herself between her father and the swords of the assassins, received one or two wounds in the scuffle. They rifled the coach of such arms and papers as it contained. They found some trinkets, which they conceived were magical; and also, as they pretended, a bee in a box, which they concluded was a familiar spirit.

Such was the progress and termination of a violent and wicked deed, committed by blinded and desperate men. It brought much scandal on the Presbyterians, though unjustly; for the moderate persons of that persuasion, comprehending the most numerous and by far

---

[1] Isabella, the Archbishop's eldest daughter, was afterwards married to John Cunningham, Esq. of Barns, in the county of Fife.

the most respectable of the body, disowned so cruel an action, although they might be at the same time of opinion that the Archbishop, who had been the cause of violent death to many, merited some such termination to his own existence. He had some virtues, being learned, temperate, and living a life becoming his station; but his illiberal and intolerant principles, and the violences which he committed to enforce them, were the cause of great distress to Scotland, and of his own premature and bloody end.

The Scottish Government, which the Archbishop's death had alarmed and irritated in the highest degree, used the utmost exertions to apprehend his murderers; and failing that, to disperse and subdue, by an extremity of violence greater than what had been hitherto employed, every assembly of armed Covenanters. All attendance upon field-conventicles was declared treason; new troops were raised, and the strictest orders sent to the commanding officers to act against nonconformists with the utmost rigour. On the other band, the intercommuned persons, now grown desperate, assembled in more numerous and better armed parties, and many of them showed a general purpose of defiance and rebellion against the King's authority, which the moderate party continued to acknowledge, as being that of the supreme civil magistrate. These circumstances soon led to a crisis.

Several of the murderers of the Archbishop of St. Andrews found their way, through great dangers, to the west of Scotland; and their own interest, doubtless, induced them to use such influence as they had acquired among the zealots of their sect by their late action, to bring matters to extremity.

Hackston, Balfour, and others, seem to have held council with Donald Cargill, one of the most noted of the preachers at conventicles, and particularly with Robert Hamilton, brother to the Laird of Prestonfield; in consequence of which they appeared at the head of eighty horse, in the little burgh of Rutherglen, on the 29th of May, appointed to be held as a holiday, as the anniversary of the Restoration of Charles II. They quenched the bonfires, which had been kindled on account of this solemnity, and, drawing up in order at the market-cross, after prayer, and singing part of a psalm, they formally entered their protest, or testimony, as they called it, against the acts abolishing Presbytery, and establishing Episcopacy, together with the other defections of the time, all of which they renounced and disclaimed. After this bravado, they affixed a copy of their testimony to the cross, closed their meeting with prayer, and then evacuated the town at their leisure, Hamilton harbouring the Fife gentlemen, that is, those who had killed the Archbishop.

We have already mentioned John Graham of Claverhouse as a distinguished officer, who bad been singularly active against the nonconformists. He was now lying in garrison at Glasgow, and on the 1st of June drew out his own troop of dragoons, with such other cavalry as he could hastily add to it, and set off in quest of the insurgents who had offered such a public affront to Government.

In the town of Hamilton he made prisoner John King, a preacher, and with him seventeen countrymen who were attending on his ministry; and hearing of a larger assembly of insurgents who were at Loudon Hill, a short distance off, he pushed forward to that place. Here Claverhouse was opposed by a large body in point of numbers, but very indifferently armed, though there were about fifty horse tolerably appointed, as many infantry with guns, and a number of men armed with scythes, forks, pikes, and halberds. The immediate spot on which the parties met was called Drumclog.[1] It is a boggy piece of ground, unfit for the acting of cavalry, and a broad drain, or ditch, seems also to have given the insurgents considerable advantage. A short but warm engagement ensued during which Balfour, and William Cleland, to be afterwards mentioned, crossed the ditch boldly, and outflanking the dragoons, compelled them to fly. About thirty of the defeated party were slain, or died of their wounds. An officer of the name of Graham, a kinsman of Claverhouse, was among the slain. His body, mistaken, it is reported, for that of his namesake, was pitifully mangled. Claverhouse's own horse was laid open by the blow of a scythe, and was scarcely able to bear him off the field of battle. As he passed the place where he had left his prisoners, King, the preacher, when he beheld his captor in this pitiful plight, hollo'd out to him to stay and take the afternoon sermon. Some Royalist prisoners were taken, to whom quarter was given, and they were dismissed. This clemency on the part of his soldiers greatly disgusted Mr. Hamilton, who now assumed the command of the insurgents. To show a good example, he killed one of the defenceless captives with his own hand, lenity being, according to his exaggerated ideas, the setting free the brats of Babel, after they had been delivered into their

---

[1] The spot is a mile westward of the road from Kilmarnock to Strathaven, and about five miles from the last named town.

hands, that they might dash them to the stones. The insurgents lost only five or six men, one of whom, named Dingwall, had assisted at the murder of the Archbishop.

After having gained this victory, the insurgents resolved to keep the field and take such future fortune as Heaven should send them. They marched to Hamilton after the action, and the next day, strongly reinforced by the numbers which joined them on all sides, they proceeded to attack the town of Glasgow.

The city was defended by Lord Ross and Claverhouse, with a small but regular force. The insurgents penetrated into the town from two points, one column advancing up the Gallowgate, the other entering by the College and the Wynd Head. But Claverhouse, who commanded the King's troops, had formed a barricade about the cross, Townhouse, and Tolbooth, so that the Whigs, in marching to the attack, were received with a fire which they could not sustain, from an enemy who lay sheltered and in safety. But although they were beaten for the present, the numbers of the insurgents began to increase so much, that Ross and Claverhouse judged it necessary to evacuate Glasgow, and march eastward, leaving all the west of Scotland at the mercy of the rebels, whose numbers speedily amounted to five or six thousand men. There were among them, however, very few gentlemen, or persons of influence, whose presence might have prevented them from falling into the state of disunion to which, owing to the following circumstances, they were speedily reduced. They erected a huge tall gallows in the centre of their camp for the execution of such enemies as they should make prisoners, and hanged upon it at least one citizen of Glasgow, who had joined in the defence of the town against their former attack. But this vindictive mode of proceeding did not meet with general approbation in their army.

The discord was now at its height between the moderate Presbyterians, who were willing to own the King's government, under the condition of obtaining freedom of conscience; and the more hot-headed and furious partisans, who would entertain no friendship or fellowship with those who owned and supported prelacy, and who held the acknowledging the Government, or the listening to the preachers who ministered by their indulgence or connivance, as a foul compromising of the cause of Presbytery, and professed it their object to accomplish a complete revolution in church and state, and render the kirk as triumphant as it had been in 1640.

The preachers likewise differed amongst themselves. Mr. John Welsh, much famed for his zeal for Presbytery, together with Mr. David Hume, headed the Moderate, or, as it was called by their opponents, the Erastian party; whilst Donald Cargill, Thomas Douglas, and John King, espoused with all ardour the more extravagant purposes, which nothing short of a miracle could have enabled them to accomplish. These champions of the two parties preached against each other from the pulpit, harangued and voted on different sides in councils of war, and had not the sense to agree, or even to adjourn their disputes, when they heard that the forces of both England and Scotland were collecting to march against their undisciplined army, ill-provided as it was with arms, and at variance concerning the causes which had brought them into the field.

While the insurgents were thus quarrelling among themselves, and incapable of taking any care of their common cause, the Privy Council ordered out the militia, and summoned to arms the vassals of the crown; many of whom, being inclined to Presbytery, came forth with no small reluctance. The Highland chiefs who lay near the scene of action were also ordered to attend the King's host with their followers.

But when the news of the insurrection reached London, Charles II., employing for a season his own good judgment, which he too often yielded to the management of others, seems to have formed an idea of conciliating the rebels, as well as of subduing them. For this purpose, he sent to Scotland, as commander-in-chief, his natural son, James, Duke of Monmouth, at the head of a large body of the Royal guards. This young nobleman was the King's favourite, both from the extreme beauty of his person and the amiableness of his disposition. Charles had taken care of his fortune, by uniting him with the heiress of the great family of Buccleuch, whose large estates are still enjoyed by their descendants. Wealthy, popular, and his father's favourite, the Duke of Monmouth had been encouraged to oppose his own court influence to that of the King's brother, the Duke of York; and as the latter had declared himself a Roman Catholic, so Monmouth, to mark the distinction betwixt them, was supposed to be favourable to Presbyterians, as well as dissenters of any sect, and was popularly called the Protestant Duke. It was naturally supposed that, having such inclinations, he was entrusted with some powers favourable to the insurgents.

These unfortunate persons having spent a great deal of time in debating on Church polemics, lost sight of the necessity of disciplining their army or supplying it with provisions, and were still lying in the vicinity of the town of Hamilton, while numbers, despairing of their success, were every day deserting them. On the 21st of June they were alarmed by the intelligence that the Duke of Monmouth was advancing at the head of a well-disciplined army. This did not recall them to their senses; they held a council, indeed, but it was only to engage in a furious debate, which lasted until Rathillet told them his sword was drawn, as well against those who accepted the Indulgence, as against the curates, and withdrew from the council after this defiance, followed by those who professed his principles.

The moderate party, thus left to themselves, drew up a supplication to the Duke of Monmouth, and after describing their intolerable grievances, declared that they were willing to submit all controversies to a free Parliament, and a free assembly of the Church.

The Duke, in reply, expressed compassion for their condition, and a wish to alleviate it by his intercession with the King, but declared they must in the interim lay down their arms. When they received this message, the insurgent troops were in the greatest disorder, the violent party having chosen this unfortunate moment for cashiering the officers whom they had formerly appointed, and nominating others who had no taint of Erastianism or Malignity; in other words, no disposition to acknowledge any allegiance to the King, or submission to the civil power. While they were thus employed, the troops of Monmouth appeared in sight.

The insurgents were well posted for defence. They had in front the Clyde, a deep river, not easily fordable, and only to be crossed by Bothwell Bridge, which gives name to the battle. This is (or rather was, for though it still exists, it is now much altered) a high, steep, and narrow bridge, having a portal, or gateway, in the centre, which the insurgents had shut and barricaded. About three hundred men were stationed to defend this important pass, under Rathillet, Balfour, and others. They behaved well, and made a stout defence till the soldiers of Monmouth forced the pass at the point of the bayonet. The insurgents then gave way, and the Royal army advanced towards the main body, who, according to the historian Burnet, seem neither to have had the grace to submit, the courage to fight, nor the sense to run away. They stood a few minutes in doubt and confusion, their native courage and enthusiasm frozen by the sense of discord amongst themselves, and the sudden approach of an army superior in discipline. At length, as the artillery began to play upon them, and the horse and Highlanders were about to charge, they gave way without resistance, and dispersed like a flock of sheep.

The gentle-tempered Duke of Monmouth gave strict orders to afford quarter to all who asked it, and to make prisoners, but spare lives. Considerable slaughter, it is said, took place, notwithstanding his orders, partly owing to the unrelenting temper of Claverhouse, who was burning to obtain vengeance for the defeat of Drumclog, and the death of his kinsman, who was slain there, and partly to the fury of the English soldiers and the Scottish Highlanders, who distinguished themselves by their cruelty.

Four hundred men were killed at the battle of Bothwell Bridge, and about twelve hundred made prisoners. These last were marched to Edinburgh, and imprisoned in the Greyfriars' Churchyard, like cattle in a pen-fold, while several ministers and others were selected for execution. The rest, after long confinement there, and without any shelter save two or three miserable sheds, and such as they found in the tombs, were dismissed, upon giving bonds for conformity in future; the more obstinate were sent as slaves to the plantations. Many of the last were lost at sea. And yet, notwithstanding these disasters, the more remote consequences of the battle of Bothwell Bridge were even more calamitous than those which were direct and immediate.

LII

The Cameronians

1679-1685

THE efforts made by Monmouth obtained an indemnity which was ill-observed, and a limited indulgence which was speedily recalled; and instead of the healing measures which were expected, severe inquisition was made into the conduct of the western proprietors, accused of favouring the insurrection, and that of the gentlemen who had failed to join the King's host, when assembled to put it down. The excuses made for this desertion of duty were singular enough, being in many cases a frank confession of the defaulters' fear of disquiet from their wives, some of whom invoked bitter curses on their husbands, if they took either horse or man to do prejudice to the fanatics who were in arms. To these excuses the court paid no heed, but fined the absentees heavily and even threatened forfeiture of their lands.

The mild influence of Monmouth in the administration of Scotland lasted but a short while; and that of Lauderdale, though he was now loaded with age as well as obloquy, in a great measure revived, until it was superseded by the arrival in Scotland of James, Duke of York, the King's brother, and heir-presumptive of the throne.

We have already said that this prince was a Catholic, and indeed it was his religion which had occasioned his exile, first to Brussels, and now to Scotland. The King consented to his brother's banishment as an unavoidable measure, the utmost odium having been excited against all Catholics by the alleged discovery of a plot amongst the Papists, to rise upon and massacre the Protestants, depose the King, and put his brother on the throne. The whole structure of this story is now allowed to have been gross lies and forgeries, but at this period to doubt it was to be as bad as the Papists themselves. The first fury of national prejudice having begun to subside, James was recalled from Brussels to Scotland in order to be nearer his brother, though still at such a distance as should not again arouse the jealousy of the irritable Protestants.

The Duke of York was of a character very different from his brother Charles. He had neither that monarch's wit nor his levity, was fond of business, and capable of yielding strict attention to it, and, without being penurious, might be considered as an economist. He was attached to his religion with a sincerity honourable to him as a man, but unhappy for him as a prince destined to reign over a Protestant people. He was severe even to cruelty and nourished the same high idea of the divine right of kings, and the duty of complete submission on the part of subjects, which was the original cause of his father's misfortunes.

On the Duke of York's arrival in Scotland, he was received with great marks of honour and welcome by the nobles and gentry, and occupied the palace of Holyrood, which had long been untenanted by Royalty. He exerted himself much to conciliate the affections of the Scottish persons of condition; and his grave and lofty, yet courteous, manners suited well the character of a people who, proud and reserved themselves, willingly pay much respect to the etiquette of rank, providing those entitled to such deference are contented to admit their claims to respect in return.

The Duke of York, it is said, became aware of the punctilious character of the Scottish nation, from a speech of the well-known Tom Dalziel. The Duke had invited this old cavalier to dine in private with him, and his Duchess, Mary of Este, daughter of the Duke of Modena. This princess chose to consider it as a derogation from her rank to admit a subject to her table, and refused to sit down to dinner if Dalziel should remain as a visitor. "Madam," said the undismayed veteran, "I have dined at a table where your father might have stood at my back." He alluded to that of the Emperor of Germany, whom the Duke of Modena must, if summoned, have attended as an officer of the household.

The spirit of the answer is said to have determined James, while holding intercourse with the Scottish nobles and gentry, to exercise as much affability as he could command or affect, which, with the gravity and dignity of his manners, gave him great influence among all who approached his person. He paid particular attention to the chiefs of Highland clans, made himself acquainted with their different interests and characters, and exerted himself to adjust and reconcile their feuds. By such means, he acquired among this primitive race, alike sensible to kind treatment and resentful of injury or neglect, so great an ascendency that it continued to be felt in the second generation of his family.

The Duke of York, a Catholic and a prince, was in both capacities disposed to severity against fanatics and insurgents; so that his presence and interference in Scottish affairs increased the disposition to severity against Presbyterians of every shade and modification. But it was on his return, after a short visit to London, during which he had ascertained that his brother's affection for him was undiminished, that he ventured to proceed to extremities in suppressing nonconformists.

The doctrines promulgated by the more fierce and unreasonable insurgents, in their camp at Hamilton, were now adopted by the numerous and increasing sect, who separated their cause entirely from that of the moderate Presbyterians. These men disowned altogether the King's authority and that of the Government, and renounced the title of all pretenders to the throne, who would not subscribe to the Solemn League and Covenant, and govern according to its principles. These doctrines were chiefly enforced by two preachers, named Cargill and Cameron, from the last of whom their followers assumed, or acquired, the title of Cameronians.

Richard Cameron laboured and died in a manner not unworthy of his high pretensions, as the founder of a religious sect. He continued in open resistance after the battle of Bothwell Bridge; and on the 22d of June 1680 occupied the little burgh of Sauquhar with a small party of armed horsemen, and published a paper, or Testimony, formally disowning the authority of the King, and proclaiming that, by injustice and tyranny, he had forfeited the throne. After this bold step, Cameron, being closely pursued, roamed through the more desolate places of the counties of Dumfries and Ayr, with a few friends in arms, of whom Hackston of Rathillet, famous for his share in the death of Archbishop Sharp, was the principal.

But, on 22d July 1680, while lying at a desolate place called Airs Moss,[1] they were alarmed with the news, that Bruce of Earlshall was coming upon them with a superior force of infantry and dragoons. The Wanderers resolved to stand their ground, and Cameron pronounced a prayer, in which he three times repeated the pathetic expression, "Lord, spare the green and take the ripe." He then addressed his followers with great firmness, exhorting them to fight to the very last, "For I see," he added, "heaven's gates open to receive all such as shall die this day."

Rathillet divided their handful of twenty-three horse upon the two flanks of about forty half-armed infantry. The soldiers approached, and charged with fury. Cameron and eight others were killed on the spot. Of the Royalist party twenty-eight were either there killed, or died of their wounds shortly after. Rathillet fought with great bravery but was at length overpowered, struck down, and made prisoner.

In the barbarous spirit of the age, the seizure of Hackston was celebrated as a kind of triumph, and all possible insult was heaped on the unhappy man. He was brought into Edinburgh, mounted on a horse without a saddle, and having his face to the tail. The head and hands of Richard Cameron were borne before him on pikes. But such insults rather arouse than break the spirits of brave men. Hackston behaved with great courage before the Council. The Chancellor having upbraided him as a man of libertine habits, "While I was so," he replied, "I was acceptable to your lordship; I only lost your favour when I renounced my vices." The Archbishop's death being alleged against him as a murder, he replied that Heaven would decide which were the greatest murderers, himself, or those who sat in judgment on him. He was executed with circumstances of protracted cruelty. Both his hands were cut off before execution, and his heart torn from his bosom before he was quite dead. His head, with that of Cameron, was fixed on the Netherbow port, the hands of the former being extended, as if in the act of prayer. One of the enemies of his party gave Cameron this testimony on the occasion: "Here are the relics of a man who lived praying and preaching and died praying and fighting."

Daniel, or Donald Cargill, took up the banner of the sect, which had fallen from Cameron's dying hand. He avouched its tenets as boldly as his predecessor, and at a large conventicle of Cameronians,

---

[1] *Airs* or *Aird's Moss*, is a large morass in the centre of the parish of Auchinleck, county of Ayr.

held in the Torwood, September 1680, had the audacity to pronounce sentence of excommunication against the King, the Duke of York, the Dukes of Monmouth, Lauderdale, and Rothes, the Lord Advocate, and General Dalziel. This proceeding was entirely uncanonical, and contrary to the rules of the Scottish Presbyterian Church, but it assorted well with the uncompromising spirit of the Hillmen, or Cameronians, who desired neither to give favours to, nor receive favours from, those whom they termed God's enemies.

A high reward being put upon Cargill's head, he was, not long afterwards, taken by a Dumfriesshire gentleman,[1] and executed, along with four others, all disowning the authority of the King. The firmness with which these men met death tended to confirm the good opinion of the spectators; and though the Cameronian doctrines were too wild to be adopted by men of sense and education, yet they spread among the inferior ranks, and were productive of much mischief.

Thus, persecution, long and unsparingly exercised, drove a part of an oppressed peasantry into wild and perilous doctrines; dangerous, if acted upon, not only to the existing tyranny, but to any other form of government, how moderate soever. It was, considering the frantic severity of the Privy Council, a much greater wonder that they had not sooner stirred up a spirit of determined and avowed opposition to their government, than that such should now have arisen. Nevertheless, blind to experience, the Duke of York, who had now completely superseded Lauderdale in the management of Scottish affairs, continued to attempt the extirpation of the Cameronian sect, by the very same violent means which had occasioned its formation.

All usual forms of law, all the bulwarks by which the subjects of a country are protected against the violence of armed power, were at once broken down, and officers and soldiers received commissions not only to apprehend, but to interrogate and punish, any persons whom they might suspect of fanatical principles; and if they thought proper, they might put them to death upon the spot. All that was necessary to condemnation was that the individuals seized upon should scruple to renounce the Covenant—or should hesitate to admit that the death of Sharp was an act of murder—or should refuse to pray for the King—or decline to answer any other ensnaring or captious questions concerning their religious principles.

---

[1] James Irvine of Bonshaw.

A scene of this kind is told with great simplicity and effect by one of the writers of the period; and I am truly sorry that Claverhouse, whom, at the time of the Revolution, we shall find acting a heroic part, was a principal agent in this act of cruelty. Nor, considering the cold-blooded and savage barbarity of the deed, can we admit the excuse either of the orders under which he acted, or of the party prejudices of the time, or of the condition of the sufferer as a rebel and outlaw, to diminish our unqualified detestation of it.

There lived at this gloomy period, at a place called Preshill, or Priesthill, in Lanarkshire, a man named John Brown, a carrier by profession, and called, from his zealous religious principles, the Christian Carrier. This person had been out with the insurgents at Bothwell Bridge, and was for other reasons amenable to the cruelty of the existing laws. On a morning of May 1685 Peden, one of the Cameronian ministers, whom Brown had sheltered in his house, took his leave of his host and his wife, repeating twice,—"Poor woman! a fearful morning—a dark and misty morning!"—words which were afterwards believed to be prophetic of calamity. When Peden was gone, Brown left his house with a spade in his hand for his ordinary labour, when he was suddenly surrounded and arrested by a band of horse, with Claverhouse at their head. Although the prisoner had a hesitation in his speech on ordinary occasions, he answered the questions which were put to him in this extremity with such composure and firmness, that Claverhouse asked whether he was a preacher. He was answered in the negative. "If he has not preached," said Claverhouse, "mickle hath he prayed in his time.—But betake you now to your prayers for the last time" (addressing the sufferer), "for you shall presently die." The poor man kneeled down and prayed with zeal; and when he was touching on the political state of the country, and praying that Heaven would spare a remnant, Claverhouse, interrupting him, said, "I gave you leave to pray, and you are preaching."—"Sir," answered the prisoner, turning towards his judge on his knees, "you know nothing either of preaching or praying if you call what I now say preaching;"— then continued without confusion. When his devotions were ended, Claverhouse commanded him to bid good-night to his wife and children. Brown turned towards them, and, taking his wife by the hand, told her that the hour was come which he had spoken of, when he first asked her consent to marry him. The poor woman answered firmly,—"In this cause I am willing to resign you."—"Then have I nothing to do save to die," he replied; "and I thank God I have been in a frame to meet death for many years." He was shot dead by a party of soldiers at the end of his own house; and although his wife was of a nervous habit and used to become sick at the sight of blood, she had on this occasion strength enough to support the dreadful scene without fainting or confusion; only her eyes dazzled when the carabines were fired. While her husband's dead body lay stretched before him, Claverhouse asked her what she thought of her husband now. "I ever thought much of him," she replied, "and now more than ever."—"It were but justice," said Claverhouse, "to lay thee beside him."—"I doubt not," she replied, "that if you were permitted, your cruelty would carry you that length. But how will you answer for this morning's work?"—"To man I can be answerable," said Claverhouse, "and Heaven I will take in my own hand." He then mounted his horse and marched, and left her with the corpse of her husband lying beside her, and her fatherless infant in her arms. "She placed the child on the ground," says the narrative with scriptural simplicity, "tied up the corpse's head, and straighted the limbs, and covered him with her plaid, and sat down and wept over him."

The persecuted and oppressed fanatics showed on all occasions the same undaunted firmness, nor did the women fall short of the men in fortitude. Two of them, of different ages, underwent the punishment of death by drowning; for which purpose they were chained to posts within the flood mark, and exposed to the fury of the advancing tide; while, at the same time, they were offered rescue from the approaching billows, the sound of which was roaring in their ears, if they would but condescend so far as to say, God save the King. "Consider," said the well-meaning friends around them, "it is your duty to pray even for the greatest sinner."—"But we are not to do so," said the elder female, "at the bidding of every profligate." Her place of execution being nearer the advancing tide, she was first drowned; and her younger companion having said something, as if she desired the King's salvation, the bystanders would have saved her; but when she was dragged out of the waves, half strangled, she chose to be replunged into them rather than abjure the Covenant. She died accordingly.[1]

---

[1] Their names were Margaret MacLauchlan, a widow aged sixty-three, and Margaret Wilson, eighteen years. They were thus executed 11th May 1685, within the flood mark in the water of Blednoch, near Wigtown in Galloway.

But it was not the common people and the fanatics alone who were vexed and harassed with unreasonable oaths. Those of higher rank were placed in equal danger, by a test oath, of a complex and puzzling nature, and so far inconsistent with itself, that while, on the one hand, the person who took it was to profess his full belief and compliance with the Confession of Faith adopted by the Scottish Church in the first Parliament of King James VI., he was in the next clause made to acknowledge the King as supreme head of the Church; a proposition entirely inconsistent with that very Confession which he had just recognised. Nevertheless, this test was considered as a general pledge of loyalty to be taken by every one to whom it should be tendered, under pain of ruinous fines, confiscations, and even death itself. The case of the Earl of Argyle was distinguished, even in those oppressive times, for its peculiar injustice.

This nobleman was the son of the Marquis who was beheaded at the commencement of this reign, and he himself, as we have already mentioned, had been placed in danger of losing life and lands by a most oppressive proceeding on the obsolete statute of leasing-making. He was now subjected to a severer storm. When the oath was tendered to him, as a Privy Councillor, he declared he took it so far as it was consistent with itself, and with the Protestant religion. Such a qualification it might have been thought, was entirely blameless and unexceptionable. And yet for having added this explanation to the oath which he was required to take, Argyle was thrown into prison, brought to the bar, tried and found guilty of high treason and leasing-making. It has been plausibly alleged that Government only used this proceeding to wring from the unfortunate Earl a surrender of his jurisdictions; but, very prudently, he did not choose to trust his life on so precarious a tenure. He was one of the few peers who still professed an attachment to the Presbyterian religion; and the enemies who had abused the laws so grossly to obtain his condemnation, were sufficiently likely to use the advantage to the uttermost. He escaped from the castle of Edinburgh, disguised in the livery of a page, holding up the train of Lady Sophia Lindsay, his step-daughter, and went over to Holland. Sentence of attainder was immediately pronounced. His honours, estate, and life were forfeited in absence; his arms were reversed and torn; his posterity incapacitated; and a large reward offered for his head.

This extravagant proceeding struck general terror, from its audacious violation of justice, while the gross fallacy on which it rested was the subject of general contempt. Even the children educated in George Heriot's Hospital (a charity on a plan similar to that of Christ Church in London), turned into ridicule the proceedings on this iniquitous trial. They voted that their yard dog was a person under trust, and that the test, therefore, should be tendered to him. Poor Watch, you may believe, only smelt at the paper held out to him, on which the oath was printed, and would pay no more attention to it. Upon this, the paper was again offered, having been previously rubbed over with butter, which induced the mastiff to swallow it. This was called taking the test with a qualification, and the dog was adjudged to be hanged as a leasing-maker and perverter of the laws of the kingdom.

The extreme violence of these proceedings awakened resentment as well as fear. But fear was at first predominant. Upwards of thirty-six noblemen and gentlemen, attached to the Presbyterian religion, resolved to sell their property in Scotland, and remove themselves to America where they might live according to the dictates of their conscience. A deputation of their number, Lord Melville, Sir John Cochrane, Baillie of Jerviswood, and others, went to London to prepare for this emigration. Here the secret was imparted to them, of an enterprise formed by Monmouth, Shaftesbury, Lord Russell, and Algernon Sidney, to alter the government under Charles II.; and, at all events, to prevent, by the most forcible means, the Duke of York's ascent to the throne in case of the King's death. The Scottish malcontents abandoned their plan of emigration, to engage in this new and more adventurous scheme. Walter Scott, Earl of Tarras, brother-in-law of the Duke of Monmouth, undertook for a rising in the south of Scotland; and many of his name and kindred, as well as other gentlemen of the Borders of Scotland, engaged in the plot. One gentleman who was invited to join excused himself, on account of the ominous sound of the titles of two of the persons engaged. He did not, he said, like such words as Gallowshiels and Hangingshaw.

Besides the Scottish plot, and that which was conducted by Russell and Sidney in London, there were in that city some desperate men, of a subordinate description, who proposed to simplify the purpose of both the principal conspiracies by putting the King to death as he passed by a place called the Ryehouse. This last plot becoming public, was the means of defeating the others. But although Campbell of Cessnock, Baillie of Jerviswood, and some conspirators of less consequence, were arrested, the escape of most of the persons concerned

partly disappointed the revenge of the Government. The circumstances attending some of these escapes were singular.

Lord Melville was about to come to Edinburgh from his residence
in Fife, and had sent his principal domestic, a Highlander named
MacArthur, to make preparations for his arrival in town. The Justice-
General was friendly to Lord Melville. He had that morning issued
warrants for his arrest, and desired to put him on his guard, but durst
take no steps to do so. Happening to see Lord Melville's valet on the
street, he bent his eyes significantly on him and asked, "What are you
doing here? Get back, you Highland dog!" The man began to say he
was making preparations for his master coming to town, when the Justice again interrupted him, saying angrily, "Get home, you Highland
dog!" and then passed on. MacArthur was sensible of the dangerous
temper of the times, and upon receiving such a hint, slight as it was,
from such a man, he resolved to go back to his master. At the Ferry he
saw a party of the guards embarking on the same voyage. Making every
exertion, he got home time enough to alarm his lord, who immediately
absconded, and soon after got over to Holland.

Sir Patrick Hume of Polwarth, afterwards Lord Marchmont, had a
still more narrow escape. The party of guards sent to arrest him had
stopped at the house of a friend to the Government to get refreshments, which were amply supplied to them. The lady of the house,
who secretly favoured the Presbyterian interest, connected the appearance of this party and the inquiries which they made concerning the
road to Polwarth Castle, with some danger threatened to Sir Patrick
Hume. She dared not write to apprise him, and still less durst she trust
a messenger with any verbal communication. She therefore wrapt up a
feather in a blank piece of paper, and sent it over the hills by a boy,
while she detained the military party as long as she could, without
exciting suspicion. In the meantime, Sir Patrick received the token, and
his acute apprehension being rendered yet more penetrating by a sense
of danger, he at once comprehended that the feather was meant to
convey a hint to him that he should fly.

Having been long peculiarly odious to the Government, Sir Patrick
could think of no secure retreat above ground. A subterranean vault in
Polwarth Churchyard, being that in which his ancestors were buried,
seemed the only safe place of refuge. The sole light admitted into this
dreary cell was by a small slit at one end. A trusty domestic contrived
to convey a bed and bed-clothes to this dismal place, and here Sir

Patrick lay concealed during the strict search which was made for him in every direction. His daughter, Grizell Hume, then about eighteen years of age, was entrusted with the task of conveying him food, which could only be brought to the vault at midnight. She had been bred up in the usual superstitions of the times, about ghosts and apparitions, but the duty which she was discharging to her father banished all such childish fears. When she returned from her first journey, her mother asked her if she was not frightened in going through the churchyard. She answered, that she had felt fear for nothing excepting the minister's dogs (the manse[1] being nigh the church), which had kept such a barking as to alarm her for a discovery. Her mother sent for the clergyman next morning, and by pretending an alarm for mad dogs, prevailed on him to destroy them, or shut them up.

But it was not enough to have a faithful messenger; much precaution was also necessary, to secure secretly, and by stealth, the provisions for the unfortunate recluse, since, if the victuals had been taken openly, the servants must naturally have suspected the purpose to which they were to be applied. Grizell Hume used, therefore, to abstract from the table, as secretly as she could, a portion of the family dinner. Sir Patrick Hume was fond of sheep's head (being a good Scotsman in all respects), and Grizell, aware of her father's taste, had slipt into her napkin a large part of one which was on the table, when one of her brothers, a boy too young to be trusted with the secret, bawled out in his surprise at the disappearance of the victuals, "Mamma, look at Grizzy—while we were supping the broth, she has eaten up all the sheep's head!"

While in this melancholy abode, Sir Patrick Hume's principal amusement was reading and reciting Buchanan's translation of the Psalms. After lurking in his father's tomb, and afterwards in his own house, for three or four weeks, he at length ventured abroad, and through many dangers made his escape to Holland, like other fugitives.

In the meantime Baillie of Jerviswood, though in a very infirm state of health, was brought to that trial from which Polwarth and others had escaped so marvellously. This gentleman had been offered his life, on condition of his becoming a witness against Lord Russell, a proposal which he rejected with disdain, saying, those who uttered it knew neither him nor his country. It does not appear that there was

---

[1] *Anglice,* Parsonage.

the slightest evidence of the Scottish gentlemen having any concern in the scheme for assassinating the King; but there is no doubt that they had meditated an insurrection, as the only mode of escaping the continued persecution of the Government.

When Baillie received sentence of death, he only replied, "My lords, the sentence is sharp, and the time is short; but I thank God, who has made me as fit to die as you are to live." He suffered death with the same firmness; his sister-in-law, a daughter of Warriston, had voluntarily shared his imprisonment and supported his exhausted frame during his trial. She attended his last moments on the scaffold and with Roman fortitude witnessed the execution of a horrid sentence. It is worthy of mention, that the son and heir of this gentleman afterwards married the same young lady who so piously supported her father, Sir Patrick Hume, while concealed in the tomb.[1] No other person was executed for accession to what was called the Jerviswood Plot; but many gentlemen were tried in absence, and their estates being declared forfeited, were bestowed on the most violent tools of the Government.

Upwards of two thousand individuals were denounced outlaws, or fugitives from justice. Other persons obnoxious to the rulers were exorbitantly fined. One of these was Sir William Scott of Harden, from whose third brother your mother is descended. This gentleman, in his early years, had been an active member of the Committee of Estates, but was now upwards of seventy and much retired from public life.

But his nephew, Walter, Earl of Tarras, was deeply concerned in the Jerviswood plot; more than one of Harden's sons were also implicated, and hence he became obnoxious to the Government. He attended only on the Indulged, that is, licensed preachers, and had kept himself free of giving any offence that could be charged against him. The celebrated Richard Cameron was for some time his chaplain, but had been dismissed as soon as he declared against the Indulgence, and afforded other symptoms of the violent opinions of his sect. But the Privy Council had determined that husbands should be made responsible for the penalties and fines incurred by their wives. Lady

---

[1] Of the marriage between Mr. George Baillie and Lady Grizell Hume, there were two daughters, Grizell and Rachel. The former was married to Mr. Murray, afterwards Sir Alexander Murray of Stanhope; the latter, to Charles Lord Binning, eldest son of Thomas, sixth Earl of Haddington, from whom are descended the present families of Haddington and of Baillie of Jerviswood.

Scott of Harden had become liable for so many transgressions of this kind, that the sum total, amounting to almost two thousand pounds, was, with much difficulty, limited to fifteen hundred, an immense sum for a Scottish gentleman of that period; but which was extorted from this aged person by imprisonment in the castle of Edinburgh.

Whilst these affairs were going on in Scotland, the Duke of York was suddenly recalled to London by the King, whose health began to fail. Monmouth, his favourite son, had been obliged to retire abroad in consequence of the affair of the Ryehouse plot. It was said that the King still nourished a secret wish to recall his son, and to send the Duke of York back to Scotland. But if he meditated such a change of resolution, which seems rather improbable, fate left him no opportunity to execute it.

Charles II. died of a stroke of apoplexy, which summoned him from the midst of a distracted country, and a gay and luxurious court, on the 6th of February 1685, in the fifty-fourth year of his age.

LIII

Whigs and Tories

1685

WHEN the Duke of York ascended the throne on the death of his brother Charles, he assumed the title of James II. of England and James VII. of Scotland. His eldest daughter, Mary (whom he had by his first wife), was married to William, Prince of Orange, the Stadtholder or President of the Dutch United Provinces; a prince of great wisdom, sense, and courage, distinguished by the share he had taken in opposing the ambition of France. He was now next heir to the crown of England, unless the King, his father-in-law, should have a surviving son by his present Queen, Mary of Este. It was natural to conclude that the Prince of Orange viewed with the most intense interest the various revolutions and changes which took place in a kingdom where he possessed so deep a stake. It did not escape remark that the Duke of Monmouth, the Earl of Argyle, and the various malcontents who were compelled to fly from England or Scotland, seemed to find support, as well as refuge, in Holland. On this subject James made several remonstrances to his son-in-law, which the Prince evaded, by alleging that a free state, like the Dutch republic, could not shut its ports against fugitives, of whatever description; and with such excuses James was obliged to remain satisfied. Nevertheless, the enemies of the monarch were so completely subdued, both in Scotland and England, that no prince in Europe seemed more firmly seated upon his throne.

In the meanwhile there was no relaxation in the oppressive measures carried on in Scotland. The same laws for apprehending, examining, and executing in the fields those suspected of nonconformity, were enforced with unrelenting severity; and as the refusal to bear evidence against a person accused of treason was made to amount to a crime equal to treason itself, the lands and life of every one seemed to be exposed to the machinations of the corrupt ministry of an arbitrary prince. To administer or receive the Covenant, or even to write in its defence, was declared treasonable, and many other delinquencies were screwed up to the same penalty of death and confiscation. Those whom the law named traitors were thus rendered so numerous, that it seemed to be impossible for the most cautious to avoid coming in contact with them, and thereby subjecting themselves to the severe penalties denounced on all having intercourse with such delinquents. This general scene of oppression would, it was supposed, notwithstanding the general show of submission, lead to a universal desire to shake off the yoke of James, should an opportunity be afforded.

Under this conviction. the numerous disaffected persons who had retreated to Holland resolved upon a double invasion of Britain, one part of which was to be directed against England, under command of the popular Duke of Monmouth, whose hopes of returning in any other peaceful fashion had been destroyed by the death of his father, Charles II. The other branch of the expedition was destined to invade Scotland, having at its head the Earl of Argyle (who had been the victim of so much unjust persecution), with Sir Patrick Hume, Sir John Cochrane, and others, the most important of the Scottish exiles, to assist and counsel him.

As these Tales relate exclusively to the history of Scotland, I need only notice that Monmouth's share of the undertaking seemed, for a time, to promise success. Having landed at Lyme, in Dorsetshire, he was joined by greater numbers of men than he had means of arming, and his rapid progress greatly alarmed James's Government. But his adherents were almost entirely of the lower order, whose zeal and courage might be relied on, but who had no advantages of influence from education or property. At length the unfortunate Duke hazarded a battle near Sedgemoor in which his cavalry, from the treachery or cowardice of their leader, Lord Grey, fled and left the infantry unprotected.

The sturdy peasants fought with the utmost resolution, until they were totally broken and dispersed, with great slaughter. But the carnage made among the fugitives was forgotten, in comparison with the savage and unsparing prosecutions which were afterwards carried on before Judge Jefferies, a man whose cruelty was a disgrace to his profession, and to mankind.

Monmouth himself had no better fortune than his adherents. He fell into the hands of the pursuers, and was brought prisoner to the Tower of London. He entreated to be permitted to have an interview with the King, alleging he had something of consequence to discover to him. But when this was at length granted, the unhappy Duke had nothing to tell, or at least told nothing, but exhausted himself in asking mercy at the hands of his uncle, who had previously determined not to grant it. Monmouth accordingly suffered death on Tower Hill, amid the lamentations of the common people, to whom he was endeared by his various amiable qualities and the beauty of his person, fitting him to be the delight and ornament of a court, but not to be the liberator of an oppressed people.

While the brief tragedy of Monmouth's invasion, defeat, and death was passing in England, Argyle's invasion of Scotland was brought to as disastrous a conclusion. The leaders, even before they left their ships, differed as to the course to be pursued. Argyle, a great chieftain in the Highlands, was naturally disposed to make the principal efforts in that part of the country which his friends and followers inhabited. Sir Patrick Hume and Sir John Cochrane, while they admitted that they were certain to raise the clan of Campbell by following the Earl's counsel, maintained, nevertheless, that this single clan, however brave and numerous, could not contend with the united strength of all the other western tribes, who were hostile to Argyle, and personally attached to James II. They complained that by landing in the West Highlands, they should expose themselves to be shut up in a corner of the kingdom, where they could expect to be joined by none save Argyle's immediate dependents; and where they must necessarily be separated from the western provinces in which the oppressed Covenanters had shown themselves ready to rise, even without the encouragement of money or arms, or of a number of brave gentlemen to command and lead them on.

These disputes augmented, when, on landing in Kintyre, the Earl of Argyle raised his clan to the number of about a thousand men. Joined to the adventurers embarked from Holland, who were about three hundred, and to other recruits, the insurgent army might amount in all to fifteen hundred, a sufficient number to have struck a severe blow before the Royal forces could have assembled, if the invaders could have determined among themselves where to aim at.

Argyle proposed marching to Inverary, to attack the Laird of Ballechan, who was lying there for the King with six hundred Highlanders, waiting the support of the Marquis of Athole, then at the head of several clans, and in motion towards Argyleshire. But Sir John Cochrane, having had some communications in the west, which promised a general rising in that country, insisted that the main effort should be made in that quarter. He had a letter also from a gentleman of Lanarkshire, named William Cleland, undertaking that if the Marquis of Argyle would declare for the work of Reformation, carried on from the year 1638 to 1648, he should be joined by all the faithful Presbyterians in that county. Sir John, therefore, demanded from Argyle a supply of men and ammunition, that he might raise the western shires; and was so eager in the request, that he said if nobody would support him, he would go alone, with a pitchfork in his hand.

Either project was hopeful, if either had been rapidly executed, but the loss of time in debating the question was fatal. At length the Lowland expedition was determined on; and Argyle, with an army augmented to two thousand five hundred men, descended into Lennox, proposing to cross the Clyde, and summon to arms the Covenanters of the west country. But the various parties among the Presbyterians had already fallen into debates, whether or not they should own Argyle and unite under his standard; so that, when that unhappy, and, it would seem, irresolute nobleman had crossed the river Leven, near to Dumbarton, he found his little army, without any prospect of reinforcement, nearly surrounded by superior forces of the King, assembling from different points, under the Marquis of Athole, the Duke of Gordon, and the Earl of Dumbarton.

Argyle, pressed on all sides, proposed to give battle to the enemy; but the majority of the council of war which he convoked were of opinion, that it was more advisable to give the Royalists the slip, and leaving their encampment in the night, to march for Glasgow, or for Bothwell Bridge; and thus at the same time get into a friendly country, and place a large and unfordable river betwixt them and a superior enemy. Lighting, therefore, numerous fires in the camp as if it were still occupied by them, Argyle and his troops commenced their projected manœuvre; but a retreat is always a discouraging movement, a night-march commonly a confused one, and the want of discipline in these hasty levies added to the general want of confidence and the universal disorder. Their guides, also, were either treacherous or ignorant, for, when morning dawned on the disspirited insurgents, instead of finding themselves near Glasgow, they perceived they were much lower on the banks of the Clyde, near Kilpatrick. Here the leaders came to an open rupture. Their army broke up and separated; and when the unfortunate Earl, being left almost alone, endeavoured to take refuge in the house of a person who had been once his servant, he was inhospitably refused admittance. He then crossed the Clyde accompanied by a single friend, who, perceiving that they were pursued, had the generosity to halt and draw upon himself the attention of the party who followed them. This was at Inchinnan ford, upon the river Cart, close to Blythswood House.

But Argyle was not more safe alone than in company. It was observed by some soldiers of the militia, who were out in every direction, that the fugitive quitted his horse and waded through the river on foot, from which they argued he must be a person of importance, who was careless about losing his horse, so that he himself made his escape. As soon, therefore, as he reached the bank, they fell upon him, and though he made some defence, at length struck him down. As he fell he exclaimed,—"Unfortunate Argyle!"—thus apprising his captors of the importance of their prisoner. A large fragment of rock, still called Argyle's Stone, marks the place where he was taken.

Thus terminated this unfortunate expedition, in which Argyle seems to have engaged, from an over estimation both of his own consequence and military talents, and which the Lowland gentlemen seem to have joined, from their imperfect knowledge of the state of the country, as reported to them by those who deeply felt their own wrongs, and did not consider that the majority of their countrymen was overawed and intimidated, as well as discontented.

By way of retaliating upon this unhappy nobleman the severities exercised towards Montrose, which he is said to have looked upon in triumph, the same disgraceful indignities were used towards Argyle, to which his enemy had been subjected. He was carried up the High Street bareheaded, and mounted on an unsaddled horse, with the hangman preceding him, and was thus escorted to the tolbooth. In both cases the disgrace lay with those who gave such orders, and did not attach to the objects of their mean malevolence.

The Council debated whether Argyle should be executed on the extravagant sentence which had condemned him for a traitor and *depraver* of the laws, on account of his adding a qualification to the test, or whether it were not better to try him anew, for the undoubted treason which he had committed by this subsequent act of invasion, which afforded a more legal and unchallengeable course of procedure. It was resolved, nevertheless, they should follow the first course, and hold Argyle as a man already condemned, lest, by doing otherwise, they should seem to throw doubt upon, if not indirectly admit, the illegality of the first sentence. The unfortunate Earl was appointed to be beheaded by the Maiden, an instrument resembling the Guillotine of modern France. He mounted the scaffold with great firmness, and embracing the engine by which he was to suffer, declared it the sweetest maiden he ever kissed, and submitted with courage to the fatal accomplishment of his sentence. When this nobleman's death is considered as the consequence of a sentence passed against him for presuming to comment upon and explain an oath which was self-contradictory, it can only be termed a judicial murder. Upwards of twenty of the most considerable gentlemen of his clan were executed in consequence of having joined him. His estate was wasted and confiscated; his brother, Lord Niel Campbell, was forced to fly to America, and his name doomed to extirpation.

Several of Argyle's Lowland followers were also condemned to death. Amongst these was Richard Rumbold, an Englishman, the principal conspirator in what was called the Ryehouse Plot. He was a republican of the old stamp, who might have ridden right-hand man to Cromwell himself. He was the most active in the scheme for assassinating the two Royal brothers, which was to have been executed at his farm called the Ryehouse, by one party firing on the Royal guards, and another pouring their shot into the King's carriage. Rumbold, who was to head the latter party, expressed some scruple at shooting the innocent postilion, but had no compunction on the project of assassinating the King and Duke of York.

Escaping from England when the discovery took place, this stern republican had found refuge in Holland, until he was persuaded to take part in Argyle's expedition. When the Scottish leaders broke up in confusion and deserted each other, a stranger and an Englishman was not likely to experience much aid or attention. Rumbold, left to shift for himself amid the general dispersion and flight, was soon beset by a party of the Royalists, and while he stoutly defended himself against two men in front, a third came behind him with a pitchfork, put it behind his ear, and turned off his steel cap, leaving his head exposed; on which Rumbold exclaimed, "O cruel countryman, to use me thus when my face was to mine enemy!"

He died the death of a traitor, as his share in the Ryehouse conspiracy justly merited. But on the scaffold, Rumbold maintained the same undaunted courage he had often shown in the field. One of his dying observations was "That he had never believed that the generality of mankind came into the world bridled and saddled, and a few booted and spurred to ride upon them."

This man's death was afterwards avenged on one Mark Kerr, the chief of those who took him: he was murdered before his own door by two young men, calling themselves Rumbold's sons, who ripped out his heart, in imitation of what their father had suffered on the scaffold. Thus does crime beget crime, and cruelty engender cruelty. The actors in this bloody deed made their escape, not so much as a dog baying at them.

Before quitting the subject of Argyle's rebellion, I may mention a species of oppression practised on the nonconformists, of a nature differing from those I have already mentioned. When the alarm of invasion arose, it was resolved by the Privy Council, that all such persons as were in prison on account of religion should be sent to the north, for their more safe custody. After a toilsome march, rendered bitter by want of food and accommodation, as well as by the raillery of the pipers, who insulted with ridiculous tunes a set of persons who held their minstrelsy to be sinful, the Wanderers, to the number of a hundred and sixty persons, of whom there were several women, and even some children, reached the place of their destination. This proved to be the castle of Dunottar, a strong fortress, almost surrounded by the German Ocean, the same in which, as I have told you, the Regalia of Scotland were preserved for some time. Here the prisoners were, without distinction, packed into a large dungeon, having a window open to the sea, in front of a huge precipice. They were neither allowed bedding nor provisions, excepting what they bought, and were treated by keepers with the utmost rigour.[1] The walls of this place, still called the

---

[1] "The guards made them. pay for every indulgence, even that of water; and when some of the prisoners resisted a demand so unreasonable, and insisted on their right to have this necessary of life untaxed, their keepers emptied the water on the prison floor, saying, 'If they were obliged to bring water for the canting Whigs, they were not bound to afford them the use of bowls or pitchers gratis.'"—*Introduction to Old Mortality.*

Whigs' vault, bear token to the severities inflicted on these unhappy persons. There are, in particular, a number of apertures cut in the wall about a man's height, and it was the custom, when such was the jailor's pleasure, that any prisoner who was accounted refractory, should be obliged to stand up with his arms extended, and his fingers secured by wedges in the crevices I have described. It appears that some of these apertures or crevices, which are lower than the others, have been intended for women, and even for children. In this cruel confinement many died, some were deprived of the use of their limbs by rheumatism and other diseases, and several lost their lives by desperate attempts to descend from the rock on which the castle is founded. Some who tried to escape by descending the precipice,were retaken, and so cruelly tortured by lighted matches tied between their fingers, that mutilation, and in some instances even death ensued.

The survivors, after enduring this horrid imprisonment for six weeks or two months, had the test offered to them. Those who, overcome by bodily anguish and the hopeless misery of their condition, agreed to take this engagement, were discharged, and the others transported to the plantations. A tombstone in Dunottar Churchyard still preserves the names of such as died in this cruel captivity in the various modes we have mentioned.

The failure of the invasions of Monmouth and Argyle, with the revenge which had been taken on their unfortunate leaders, was by James, in his triumph, recorded by two medals struck for the occasion, which bore on one side two severed heads, on the other two headless trunks; a device as inhuman as the proceedings by which these advantages had been followed up, and as the Royal vengeance which had been so unsparingly executed.

The part of the nation which inclined to support the King in all political discussions now obtained a complete superiority over the rest. They were known by the name of Tories, an appellation borrowed from Ireland, where the irregular and desultory bands, which maintained a sort of skirmishing warfare after Cromwell had suppressed every national and united effort, were so called. Like the opposite term of Whig, Tory was at first used as an epithet of scorn and ridicule, and both were at length adopted as party distinctions, coming in place of those which had been used during the Civil War, the word Tory superseding the term of Cavalier, and Whig being applied instead of Roundhead. The same terms of distinction have descended to our time as expressing the outlines of the two political parties which divide the Houses of Parliament, and, viewed politically, the whole mass of the community. A man who considers that, in the general view of the constitution, the monarchical power is in danger of being undermined by the popular branches, and who therefore supports the crown in ordinary cases of dispute, is a Tory; while one who conceives the power of the crown to be more likely to encroach upon the liberties of the people, throws his weight and influence into the popular scale, and is called a Whig.

Either of these opinions may be honourably and conscientiously maintained by the party whom reflection or education has led to adopt it; and the existence of two such parties opposing each other with reason and moderation, and by constitutional means only, is the sure mode of preventing encroachment either on the rights of the crown or on the privileges of the people, and of keeping the constitution itself inviolate, as the stays and rigging of a vessel straining against each other in opposite directions tend to keep the ship's mast upright in its place. But as it is natural for men to drive favourite opinions into extremes, it has frequently happened that the Whigs, or the more violent part of that faction, have entertained opinions which tended towards democracy; and that the Tories, on the other hand, indulging in opposite prejudices, have endangered the constitution by their tendency towards absolute rule.

Thus, in the great Civil War, the friends to popular freedom began their opposition to Charles I. in the laudable desire to regain the full extent of constitutional liberty, but could not bring the war to a conclusion until the monarchy was totally overthrown, and liberty overwhelmed in the ruins. In like manner, the Tories of Charles II. and James II.'s time, remembering the fatal issue of the Civil Wars, adopted the opposite and equally mistaken opinion that no check could be opposed to the will of the sovereign without danger of overturning the throne, and by their unlimited desire to enlarge the prerogative of the crown, they not only endangered the national liberty, but conducted the deluded sovereign to his ruin. When, therefore, we speak of any particular measure adopted by the Whigs or Tories, it would be very rash to consider it as deserving of censure or applause merely on account of its having originated with the one or other of these parties. On the contrary, its real merits can only be soundly estimated when we have attentively considered its purpose and effect, compared with the general spirit of the constitution, and with the exigencies of the times when it was brought forward.

During the whole of Charles the Second's reign a violent struggle had been continued in England between the Whigs and the Tories, in the course of which both parties acted with a furious animosity which admitted of no scruple concerning the means to be resorted to for annoying their adversaries. The Whig party had availed themselves of that detestable imposture called the Popish Plot to throw upon the Tories the guilt of an attempt to massacre the Protestants, and bring England back to the Catholic faith by the sword. Under this pretext they shed no small quantity of innocent blood. The Tories regained a decided ascendency by the discovery of the Ryehouse Plot, an atrocious enterprise at which men's minds revolted, and which the court artfully improved by confounding the more moderate schemes laid by Monmouth, Lord Russell, and others, for obtaining some relief from the oppressive and unconstitutional measures of the court, with the bloody measures against the King's person which Rumbold and other desperate men had meditated. The general hatred inspired by the latter enterprise excited a widespread clamour against the conspirators, and the Tories in their turn became the instruments of sacrificing, on account of a conspiracy of which they were ignorant, Lord Russell and Algernon Sidney, two men whose names, for free and courageous sentiments, will live for ever in history.

The prejudice against the Whigs had not subsided when James ascended the throne; and the terrible mode in which the invasion of Monmouth was suppressed and punished, if it excited compassion for the sufferers, spread, at the same time, general dread of the Government. In these circumstances, the whole powers of the state seemed about to be surrendered to the King, without even a recollection of the value of national liberty, or of the blood which had been spent in its defence. The danger was the greater, that a large proportion of the national clergy were extravagant Royalists, who had adopted maxims utterly inconsistent with freedom, and with the very essence of the British constitution. They contended that the right of kings flowed from God, and that they were responsible to Him only for the manner in which they exercised it; that no misconduct, however gross, no oppression, however unjust, gave the subject any right to defend his person or his property against the violence of the sovereign; and that any attempt at resistance, however provoked, was contrary alike to religion and to law, and rendered its author liable to punishment in this world for treason or sedition, and in that which is to come to eternal condemnation, as foes of the Prince whom Heaven had made their anointed sovereign. Such were the base and slavish maxims into which many wise, good, and learned men were hurried, from the recollection of the horrors of civil war, the death of Charles I., and the destruction of the Hierarchy; and thus do men endeavour to avoid the repetition of one class of crimes and errors, by rushing into extremes of a different description.

James II. was unquestionably desirous of power; yet such was the readiness with which courts of justice placed at his feet the persons and property of his subjects, and so great the zeal with which many of the clergy were disposed to exalt his authority into something of a sacred character, accountable for his actions to Heaven alone, that it must have seemed impossible for him to form any demand for an extension of authority which would not have been readily conceded to him, on the slightest hint of his pleasure. But it was the misfortune of this monarch to conceive, that the same sophistry by which divines and lawyers placed the property and personal freedom of his subjects at his unlimited disposal, extended his power over the freedom of their consciences also.

We have often repeated, that James was himself a Roman Catholic; and, as a sincere professor of that faith, he was not only disposed, but bound, as far as possible, to bring others into the pale of the Church, beyond which, according to the Popish belief, there is no salvation. He might also flatter himself, that the indulgences of a life which had been in some respects irregular, might be obliterated and atoned for by the great and important service of ending the northern heresy. To James's sanguine hopes there appeared at this time a greater chance of so important a change being accomplished than at any former period. His own power, if he were to trust the expressions of the predominant party in the state, was at least as extensive over the bodies and minds of his subjects as that of the Tudor family, under whose dynasty the religion of England four times changed its form, at the will and pleasure of the sovereign. James might, therefore, flatter himself that as Henry VIII., by his sole fiat, detached England from the Pope, and assumed in his own person the office of Head of the Church, so a submissive clergy, and a willing people might, at a similar expression of the present sovereign's will and pleasure, return again under the dominion of the Holy Father, when they beheld their prince surrender to him, as a usurpation, the right of supremacy which his predecessor had seized upon.

But there was a fallacy in this reasoning. The Reformation presented to the English nation advantages both spiritual and temporal of which they must necessarily be deprived by a reconciliation with Rome. The former revolution was a calling from darkness into light, from ignorance into knowledge, from the bondage of priestcraft into freedom, and a mandate of Henry VIII., recommending a change fraught with such advantages, was sure to be promptly obeyed. The purpose of James, on the contrary, tended to restore the ignorance of the dark ages, to lock up the Scriptures from the use of laymen, to bring back observances and articles of faith which were the offspring of superstitious credulity, and which the increasing knowledge of more than a century had taught men to despise.

Neither would a reconciliation with Rome have been more favourable to those who looked to a change of religion only as the means of obtaining temporal advantages. The acquiescence of the nobility in the Reformation had been easily purchased by the spoils of the Church property; but their descendants, the present possessors, would have every reason to apprehend, that a return to the Catholic religion might be cemented by a resumption of the Church lands, which had been confiscated at the Reformation.

Thus the alteration which James proposed to accomplish in the national religion was a task as different from that effected by Henry VIII. as is that of pushing a stone up hill from assisting its natural impulse by rolling it downwards. Similar strength may indeed be applied in both cases, but the result of the two attempts must be materially different. This distinction James did not perceive; and he persevered in his rash attempt, in an evil hour for his own power, but a fortunate one for the freedom of his subjects, who being called on to struggle for their religion, reasserted their half-surrendered liberty, as the only mode by which they could obtain effectual means of resistance.

LIV

The Great Revolution

1685-1688

I N attempting the rash plan which doubtless had for its object the re-establishment of the Catholic religion in his dominions, James II., in his speech to the first English Parliament after Monmouth's defeat, acquainted them with his intentions in two particulars, both highly alarming in the existing temper of the public. The first was that having seen, as he said, from the example of the last rebellion, that the militia were not adequate to maintain the defence of the kingdom, it was the King's purpose in future to maintain a body of regular troops, for whose pay he requested the House of Commons would make provision. The second point was no less ominous. The King desired that no man should object if he employed some officers in the army who were not qualified according to the Test Act. "They were persons," he said, "well known to him, and having had the benefit of their assistance in a time of need and danger, he was determined neither to expose them to disgrace nor himself to the want of their services on a future occasion."

To understand what is alluded to, you must be informed that the Test Act was contrived to exclude all persons from offices of public trust, commissions in the army, and the like, who should not previously take the test oath, declaring themselves Protestants, according to the Church of England. King James's speech from the throne, therefore, intimated first, that he intended to maintain a standing military force, and, secondly, that it was his purpose to officer these in a great measure with Papists, whom he designed thus to employ, although they could not take the test.

Both these suspicious and exceptionable measures being so bluntly announced created great alarm. When it was moved in the House of Lords, that thanks be returned for the King's speech, Lord Halifax said that thanks were indeed due to his Majesty, but it was because he had frankly let them see the point he aimed at. In the House of Commons, the reception of the speech was more markedly unfavorable; and an address was voted, representing that the Papist officers lay under disabilities, which could only be removed by Act of Parliament.

This intimation was ill received by the King in his turn, who expressed himself displeased at the implied jealousy of his purposes. The House remained in profound silence for some time, until Mr. Cook stood up and said, "I hope we are all Englishmen, and not to be frightened out of our duty by a few hard words." This was considered as censurable language, and the gentleman who used it was sent to the Tower. The King presently afterwards prorogued the Parliament, which never met again during the short remainder of his reign.

Highly exasperated and disappointed at the unexpected and unfavourable reception which his propositions in favour of the Roman Catholics had received from the English Parliament, James determined that the legislature of Scotland, which till now had studied to fulfil, and even anticipate, his slightest wishes, should show their southern neighbours, in this instance also, the example of submission to the will of their sovereign. In order to induce them, and particularly the representatives of the burghs, to consent without hesitation, he promised a free intercourse of trade with England, and an ample indemnity for all past offences; measures which he justly regarded as essential to the welfare of Scotland. But these highly desirable favours were clogged by a request, proposed as a sort of condition, that the penal laws should be abolished, and the test withdrawn. The Scottish Parliament, hitherto so submissive, were alarmed at this proposal, which although it commenced only by putting Popery on a level with the established religion, was likely, they thought, to end in overturning the Reformed doctrines, and replacing those of the Church of Rome.

It is true that the Scottish penal laws respecting the Roman Catholics were of the most severe and harsh character. The punishments for assisting at the celebration of the mass were, for the first offence, confiscation and corporal punishment; for the second, banishment, and to the third, the pains of treason were annexed. These tyrannical laws had been introduced at a violent period, when those who had just shaken off the yoke of Popery were desirous to prevent, by every means, the slightest chance of its being again imposed on them, and when, being irritated by the recollection of the severities inflicted by the Roman Catholics on those whom they termed heretics, the Protestants were naturally disposed to retaliate upon the sect by whom intolerant cruelties had been practised.

But although little could be said in defence of these laws, when the Catholics were reduced to a state of submission, the greater part by far of the people of Scotland desired that they should continue to exist, as a defence to the Reformed religion, in case the Papists should at some future period attempt to recover their ascendency. They urged that while the Catholics remained quiet there had been no recent instance of the penal laws being executed against them and that, therefore, since they were already in actual enjoyment of absolute freedom of conscience, the only purpose of the proposed abolition of the penal laws must be, to effect the King's purpose of bringing the Catholics forward into public situations, as the favoured ministers of the King, and professing the same religion with his Majesty.

Then in respect to the test oath, men remembered that it had been the contrivance of James himself, deemed so sacred, that Argyle had been condemned to death for even slightly qualifying it; and declared so necessary to the safety, nay existence, of the Episcopal Church of Scotland, that it was forced upon Presbyterians at the sword's point. The Protestants, therefore, of every description, were terrified at the test's being dispensed with in the case of the Roman Catholics, who supported as they were by the King's favour, were justly to be regarded as the most formidable enemies of all whom their Church termed heretics.

The consequence of all this reasoning was that the Episcopal party in Scotland, who had hitherto complied with every measure which James had proposed, now stopped short in their career and would no longer keep pace with his wishes. He could get no answer from the Scottish Parliament, excepting the ambiguous expression that they would do as much for the relief of the Catholics as their consciences would permit.

But James, although he applied to Parliament in the first instance, had, in case he found that assembly opposed to his wishes, secretly formed the resolution of taking away the effect of the penal laws, and removing the Test Act, by his own royal prerogative; not regarding the hatred and jealousy which he was sure to excite by a course of conduct offensive at once to the liberties of his subjects and threatening the stability of the Reformed religion.

The pretence on which this stretch of his royal prerogative was exerted was very slender. The right indeed had been claimed, and occasionally exercised, by the kings of England, of dispensing with penal statutes in such individual cases as might require exception or indulgence. This right somewhat resembled the crown's power of pardoning criminals whom the law has adjudged to death; but, like the power of pardon, the dispensing privilege could only be considered as extending to cases attended with peculiar circumstances. So that when the King pretended to suspend the effect of the penal laws in all instances whatever, it was just as if, being admitted to be possessed of the power of pardoning a man convicted of murder, he had claimed the right to pronounce that murder should in no case be held a capital crime. This reasoning was unanswerable. Nevertheless, at the risk of all the disaffection which such conduct was certain to excite, James was rash enough to put forth a Royal proclamation in which, by his own authority, he dispensed at once with all the penal laws affecting Catholics, and annulled the oath of Supremacy and the Test, so that a Catholic became as eligible for public employment as a Protestant. At the same time, to maintain some appearance of impartiality, an indulgence was granted to moderate Presbyterians, while the laws against the conventicles which met in arms, and in the open fields, were confirmed and enforced.

In this arbitrary and violent proceeding, James was chiefly directed by a few Catholic counselors, none of whom had much reputation for talent, while most of them were inspired by a misjudging zeal for their religion, and imagined they saw the restoration of Popery at hand. To these must be added two or three statesmen, who, being originally Protestants, had adopted the Catholic religion in compliance with the wishes of the King. From these men, who had sacrificed conscience and decency to court favour, the very worst advice was to be apprehended, since they were sure to assert to extremity the character which they had adopted on the ground of self-interest. Such a minister was the Earl of Perth, Chancellor of Scotland, who served the King's pleasure to the uttermost in that kingdom; and such, too, was the far more able and dangerous Earl of Sunderland in England, who, under the guise of the most obsequious obedience to the King's pleasure, made it his study to drive James on to the most extravagant measures, with the secret resolution of deserting him as soon as he should see him in danger of perishing by means of the tempest which he had encouraged him wantonly to provoke.

The sincerity of those converts who change their faith at a moment, when favour and power can be obtained by the exchange, must always be doubtful, and no character inspires more contempt than that of an apostate who deserts his religion for love of gain. Not, however, listening to these obvious considerations, the King seemed to press on the conversion of his subjects to the Roman Catholic faith, without observing that each proselyte, by the fact of becoming so, was rendered generally contemptible, and lost any influence he might have formerly possessed. Indeed the King's rage for making converts was driven to such a height by his obsequious ministers, that an ignorant negro, the servant or slave of one Reid, a mountebank, was publicly baptized after the Catholic ritual upon a stage in the High Street of Edinburgh, and christened James, in honour, it was said, of the Lord Chancellor James Earl of Perth, King James himself, and the Apostle James.

While the King was deserted by his old friends and allies of the Episcopal Church, he probably expected that his enemies, the Presbyterians, would have been conciliated by the unexpected lenity which they experienced. To bring this about, the Indulgence was gradually extended until it comprehended almost a total abrogation of all the oppressive laws respecting fanatics and conventicles, the Cameronians alone being excepted, who disowned the King's authority. But the Protestant nonconformists, being wise enough to penetrate into the schemes of the Prince, remained determined not to form a union with the Catholics, and generally refused to believe that the King had any other object in view than the destruction of Protestants of every description.

Some ministers, indeed, received the toleration with thanks and flattery; and several Presbyterians of rank accepted offices under Government in the room of Episcopalians, who had resigned rather than acquiesce in the dispensation of the penal laws. But, to use their own expressions, the more clear-sighted Presbyterians plainly saw that they had been less aggrieved with the wounds, stabs, and strokes, which the Church had formerly received, than by this pretended Indulgence, which they likened to the cruel courtesy of Joab, who gave a salute to Abner, while at the same time he stabbed him under the fifth rib. This was openly maintained by one large party among the Presbyterians, while the more moderate admitted that Heaven had indeed made the King its instrument to procure some advantage to the Church; but that being convinced the favour shown to them was not sincere, but bestowed with the purpose of disuniting Protestants amongst themselves, they owed James little gratitude for that which he bestowed, not from any good-will to them, but to further his own ends.

These discords between the King and his former friends in Scotland occasioned many changes in the administration of the country. The Duke of Queensberry, who had succeeded Lauderdale in his unlimited authority, and had shown the same disposition to gratify the King on all former occasions, was now disgraced on account of his reluctance to assent to the rash measures adopted in favour of the Catholics. Perth and Melfort, the last also a convert to the Catholic faith, were placed at the head of the administration. On the other hand, Sir George MacKenzie, long King's advocate, and so severe against the Covenanters that he received the name of the Bloody MacKenzie, refused to countenance the revocation of the penal laws, and was, like Queensberry, deprived of his office. Sir James Stewart of Goodtrees, named in his stead, was a Presbyterian of the more rigid sort, such as were usually called fanatics. Judges were also created from the same oppressed party. But none of the nonconformists so promoted, however gratified with their own advancement, either forgot the severity with which their sect had been treated, through the express interference and influence of James, or gave the infatuated monarch credit for sincerity in apparent change of disposition towards them.

Insensible to the general loss of his friends and partisans, James proceeded to press the exercise of his dispensing power. By a new order from court, the most ridiculous and irritating that could well be imagined, all persons in civil employment, without exception, were ordered to lay down their offices, and resume them again by a new commission, without taking the test, which reassumption, being an act done against the existing laws, they were required instantly to wipe out by taking out a remission from the crown for obeying the Royal command. And it was declared, that such as did not obtain such a remission should be afterwards incapable of pardon, and subjected to all the penalties of not having taken the test. Thus the King laid his commands upon his subjects to break one of the standing laws of the kingdom, and then stood prepared to enforce against them the penalty which they had incurred (a penalty due to the crown itself), unless they consented to shelter themselves by accepting a pardon from the King for a crime which they had committed by his order, and thus far acknowledge his illegal power to suspend the laws. In this manner, it was expected that all official persons would be compelled personally to act under and acknowledge the King's power of dispensing with the constitution.

In England the same course of misgovernment was so openly pursued that no room was left the people to doubt that James designed to imitate the conduct of his friend and ally, Louis XIV. of France, in the usurpation of despotic power over the bodies and consciences of his subjects. It was just about this time that the French monarch revoked the toleration which had been granted by Henry IV. to the French Protestants, and forced upwards of half a million of his subjects, offending in nothing excepting their worshipping God after the Protestant manner, into exile from their native country. Many thousands of these persecuted men found refuge in Great Britain, and by the accounts they gave of the injustice and cruelty with which they had been treated, increased the general hatred and dread of the Catholic religion, and in consequence the public jealousy of a prince who was the bigoted follower of its tenets.

But James was totally blind to the dangerous precipice on which he stood, and imagined that the murmurs of the people might be suppressed by the large standing army which he maintained, a considerable part of which, in order to overawe the city of London, lay encamped on Hounslow Heath.

To be still more assured of the fidelity of his army, the King was desirous to introduce amongst them a number of Catholic officers, and also to convert as many of the soldiers as possible to that religion. But even among a set of men, who from their habits are the most disposed to obedience, and perhaps the most indifferent about religious distinctions, the name of Papist was odious; and the few soldiers who embraced that persuasion were treated by their comrades with ridicule and contempt.

In a word, any prince less obstinate and bigoted than James might easily have seen that the army would not become his instrument in altering the laws and religion of the country. But he proceeded with the most reckless indifference to provoke a struggle which it was plain must be maintained against the universal sentiments of his subjects. He had the folly not only to set up the Catholic worship in his Royal chapel, with the greatest pomp and publicity, but to send an ambassador, Lord Castlemaine, to the Pope, to invite his Holiness to countenance his proceedings, by affording him the presence of a nuncio from the See of Rome. Such a communication was, by the law of England, an act of high treason and excited the deepest resentment in England, while abroad it was rather ridiculed than applauded. Even the Pope himself afforded the bigoted monarch very little countenance in his undertaking, being probably of opinion that James's movements were too violent to be secure. His Holiness was also on indifferent terms with Louis XIV., of whom James was a faithful ally, and, on the whole, the Pope was so little disposed to sympathise with the imprudent efforts of the English monarch in favour of the Catholic religion, that he contrived to evade every attempt of Lord Castlemaine to enter upon business, by affecting a violent fit of coughing whenever the conversation took that turn. Yet even this coldness, on the part of the head of his own Church, who might be supposed favourable to James's views, and so intimately concerned in the issue of his attempt, did not chill the insane zeal of the English monarch.

To attain his purpose with some degree of grace from Parliament, which, though he affected to despise it, he was still desirous of conciliating, the King took the most unconstitutional measures to influence the members of both Houses. One mode was by admitting individuals to private audiences, called Closetings, and using all the personal arguments, promises, and threats which his situation enabled him to enforce, for the purpose of inducing the members to comply with his views. He extorted also, from many of the Royal burghs, both in England and Scotland, the surrender of their charters, and substituted others which placed the nomination of their representatives to Parliament in the hands of the crown; and he persisted obstinately in removing Protestants from all offices of honour and trust in the Government, and in filling their situations with Papists. Even his own brothers-in-law, the Earls of Clarendon and Rochester were disgraced, or at least dismissed from their employments, because they would not sacrifice their religious principles to the King's arguments and promises.

Amid so many subjects of jealousy, all uniting to show that it was the purpose of the King to assume arbitrary power, and by the force of tyranny over the rights and lives of his subjects, to achieve a change in the national religion, those operations which immediately affected the Church were the objects of peculiar attention.

As early in his unhappy career as 1686, the year following that of his accession to the throne, James had ventured to re-establish one of the most obnoxious institutions in his father's reign, namely, the Court of High Ecclesiastical Commission, for trying all offences of the clergy. This oppressive and vexatious judicature had been abolished in Charles the First's time, along with the Star Chamber, and it was declared by act of Parliament that neither of them should ever be again erected. Yet the King, in spite of experience and of law, recalled to life this oppressive Court of Ecclesiastical Commission, in order to employ its arbitrary authority in support of the cause of Popery. Sharpe, a clergyman of London, had preached with vehemence in the controversy between Protestants and Catholics, and some of the expressions he made use of were interpreted to reflect on the King. Sharpe endeavoured to apologise, but, nevertheless, the Bishop of London received orders to suspend the preacher from his functions. That prelate excused himself from obedience because he had no power to proceed thus summarily against a person not convicted of any offence. The Bishop's excuse, as well as Sharpe's apology, were disregarded, and both were suspended from their functions by this illegal court; the preacher, because he exerted himself, as his profession required, in combating the arguments by which many were seduced from the Protestant faith; the prelate, because he declined to be an instrument of illegal oppression. The people saw the result of this trial with a deep sense of the illegality shown and the injustice inflicted.

The Universities were equally the object of the King's unprovoked aggressions. It was in their bosom that the youth of the kingdom, more especially those destined for the clerical profession, were educated, and James naturally concluded that to introduce the Catholic influence into these two great and learned bodies would prove a most important step in his grand plan of re-establishing that religion in England.

The experiment upon Cambridge was a slight one. The King, by his mandate, required the University to confer a degree of master of arts upon Father Francis, an ignorant Benedictine monk. Academical honours of this kind are generally conferred without respect to the religion of the party receiving them; and indeed the University had, not very long before, admitted a Mahommedan to the degree of master of arts; but that was an honorary degree only, whereas the degree demanded for the Benedictine monk inferred a right to sit and vote in the elections of the University, whose members, considering that the Papists so introduced might soon control the Protestants, resolved to oppose the King's purpose in the commencement, and refused to grant the degree required. The Court of High Commission suspended the vice-chancellor, but the University chose a man of the same determined spirit in his room; so that the King was not the nearer to his object, which he was compelled for the present to abandon.

Oxford, however, was attacked with more violence, and the consequences were more important. That celebrated University had been distinguished by its unalterable attachment to the Royal cause. When Charles I. was compelled to quit London, he found a retreat at Oxford where the various colleges expended in supporting his cause whatever wealth they possessed, while many members of the University exposed their lives in his service. In Charles the Second's time, Oxford, on account of its inflexible loyalty, had been chosen as the place where the King convoked a short Parliament, when the interest of the Whigs in the city of London was so strong as to render him fearful of remaining in its vicinity. It was less to the honour of this University, that it had shown itself the most zealous in expressing, and enforcing by its ordinances, the slavish tenets of passive obedience and non-resistance to the Royal authority which were then professed by many of the members of the Church of England; but it was an additional proof that their devotion to the King was almost unlimited.

But if James recollected anything whatever of these marks of loyalty to the crown, the remembrance served only to encourage him in his attack upon the privileges of the University, in the belief that they would not be firmly resisted. With ingratitude, therefore, as well as folly, he proceeded to intrude his mandate on the society of Magdalen College, commanding them to choose for their president one of the new converts to the Catholic religion, and on their refusal, expelled them from the college; thus depriving them of their revenues and endowments, because they would not transgress the statutes, to the observance of which they had solemnly sworn.

A still more fatal error, which seems indeed to have carried James's imprudence to the uttermost, was the ever memorable prosecution of the bishops, which had its origin in the following circumstances. In 1688 James published a second declaration of indulgence, with an order subjoined, by which it was appointed to be read in all the churches. The greater part of the English bishops, disapproving of the King's pretended prerogative of dispensing with the test and penal laws, resolved to refuse obedience to this order, which, as their sentiments were well known, could only be intended to disgrace them in the eyes of the people. Six of the most distinguished of the prelates joined with [Sancroft] the Archbishop of Canterbury, in a humble petition to the King, praying his Majesty would dispense with their causing to be published in their dioceses a declaration founded upon the claim of Royal dispensation, which claim having been repeatedly declared illegal, the petitioners could not, in prudence, honour, or conscience, be accessary to distributing a paper which asserted its validity in so solemn a manner all over the nation.

The King was highly incensed at this remonstrance, and summoning the seven prelates before his Privy Council, he demanded of them if they owned and adhered to their petition. They at once acknowledged that they did so, and were instantly committed to the Tower on a charge of sedition. The rank and respectability of these distinguished men, the nature of' the charge against whom, in the popular apprehension, was an attempt to punish them for a bold yet respectful discharge of their high duties, coupled with the anxious dread of what might be expected to follow such a violent procedure, wrought up the minds of the people to the highest pitch.

An immense multitude assembled on the banks of the Thames, and beheld with grief and wonder those fathers of the Church conveyed to prison in the boats appointed for that purpose. The enthusiasm was extreme. The spectators wept, they kneeled, they prayed for the safety of the prisoners, which was only endangered by the firmness with which they had held fast their duty; and the benedictions which the persecuted divines distributed on every side were answered with the warmest wishes for their freedom, and the most unreserved avowal of their cause. All this enthusiasm of popular feeling was insufficient to open James's eyes to his madness. He urged on the proceedings against the prelates, who, on the 17th June 1688, were brought to trial, and, after a long and most interesting hearing of their cause, were fully acquitted. The acclamations of the multitude were loud in proportion to the universal anxiety which prevailed while the case was in dependence; and when the news reached the camp at Hounslow, the extravagant rejoicings of the soldiers, unchecked by the King's own presence, showed that the army and the people were animated by the same spirit.

Yet James was so little influenced by this universal expression of adherence to the Protestant cause, that he continued his headlong career with a degree of rapidity which compelled the reflecting part of the Catholics themselves to doubt and fear the event. He renewed his violent interference with the universities, endeavoured to thrust on Magdalen College a Popish bishop, and resolved to prosecute every clergyman who should refuse to read his declaration of indulgence, that is to say, with the exception of an inconsiderable minority, the whole clergy of the Church of England.

While the kingdoms of Scotland and England were agitated by these violent attempts to establish the Roman Catholic religion, their fears were roused to the highest pitch by observing with what gigantic strides the King was advancing to the same object in Ireland, where, the great body of the people being Catholics, he had no occasion to disguise his purposes. Lord Tyrconnell, a headstrong and violent man, and a Catholic of course, was appointed Viceroy, and proceeded to take every necessary step by arming the Papists and depressing the Protestants, to prepare for a total change, in which the latter should be subjugated by a Catholic Parliament. The violence of the King's conduct in a country where he was not under the necessity of keeping any fair appearances, too plainly showed the Protestants of England and Scotland that the measure presented to them as one of general toleration for all Christian sects, was in fact designed to achieve the supremacy of the Catholic faith over heresy of every denomination.

During all this course of mal-administration, the sensible and prudent part of the nation kept their eyes fixed on William, Prince of Orange, married, as I have before told you, to James's eldest daughter, Mary, and heir to the throne, unless it happened that the King should have a son by his present Queen. This was an event which had long been held improbable, for the children which the Queen had hitherto borne were of a very weak constitution, and did not long survive their birth; and James himself was now an elderly man.

The Prince of Orange, therefore, having a fair prospect of attaining the throne after his father-in-law's death, observed great caution in his communications with the numerous and various factions in England and Scotland; and even to those who expressed the greatest moderation and the purest sentiments of patriotism, he replied with a prudent reserve, exhorting them to patience, dissuading from all hasty insurrections, and pointing out to them, that the death of the King must put an end to the innovations which he was attempting on the constitution.

But an event took place which entirely altered the Prince of Orange's views and feelings, and forced him upon an enterprise, one of the most remarkable in its progress and consequences of any which the history of the world affords. Mary, Queen of England, and wife of James II., was delivered of a male child on the 10th June 1688. The Papists had long looked forward to this event as one which should perpetuate the measures of the King in favour of the Roman Catholics after his own death. They had, therefore, ventured to prophesy that the expected infant would be a son, and they imputed the fulfillment of their wishes to the intervention of the Virgin Mary of Loretto, propitiated by prayers and pilgrimages.

The Protestant party, on the other hand, were disposed to consider the alleged birth of the infant, which had happened so seasonably for the Catholics, as the result not of a miracle of the Popish saints, but of a trick at court. They affirmed that the child was not really the son of James and his wife, but a supposititious infant, whom they were desirous to palm upon their subjects as the legal heir of the throne, in order to defeat the claims of the Protestant successors. This assertion, though gravely swallowed by the people, and widely spread amongst them, was totally without foundation; nor was it possible that there could exist more complete proof of such a fact, than James himself published to the world concerning the birth of this young Prince of Wales. But the King's declarations, and the evidence which he at length made public, were unable to bear down the calumny which was so widely and anxiously circulated. The leaders of the Protestant party, whatever they might themselves believe, took care to make the rumour of the alleged imposture as general as possible; and many whose Tory principles would not have allowed them to oppose the succession of a prince really descended of the blood royal, stood prepared to dispute the right of the infant to succeed to the throne, on account of the alleged doubtfulness of his birth.

One thing, however, was certain, that whether the child was supposititious or not, his birth was likely to prolong the misgovernment under which the country groaned. There now no longer existed the prospect that James would be, at no distant date, succeeded by his son-in-law, the Prince of Orange, with whom the Protestant religion must necessarily recover its predominance. This infant was, of course, to be trained up in the religion and principles of his father; and the influence of the dreaded spirit of Popery, instead of terminating with the present reign, would maintain and extend itself through that of a youthful successor. The Prince of Orange, on his part, seeing himself, by the birth and rights of this infant, excluded from the long-hoped-for succession to the crown of England, laid aside his caution, with the purpose of taking a bold and active interference in British politics.

He now publicly, though with decency, declared that his sentiments were opposite to those on which his father-in-law acted, and that though he was disposed to give a hearty consent to repealing penal statutes in all cases, being of opinion that no one should be punished for his religious opinions, yet he could not acquiesce in the King's claim to dispense with the test, which only excluded from public offices those whose conscience would not permit them to conform to the established religion of the country in which they lived. Having thus openly declared his sentiments, the Prince of Orange was resorted to openly or secretly, by all those, of whatever political opinions, who joined in the general fear for the religious and civil liberties of the country, which were threatened by the bigotry of James. Encouraged by the universal sentiments of the English nation, a few Catholics excepted, and by the urgent remonstrances of many of the leading men of all the various parties, the Prince of Orange resolved to appear in England at the head of an armed force, with the purpose of putting a stop to James's encroachments on the constitution in Church and State.

Under various plausible pretexts, therefore, the Prince began to assemble a navy and army adequate to the bold invasion which he meditated; while neither the warning of the King of France, who penetrated the purpose of these preparations, nor a sense of the condition in which he himself stood, could induce James to take any adequate measures of defence.

The unfortunate Prince continued to follow the same measures which had lost him the hearts of his subjects, and every step he took encouraged and prompted disaffection. Dubious of the allegiance of his army, he endeavoured, by introducing Irish Catholics amongst them, to fill their ranks, in part at least, with men in whom he might repose more confidence. But the lieutenant-colonel and five captains of the regiment in which the experiment was first tried, refused to receive the proposed recruits; and though these officers were cashiered for doing so, yet their spirit was generally applauded by those of their own profession.

Another experiment on the soldiery had a still more mortifying result. Although it is contrary to the British constitution to engage soldiers under arms in the discussion of any political doctrine, since they must be regarded as the servants, not the counsellors of the state, nevertheless James resolved, if possible, to obtain from the army their approbation of the repeal of the test and the penal statutes. By way of experiment, a single battalion was drawn up in his own presence, and informed that they must either express their hearty acquiescence in the King's purposes in respect to these laws, or lay down their arms, such being the sole condition on which their services would be received. On hearing this appeal, the whole regiment, excepting two officers and a few Catholic soldiers, laid down their arms. The King stood mute with anger and disappointment, and at length told them, in a sullen and offended tone, to take up their arms and retire to their quarters, adding that he would not again do them the honour to ask their opinions.

While James was thus extorting from his very soldiers opinions the most unfavourable to his measures, he suddenly received intelligence from his ambassador in Holland, that the Prince of Orange was about to put to sea with an army of fifteen thousand men, supplied by the States of Holland, and a fleet of five hundred sail.

Conscious that he had lost the best safeguard of a monarch—namely, the love and affections of his subjects, this news came upon James like a thunder-clap. He hastened to retract all the measures which had rendered his reign so unpopular; but it was with a precipitation which showed fear, not conviction, and the people were persuaded that the concessions would be recalled as soon as the danger was over.

In the meantime the Dutch fleet set sail. At first it encountered a storm, and was driven back into harbour. But the damage sustained by some of the vessels being speedily repaired, they again put to sea, and with so much activity, that the short delay proved rather of service than otherwise; for the English fleet, which had also been driven into harbour by the storm, could not be got ready to meet the invaders. Steering for the west of England, the Prince of Orange landed in Torbay on the 5th November 1688, being the anniversary of the Gunpowder Plot, a circumstance which seemed propitious to an enterprise commenced in opposition to the revival of Popery in England.

Immediately on his landing the Prince published a manifesto, setting forth, in plain and strong terms, the various encroachments made by the reigning monarch upon the British constitution, and upon the rights as well of the Church as of private persons and corporate bodies. He came, he said, with an armed force, to protect his person from the King's evil counsellors, but declared that his only purpose was to have a full and free Parliament assembled in order to procure a general settlement of religion, liberty, and property.

Notwithstanding that so many persons of rank and influence had privately encouraged the Prince of Orange to this undertaking, there appeared at first very little alacrity to support him in carrying it through. The inhabitants of the western counties, where the Prince landed, were overawed by recollection of the fearful punishment inflicted upon those who had joined Monmouth, and the Prince had advanced to Exeter ere he was joined by any adherent of consequence. But from the time that one or two gentlemen of consideration joined him, a general commotion took place all over England, and the nobility and gentry assumed arms on every side for redress of the grievances set forth in the Prince's manifesto.

In the midst of this universal defection, King James gave orders to assemble his army, assigned Salisbury for his headquarters, and announced his purpose of fighting the invaders. But he was doomed to experience to what extent he had alienated the affections of his subjects by his bigoted and tyrannical conduct. Several noblemen and officers of rank publicly deserted, and carried off to the Prince's army numbers of their soldiers. Amongst these was Lord Churchill, afterwards the celebrated Duke of Marlborough. He was a particular favourite of the unhappy King, who had bestowed a peerage on him, with high rank in the army; and his desertion to the Prince on this occasion showed that the universal aversion to King James's measures had alienated the affections of those who would otherwise have been most devotedly attached to him.

A still more striking defection seems to have destroyed the remains of the unhappy monarch's resolution. His second daughter, the Princess Anne, who was married to a younger son of the King of Denmark, called Prince George, escaped by night from London, under the protection of the Bishop of that city, who raised a body of horse for her safeguard, and rode armed at their head. She fled to Nottingham, where she was received by the Earl of Dorset, and declared for a free

Protestant Parliament. Her husband, and other persons of the first distinction, joined the Prince of Orange.

The sudden and unexpected dissolution of his power, when every morning brought intelligence of some new defection or insurrection, totally destroyed the firmness of James, who, notwithstanding his folly and misconduct, becomes, in this period of unmitigated calamity, an object of our pity. At the tidings of his daughter's flight, he exclaimed, with the agony of paternal feeling, "God help me, my own children desert me!" In the extremity and desolation of his distress, the unfortunate monarch seems to have lost all those qualities which had gained him in earlier life the character of courage and sagacity; and the heedless rashness with which he had scorned the distant danger was only equalled by the prostrating degree of intimidation which now overwhelmed him.

He disbanded his army, to the great increase of the general confusion; and finally, terrified by the recollection of his father's fate, he resolved to withdraw himself from his kingdom. It is probable that he could not have taken any resolution which would have been so grateful to the Prince of Orange. If James had remained in Britain, the extremity of his misfortunes would probably have awakened the popular compassion; and the tenets of the High Churchmen and Tories, although they had given way to their apprehensions for the safety of religion and liberty, might, when these were considered as safe, have raised many partisans to the distressed monarch. Besides, while King James remained in his dominions, it would have been an obnoxious and odious attempt, on the part of the Prince of Orange, to have plucked the crown forcibly from the head of his father-in-law, in order to place it upon his own. On the other hand, if the flight of the King into foreign countries should leave the throne unoccupied, nothing could be so natural as to place there the next Protestant heir of the crown, by whose providential interference the liberties and constitution of the country had been rescued from such imminent danger.

Fortune seemed at first adverse to an escape, which was desired by King James, owing to his fears, and by the Prince of Orange, in consequence of his hopes. As the King, attended by one gentleman, endeavoured to get on board of a vessel prepared for his escape, they were seized by some rude fishermen, who were looking out to catch such priests and Catholics as were flying from the kingdom. At the hands of these men the unfortunate monarch received some rough treatment, until the gentry of the country interposed for the protection of his person, but still refused to permit him to depart the kingdom. He was allowed, however, to return to London, where the rabble, with their usual mutability, and moved with compassion for the helpless state to which they beheld the King reduced, received him with acclamations of favour.

The Prince of Orange, not a little disappointed by this incident, seems to have determined to conduct himself towards his father-in-law with such a strain of coldness and severity as should alarm James for his personal safety, and determine him to resume his purpose of flight. With such a view the Prince refused to receive the nobleman whom the King had sent to him to desire a conference, and ordered the messenger to be placed under arrest. In reply to the message he issued a command, transmitted at midnight, that the King should leave his palace the next morning. The dejected sovereign yielded to the mandate, and, at his own request, Rochester was assigned for his abode. That happened which must have been foreseen, from his choosing a place near the river as his temporary habitation. James privately embarked on board of a frigate, and was safely landed at Ambleteuse, in France. He was received by Louis XIV. with the utmost generosity and hospitality, and lived for many years at St. Germains under his protection and at his expense, excepting only during a short campaign (to be afterwards noticed) in Ireland. Every effort to replace him in his dominions only proved destructive to those who were engaged in them. The exiled monarch was looked upon with reverence by sincere Catholics, who counted him as a martyr to his zeal for the form of religion which he and they professed; but by others he was ridiculed as a bigot who had lost three kingdoms for the sake of a mass.

A Convention, as it was called (in effect a Parliament, though not such in form, because it could not be summoned in the King's name), was convoked at Westminster; and, at their first meeting, they returned their unanimous thanks to the Prince of Orange for the deliverance which he had achieved for the nation. The House of Commons then proceeded, by a great majority, to vote that King James had forfeited his regal title by a variety of encroachments on the constitution; that, by his flight, he had abdicated the government; and that the throne was vacant. But as great part of this resolution was adverse to the doctrine of the Tories, who refused to adopt it, the mention of forfeiture was omitted; and it was finally settled that by his evil administration, and subsequent flight from Britain, King James had *abdicated* the throne. And I cannot forbear to point out to you the singular wisdom of both the great parties in the state, who, by keeping the expressions of their resolution so general as to clash with the sentiments of neither, concurred in a measure so important, without starting any theoretical disputes to awaken party contention at a moment when the peace of England depended on unanimity.

The throne being thus declared vacant, the important question remained, by whom it should be filled. This was a point warmly disputed. The Tories were contented that the Prince of Orange should exercise the regal power, but only under the title of Regent. They could not reconcile themselves to the dethroning a King and electing his successor; and contended that James's course of misconduct did not deprive him of his kingly right and title, but only operated like some malady, which rendered him unfit to have the exercise of regal power. The Whigs replied that this doctrine would prevent the nation from deriving the desired advantages from the Revolution, since, if James was in any respect to be acknowledged as a sovereign, he might return and claim the power which is inalienable from the Royal right. Besides, if James was still King, it was evident that his son, who had been carried abroad, in order that he might be bred up in Popery, and in arbitrary doctrines, must be acknowledged after the death of James himself. They, therefore, declared for the necessity of filling up the vacant sovereignty. A third party endeavoured to find a middle opinion, with regard to which the objections applicable to those we have just expressed should not hold good. They proposed that the crown should be conferred on Mary, Princess of Orange, in her own right; thus passing over the infant Prince of Wales, and transferring their allegiance to Mary as the next Protestant heir of the crown.

The Prince of Orange, who had listened to, and watched these debates in silence, but with deep interest, now summoned a small council of leading persons, to whom he made his sentiments known.

He would not, he said, interfere in any respect with the right of the English Parliament to arrange their future government according to their own laws, or their own pleasure. But he felt it necessary to acquaint them, that if they chose to be governed by a Regent, he would not accept that office. Neither was he disposed to take the government of the kingdom under his wife, supposing she was chosen Queen. If either of these modes of settlement were adopted, he informed them he would retire entirely from all interference with British affairs. The Princess, his wife, seconded her husband's views, to whom she always paid the highest degree of conjugal deference.

The wisdom and power of the Prince of Orange, nay even the assistance of his military force, were absolutely indispensable to the settlement of England, divided as it was by two rival political parties, who had indeed been forced into union by the general fear of James's tyranny, but were ready to renew their dissensions the instant the overwhelming pressure of that fear was removed. The Convention were, therefore, obliged to regulate the succession to the throne upon the terms agreeable to the Prince of Orange. The Princess and he were called to the throne jointly, under the title of King William and Queen Mary, the survivor succeeding the party who should first die. The Princess Anne of Denmark was named to succeed after the death of her sister and brother-in-law, and the claims of James's infant son were entirely passed over.

The Convention did not neglect this opportunity to annex to the settlement of the crown a Declaration of Rights, determining in favour of the subject those rights which had been contested during the late reigns, and drawing with more accuracy and precision than had hitherto been employed the lines which circumscribe the Royal authority.

Such was this memorable Revolution, which (saving a petty and accidental skirmish) decided the fate of a great kingdom without bloodshed, and in which, perhaps for the only time in history, the heads of the discordant factions of a great empire laid aside their mutual suspicion and animosity, and calmly and dispassionately discussed the great concerns of the nation, without reference to their own interests or those of their party. To the memory of this Convention, or Parliament, the Britannic kingdoms owe the inestimable blessing of a constitution, fixed on the decided and defined principles of civil and religious liberty.

LV

The Jacobite Cause

1688-1689

THE necessity of explaining the nature and progress of the Revolution of England, without which it would be impossible for you to comprehend what passed in the northern part of the kingdom, has drawn us away from the proper subject of this little book, and makes it necessary that we should return to our account of Scottish affairs during the time that these important events were taking place in England.

We have mentioned the discontents which existed among King James's most zealous friends in Scotland, on account of his pressing the revocation of the Test, and that several of the crown officers and crown lawyers, and even two or three of the judges, had been displaced for demurring to that measure, the vacancies being filled with Catholics or Presbyterians. You have also been told that by this false policy, James lost the affection of his friends of the Episcopal Church, without being able to conciliate his ancient enemies, the nonconformists.

Thus stood matters in Scotland, when, in September 1688, King James sent down to his council in Scotland an account of the preparations making in Holland to invade England. Upon this alarming news the militia were ordered to be in readiness; the Highland chiefs were directed to prepare their clans to take the field; and the vassals of the crown were modelled into regiments, and furnished with arms. These forces, joined to the standing army, would have made a considerable body of troops.

But unanimity, the soul of national resistance, was wanting. The Scottish Royalists were still so much attached to the crown, and even to the person of James, that, notwithstanding the late causes of suspicion and discord which had occurred betwixt them and the King, there remained little doubt that they would have proved faithful to his cause. But the Presbyterians, even of the most moderate party, had suffered so severely at James's hand, both during his brother's reign and his own, that it was hardly to be expected that a few glances of Royal favour, to which they appeared to be admitted only because they could not be decently excluded from the toleration designed for the benefit of the Catholics, should make them forget the recent terrors of the storm. Several of the gentry of this persuasion, however, seemed ready to serve the King, and obtained commissions in the militia; but the event showed that this was done with the purpose of acting more effectually against him.

The Earl of Perth endeavoured to ascertain the real sentiments of that numerous party, by applying to them through the medium of Sir Patrick Murray, a person who seemed attached to no particular sect, but who was esteemed by all. This gentleman applied to such leading Presbyterian ministers as were in Edinburgh, reminding them of the favours lately shown them by the King, and requesting they would now evince their gratitude by influencing their hearers to oppose the unnatural invasion threatened by the Prince of Orange. The clergymen received the overture coldly, and declined to return an answer till there should be more of their brethren in town. Having in the interim obtained information which led them to expect the ultimate success of the Prince of Orange, they sent as their answer to the Earl of Perth, through Sir Patrick Murray, "That they owned the King had of late been used as Heaven's instrument to show them some favour; but being convinced that he had done so only with a design to ruin the Protestant religion, by introducing dissension among its professors of different denominations, and observing that the persons whom he voluntarily raised to power were either Papists or persons popishly inclined, they desired to be excused from giving any further answer, saving that they would conduct themselves in this juncture as God should inspire them."

From this answer, it was plain that James was to expect nothing from the Presbyterians; yet they remained silent and quiet, waiting the event, and overawed by the regular troops, who were posted in such places as to prevent open insurrection.

The disaffection of the English soldiery having alarmed James's suspicions, he sent orders that his Scottish army should be drawn together, and held in readiness to march into England. The Scottish administration answered by a remonstrance, that this measure would leave the government of Scotland totally defenceless, and encourage the disaffected, who could not but think the affairs of King James were desperate, since he could not dispense with the assistance of so small a body of troops. To this remonstrance the King replied by a positive order that the Scottish army should advance into England.

This little army might consist of six or seven thousand excellent troops, commanded by James Douglas, brother to the Duke of Queensberry, as General-in-Chief, and by the more celebrated John Graham of Claverhouse, recently created Viscount of Dundee, as Major-General. The former was secretly a favourer of the Prince of Orange's enterprise. Viscount Dundee, on the other hand, was devotedly attached to the cause of King James, and redeemed some of his fiercer and more cruel propensities by the virtue of attaching himself to his benefactor, when he was forsaken by all the world besides. It is said that the march was protracted by Douglas, lest the steadiness of the Scottish army should have served as an example to the English. At length, however, they reached London, where the Viscount of Dundee claimed a right to command, as eldest Major-General; but the English officers of the same rank, whether out of national jealousy, or that Dundee's obtaining so high a rank might have interfered with their private schemes, positively refused to serve under him. It is said, that, in the event of his obtaining this command, his design was to assemble such English troops as yet remained faithful, and, at the head of these and the Scottish army, to have marched against the Prince of Orange and given him battle. But this scheme, which must have cost much bloodshed, was defeated by the refusal of the English officers to fight under him.

King James, amidst the distraction of his affairs, requested the advice of this sagacious and determined adherent, who pointed out to him three courses. The first, was to try the fate of war, by manfully fighting the Prince of Orange. The second alternative was, to meet him in friendship and require to know his purpose. The third was, to retire into Scotland, under protection of the little army which had marched to support him. The King, it is said, was inclined to try the third alternative; but, as he received intelligence that several Scottish peers and gentlemen were come post to London, to wait on the Prince of Orange, he justly doubted whether that kingdom would have proved a safer place of refuge than England. Indeed, he presently afterwards heard that one of Douglas's battalions had caught the spirit of desertion and gone over to the Prince.

Shortly after this untoward event, Dundee, with such of his principal officers as adhered to the cause of James, received assurances of the King's disposition to hazard battle, and were commanded to meet him at Uxbridge, to consult upon the movements to be adopted. When the Scottish officers reached the place appointed, instead of meeting with the King, they learned that their misguided monarch had fled, and received the fatal order to disband their forces. Dundee, with the Lords Linlithgow and Dunmore, shed tears of grief and mortification. In the uncertainty of the times, Dundee resolved to keep his forces together, until he had conducted them back into Scotland. With this view he took up his quarters at Watford, intending to retreat on the ensuing morning. In the meanwhile the town's people, who did not like the company of these northern soldiers, raised a report during the course of the night that the Prince of Orange was coming to attack them, hoping, by this false alarm, to frighten the Scottish troops from the place sooner than they intended. But Dundee was not a person to be so easily startled. To the great alarm of the citizens, he caused his trumpets sound to arms, and taking up a strong position in front of the town, sent out to reconnoitre, and learn the intentions of the Prince of Orange. Thus the stratagem of the citizens of Watford only brought on themselves the chance of a battle in front of their town, which was most likely to suffer in the conflict, be the event what it would.

But the Prince of Orange knew Dundee's character well. He had served his early campaigns under that Prince, and had merited his regard, not only by a diligent discharge of his duty, but also by rescuing William at the battle of Seneff in 1674, and remounting him on his own horse when that of the Prince was slain under him. Dundee had left the Dutch service on being disappointed of a regiment.

Knowing, therefore, the courage, talent, and obstinacy of the Scottish commander, the Prince of Orange took the step of assuring the Viscount of Dundee that he had not the least intention of molesting him, and that understanding he was at Watford, and was keeping his men embodied, he had to request he would remain there till further orders. When the news of the King's return to London was rumoured, Dundee went to assure his old master of his continued attachment, and to receive his orders; and it is said he even, in that moment of universal despair, offered to assemble the dispersed troops of the King, and try the fate of war. But James's spirit was too much broken to stand such a hazard.

On James's final flight to France, and the decision of the Convention, elevating the Prince and Princess of Orange to the throne, Dundee would no longer retain his command, but retired to Scotland, at the head of a bodyguard of twenty or thirty horse, who would not quit him, and without whose protection he could not perhaps have passed safely through the southern and western counties, where he had exercised so many severities. The Scottish army, or what remained of it, was put under the command of General MacKay, an officer attached to King William, and transferred to the service of the new monarch, though there were many amongst them who cast a lingering eye towards that of their old master.

In the meantime, the Revolution had been effected in Scotland, though not with the same unanimity as in England. On the contrary, the Episcopalians throughout the kingdom, in spite of all the provocations which they had received, could not prevail upon themselves to join in any measures which should be unfavourable to James's interest, and would probably have appeared in arms in his cause, had there been any one present in Scotland to raise and uphold the exiled monarch's banner.

The Scottish prelates, in particular, hastened to show, that in the extremity of King James's misfortunes they had forgotten their rupture with him, and had returned to the principles of passive obedience by which their church was distinguished. On the 3d November the whole of their number, excepting the Bishops of Argyle and Caithness, joined in a letter to the King, professing their own fixed and unshaken loyalty, promising their utmost efforts to promote among his subjects an *intemerable* and steadfast allegiance, and praying that Heaven would give the King the hearts of his subjects and the necks of his enemies.

But the defenceless state in which King James's Scottish government was left, after the march of Douglas and Dundee into England at the head of the regular forces, rendered the good wishes of the bishops of little service. It soon began to appear that the Scottish Presbyterians were determined to avail themselves of an opportunity for which the chiefs amongst them had long made preparations. The Earls of Glencairn, Crawford, Dundonald, and Tarras, with several other persons of consideration, encouraged the rising of the Presbyterians, who, hastily assuming arms, appeared in different parts of the country, in open opposition to the Government.

These desultory forces might have been put down by the militia; but a manœuvre of the Earl of Athole, whose connection with the Earl of Derby had procured him admission into the secrets of the Revolution, prevented the adherents of King James from having this support. Lord Tarbat concurred in the sentiments of Athole, and both being members of the Privy Council, had an opportunity of carrying their purpose into execution. When the news reached Scotland, that the army of King James was disbanded, and the King had fled, these two noblemen persuaded the Chancellor, Perth, and other Catholics or zealous Jacobites in the Privy Council, that, as there was now no chance of coming to a decision by force of arms, it was their duty to disband the militia, as their services could not be needed, and their maintenance was a burden to the country.

The Earl of Perth, who appears to have been a timorous man, and of limited understanding, was persuaded to acquiesce in this measure; and no sooner had he parted with the militia, his last armed defence, than his colleagues made him understand that he being a Papist, incapacitated by law from holding any public office, they did not think themselves in safety to sit and vote with him as a member of government. And, while the Protestant part of his late obsequious brethren seemed to shun him as one infected with the plague, the rabble beat drums in the streets, proclaimed him traitor, and set a price upon his head. The late Chancellor's courage could not withstand the menace, and he escaped from the metropolis with the purpose of flying beyond seas. But being pursued by armed barks, he was taken, and detained a prisoner for more than four years.

In the meantime, an act of violence of a decided character took place in Edinburgh. Holyrood House, the ancient palace of James's ancestors, and his own habitation when in Scotland, had been repaired with becoming splendour when he came to the throne. But it was within its precincts that he had established his royal chapel for the Catholic service, as well as a seminary of Jesuits, an institution which, under pretext of teaching the Latin language, and other branches of education gratis, was undoubtedly designed to carry on the work of making proselytes. At Holyrood House a printing establishment was also erected, from which were issued polemical tracts in defence of the Catholic religion, and similar productions. The palace and its inmates were on all these accounts very obnoxious to the Presbyterian party, which now began to obtain the ascendency.

The same bands, consisting of the meaner class of people, apprentices, and others, whose appearance had frightened the Chancellor out of the city, continued to parade the streets with drums beating, until, confident in their numbers, they took the resolution of making an attack on the palace, which was garrisoned by a company of regular soldiers, commanded by one Captain Wallace.

As the multitude pressed on this officer's sentinels, he at length commanded his men to fire, and some of the insurgents were killed. A general cry was raised through the city, that Wallace and his soldiers were committing a massacre of the inhabitants; and many of the citizens, repairing to the Earl of Athole and his colleagues, the only part of the Privy Council which remained, obtained a warrant from them for the surrender of the palace, and an order for the King's heralds to attend in their official habits to intimate the same. The city guard of Edinburgh was also commanded to be in readiness to enforce the order; the trained bands were got under arms, and the provost and magistrates, with a number of persons of condition, went to show their good-will to the cause. Some of these volunteers acted a little out of character. Lord Mersington, one of the Judges of the Court of Session, lately promoted to that office by James II., at the time when he was distributing his favours equally betwixt Papist and Puritan, attracted some attention from his peculiar appearance; he was girt with a buff belt above five inches broad, bore a halbert in his hand and (if a Jacobite eye-witness speaks truth) was "as drunk as ale and brandy could make him."

On the approach of this motley army of besiegers, Wallace, instead of manning the battlements and towers of the palace, drew up his men imprudently in the open court-yard in front of it. He refused to yield up his post, contending that the warrant of the Privy Council was only signed by a small number of that body. Defiance was exchanged on both sides, and firing commenced; on which most of the volunteers got into places of safety, leaving Captain Wallace and the major of the city guard to dispute the matter professionally. It chanced that the latter proved the better soldier, and finding a back way into the palace, attacked Wallace in the rear. The defenders were at the same time charged in front by the other assailants, and the palace was taken by storm. The rabble behaved themselves as riotously as might have been expected, breaking, burning, and destroying not only the articles which belonged to the Catholic service, but the whole furniture of the chapel; and, finally, forcing their way into the Royal sepulchres, and pulling about the bodies of the deceased princes and kings of Scotland. These monuments, to the great scandal of the British Government, were not closed until ten or twelve years since, before which time, the exhibition of the wretched relics of mortality which had been dragged to light on this occasion was a part of the show offered for the amusement of strangers who visited the palace.

This riot, which ascertained the complete superiority of the Presbyterian party, took place on the 10th December 1688. The houses of various Catholics, who then resided chiefly in the Canongate, were mobbed, or rabbled, as was then the phrase, their persons insulted, and their property destroyed. But the populace contented themselves with burning and destroying whatever they considered as belonging to Papists and Popery, without taking anything for their own use.

This zeal for the Protestant cause was maintained by false rumours that an army of Irish Catholics had landed in the west and were burning, spoiling, and slaying. It was even said they had reached Dumfries. A similar report had produced a great effect on the minds of the English during the Prince of Orange's advance to the capital. In Scotland it was a general signal for the Presbyterians to get to arms and, being thus assembled, they, and particularly the Cameronians, found active occupation in expelling from the churches the clergy of the Episcopal persuasion. To proceed in this work with some appearance of form, they, in most cases, previously intimated to the Episcopal curates that they must either leave their churches voluntarily or be forcibly ejected from them.

Now, since these armed nonconformists had been, to use their own language, for nearly twenty years "proscribed, forfeited, miserably oppressed, given up as sheep to the slaughter, intercommuned, and interdicted of harbour or supply, comfort or communion, hunted and slain in the fields, in cities imprisoned, tortured, executed to the death, or banished and sold as slaves;" and, as many of them avowed the same wild principles which were acted upon by the murderers of Archbishop

Sharp, it might have been expected that a bloody retaliation would take place as soon as they had the power in their own hands. Yet it must be owned that these stern Cameronians showed no degree of positive cruelty. They expelled the obnoxious curates with marks of riotous triumph, tore their gowns, and compelled them sometimes to march in a mock procession to the boundary of their parish; they plundered the private chapels of Catholics, and destroyed whatever they found belonging to their religion; but they evinced no desire of personal vengeance; nor have I found that the clergy who were expelled in this memorable month of December 1688, although most of them were treated with rudeness and insult, were, in any case, killed or wounded in cold blood.

These tumults were likely to have again excited the inhabitants of Edinburgh; but the College of Justice, under which title all the different law bodies of the capital are comprehended, assumed arms for maintaining the public peace, and resisting an expected invasion of the city by the Cameronians, who threatened in this hour of triumph a descent on the metropolis, and a second Whigamores' Raid. This species of civic guard effectually checked their advance, until, not being supposed favourable to the Prince of Orange, it was disbanded by proclamation when he assumed the management of public affairs.

Scotland may be said to have been, for some time, without a government; and, indeed, now that all prospect of war seemed at an end, men of all parties posted up to London as the place where the fate of the kingdom must be finally settled. The Prince of Orange recommended the same measure which had been found efficient in England; and a Convention of the Scottish Estates was summoned to meet in March 1689. The interval was spent by both parties in preparing for a contest.

The Episcopal party continued devoted to the late King. They possessed a superiority among the nobility, provided the bishops should be permitted to retain their seats in the Convention. But among the members for counties, and especially the representatives of burghs, the great majority was on the side of the Whigs, or Williamites, as the friends of the Prince of Orange began to be called.

If actual force were to be resorted to, the Jacobites relied on the faith of the Duke of Gordon, who was governor of the castle of Edinburgh, on the attachment of the Highland clans, and the feudal influence of the nobles and gentry of the north. The Whigs might reckon on the full force of the five western shires, besides a large proportion of the south of Scotland. The same party had on their side the talents and abilities of Dalrymple, Fletcher, and other men of strong political genius, far superior to any that was possessed by the Tories. But if the parties should come to an open rupture, the Whigs had no soldier of reputation to oppose to the formidable talents of Dundee.

The exiled King having directed his adherents to attend the Convention, and, if possible, secure a majority there, Dundee appeared on the occasion with a train of sixty horse, who had most of them served under him on former occasions. The principal Whigs, on their part, secretly brought into town the armed Cameronians, whom they concealed in garrets and cellars till the moment should come for their being summoned to appear in arms. These preparations for violence show how inferior in civil polity Scotland must have been to England, since it seemed that the great national measures which were debated with calmness, and adopted with deliberation in the Convention of England, were, in that of North Britain, to be decided, apparently, by an appeal to the sword.

Yet the Convention assembled peaceably, though under ominous circumstances. The town was filled with two factions of armed men, lately distinguished as the persecuting and the oppressed parties, and burning with hatred against each other. The guns of the castle, from the lofty rock on which it is situated, lay loaded and prepared to pour their thunders on the city; and under these alarming circumstances, the peers and commons of Scotland were to consider and decide upon the fate of her crown. Each party had the deepest motives for exertion.

The Cavaliers, or Jacobites, chiefly belonging by birth to the aristocracy, forgot James's errors in his misfortunes, or indulgently ascribed them to a few bigoted priests and selfish counsellors by whom, they were compelled to admit, the Royal ear had been too exclusively possessed. They saw, in their now aged monarch, the son of the venerated martyr, Charles I., whose memory was so dear to them, and the descendant of the hundred princes who had occupied the Scottish throne, according to popular belief, for a thousand years, and under whom their ancestors had acquired their fortunes, their titles, and their fame. James himself, whatever were the political errors of his reign, had been able to attach to himself individually many both of the nobility and gentry of Scotland, who regretted him as a friend as well as a sovereign, and recollected the familiarity with which he could temper his stately courtesy, and the favours which many had personally received from him. The compassion due to fallen majesty was in this case enhanced, when it was considered that James was to be uncrowned, in order that the Prince and Princess of Orange, his son-in-law and daughter, might be raised to the throne in his stead, a measure too contrary to the ordinary feelings of nature not to create some disgust. Besides, the Cavaliers generally were attached to the Episcopal form of worship, and to the constitution of a church which, while it supported with credit the dignity of the sacred order, affected not the rigorous discipline and vexatious interference in the affairs of private families for which they censured the Presbyterians. Above all, the Jacobites felt that they themselves must sink in power and influence with the dethronement of King James, and must remain a humbled and inferior party in the kingdom which they lately governed, hated for what had passed, and suspected in regard to the future.

The Whigs, with warmer hopes of success, had even more urgent motives for political union and exertion. They reckoned up the melancholy roll of James's crimes and errors, and ridiculed the idea that he who had already suffered so much both in his youth and middle age would ever become wiser by misfortune. Bigotry and an extravagant and inveterate love of power, they alleged, were propensities which increased with age; and his religion, they contended, while it would readily permit him to enter into any engagements which an emergency might require, would with equal ease dispense with his keeping them, and even impute it as a merit that he observed no faith with heretics. The present crisis, they justly argued, afforded a happy occasion to put an end to that course of open encroachment upon their liberty and property, of which the Scottish nation had so long had to complain; and it would be worse than folly to sacrifice the rights and liberties of the people to the veneration attached to an ancient line of princes, when their representative had forgotten the tenure by which he held the throne of his fathers. The form of the Presbyterian Church, while it possessed a vital power over the hearts and consciences of the worshippers, was also of a character peculiarly favourable to freedom, and suitable to a poor country like that of Scotland, which was unable to maintain bishops and dignitaries with becoming splendour. A great part of the nation had shown themselves attached to it, and disposed to submit to the greatest hardships, and to death itself, rather than conform to the Episcopal mode of worship; and it was fitting they should have permission to worship God in the way their consciences recommended. The character of William afforded the most brilliant arguments to his partisans in the Convention. He had been from his youth upward distinguished as the champion of public freedom, his zeal for which exceeded even his ambition. He was qualified by the doctrines of toleration, which he had deeply imbibed, to cure the wounds of nations distracted by civil faction, and his regard for truth and honour withstood every temptation to extend his power, which the unsettled circumstances of the British kingdoms might present to an ambitious prince.

Distracted by these various considerations, the Scottish Convention met. The first contest was for the nomination of a president, in which it is remarkable that both the contending parties made choice of candidates, in whom neither could repose trust as faithful partisans. The Marquis of Athole was proposed by the Jacobites, to whose side he now inclined, after having been, as I have shown you, the principal actor in displacing James's Scottish administration, and chasing from Edinburgh that King's chancellor, the Earl of Perth. The Whigs, on the other hand, equally at a loss to find an unexceptionable candidate, set up the Duke of Hamilton, although his future conduct was so undecided and dubious as to make them more than once repent of their choice.

The Duke of Hamilton attained the presidency by a majority of fifteen, which, though not a very predominating one, was sufficient to ascertain the superiority of the Whigs, who, as usual in such cases, were immediately joined by all those whom timidity or selfish considerations had kept aloof, until they should discover which was the safest, and likely to be the winning side. The majorities of the Whigs increased therefore upon every question, while the Jacobite party saw no remedy but in some desperate and violent course. The readiest which occurred was to endeavour to induce the Duke of Gordon, governor of the castle, to fire upon the town, and to expel the Convention, in which their enemies were all-powerful. The Convention, on the other hand, by a great majority, summoned the Duke to surrender the place under the pains of high treason.

The position of the Duke was difficult. The castle was strong, but it was imperfectly supplied with provisions; the garrison was insufficient, and many among them of doubtful fidelity; and as every other place of strength throughout the kingdom had been surrendered, to refuse compliance might be to draw upon himself the unmitigated vengeance of the prevailing party. The Duke was therefore uncertain how to decide when the Earls of Lothian and Tweeddale came to demand a surrender in the name of the Convention; and he at first offered to comply, on obtaining indemnity for himself and his friends. But the Viscount of Dundee, getting access to the castle while the treaty was in dependence, succeeded in inspiring the Duke with a share of his own resolution; so that when the commissioners desired to know the friends for whom he demanded immunity, he answered by delivering to them a list of all the clans in the Highlands; which being interpreted as done in scorn, the two Earls returned so indignant that they scarce could find words to give an account of their errand to the Convention.

Soon after, the Duke of Gordon was solemnly summoned by two heralds, in their ceremonial habits, to surrender the castle; and they at the same time published a proclamation, prohibiting any one to converse with or assist him, should he continue contumacious. The Duke desired them to inform the Convention that he held his command by warrant from their common master; and, giving them some money to drink King James's health, he observed that when they came to declare loyal subjects traitors, with the King's coats on their backs, they ought in decency to turn them.

But though Dundee had been able to persuade the Duke to stand a siege in the castle, he could not prevail upon him to fire on the town; an odious severity which would certainly have brought general hatred upon him, without, perhaps, having the desired effect of dislodging the Convention. This scheme having failed, the Jacobites resolved upon another, which was to break up with all their party, and hold another and rival Convention at Stirling. For this purpose it was proposed that the Earl of Mar, hereditary keeper of Stirling Castle, should join them in order that they might have the protection of the fortress, and that Athole should assist them with a body of his Highlanders. These noblemen entered into the plan; but when it came to the point of execution, the courage of both seems to have given way, and the design was postponed.

Whilst affairs were in this state, Dundee, provoked alike at the vacillation of his friends and the triumph of his enemies, resolved no longer to remain inactive. He suddenly appeared before the Convention, and complained of a plot laid to assassinate himself and Sir George MacKenzie, the late King's advocate,—a charge which was very probable, since the town was now filled with armed Cameronians, who had smarted so severely under the judicial prosecutions of the lawyer, and the military violence of the soldier. Dundee demanded that all strangers should be removed from the town; and when it was answered that this could not be done without placing the Convention at the mercy of the Popish Duke of Gordon and his garrison, he left the assembly in indignation, and returning to his lodgings, instantly took arms and mounted his horse, attended by his followers. The city was alarmed at this demonstration, so unexpected, at the same time so formidable from the active and resolute character of its leader; and the Convention, feeling or pretending personal alarm, ordered the gates of their hall to be locked, and the keys to be laid upon the table. In the meantime, the drums beat to arms, and the bands of westland-men, who had been hitherto concealed in garrets and similar lurking-holes, appeared in the streets with their arms prepared, and exhibiting, in their gestures, language, and looks, the stern hopes of the revenge which they had long panted for.

While these things were passing, Dundee, in full view of friends and enemies, rode at leisure out of the city, by the lane called Leith Wynd, and proceeded along the northern bank of the North Loch, upon which the New Town of Edinburgh is now situated. From thence, turning under the western side of the castle, he summoned the Duke of Gordon to a conference at the foot of the walls, and for that purpose scrambled up the precipitous bank and rock on which the fortress is situated. So far as is known respecting this singular interview, Dundee's advice to the Duke was to maintain the castle at all risks, promising him speedy relief.

The people of Edinburgh, who witnessed from a distance this extraordinary conference, concluded that the castle was about to fire upon the city, and the spectators of Dundee's exploit were mistaken for his adherents; while the Jacobite members of the Convention on their part, unarmed and enclosed among their political enemies, were afraid of being massacred by the armed Whigs. The Convention, when their alarm subsided, sent Major Bunting with a party of horse to pursue Dundee and make him prisoner. That officer soon overtook the Viscount, and announced his commission, to which Dundee only deigned to answer, that if he dared attempt to execute such a purpose, he would send him back to the Convention in a pair of blankets. Bunting took the hint, and suffering the dreaded commander and his party to pass unmolested, returned in peace to the city. Dundee marched towards Stirling, and in consequence of his departure, the other friends of King James left Edinburgh, and hastened to their own homes.

So soon as this extraordinary scene had passed over, the Convention, now relieved from the presence of the Jacobite members, resolved upon levying troops to defend themselves, and to reduce the castle. The Cameronians were the readiest force of whose principles they could be assured, and it was proposed to them to raise a regiment of two battalions, under the Earl of Angus, eldest son of the Marquis of Douglas, a nobleman of military talents, as colonel, and William Cleland, as lieutenant-colonel. This last had been one of the commanders at Drumclog, and besides being a brave gentleman, was a poet, though an indifferent one, and more a man of the world than most of the sect to which he belonged.

Some of the more rigid Covenanters were of opinion, that those who possessed their principles had no freedom (to use their own phraseology) to join together for the defence of a Convention, in which so many persons were in the possession both of places and power who had been deeply engaged in the violent measures of the last reign; and they doubted this the more, as no steps had been taken to resume the obligations of the Covenant. But the singular and most unexpected train of events, which had occasioned their being called to arms to defend a city, where they had never before been seen openly save when dragged to execution, seemed so directly the operation of Providence in their favour, that, giving way for once to the dictates of common sense, the Cameronians agreed to consider the military association now proposed as a necessary and prudential measure, protesting only that the intended regiment should not be employed either under or along with such officers as had given proofs of attachment to Popery, Prelacy, or Malignancy. They also stipulated for regular opportunities of public worship, and for strict punishment of unchristian conversation, swearing, and profligacy of every sort; and their discipline having been arranged as much to their mind as possible, eighteen hundred men were raised, and, immediately marching to Edinburgh, assumed the duty of defending the Convention and blockading the garrison in the castle.

The Cameronians were soon, however, relieved by troops more competent to such a task, being a part of the regular army sent down to Scotland by King William, in order to give his party the decided superiority in that kingdom. Batteries were raised against the castle, and trenches opened. The Duke of Gordon made an honourable defence, while, at the same time, he avoided doing any damage to the town, and confined his fire to returning that of the batteries, by which he was annoyed. But the smallness of his garrison, the scarcity of provisions, the want of surgical assistance and medicines for the wounded, above all, the frequency of desertion, induced the Duke finally to surrender upon honourable terms; and in June he evacuated the fortress.

The Convention, in the meantime, almost entirely freed from opposition within their own assembly, proceeded to determine the great national question arising out of the change of government. Two letters being presented to them, one from King James, the other on the part of the Prince of Orange, they opened and read the latter with much reverence, while they passed over with little notice that of his father-in-law, intimating by this that they no longer regarded him as a sovereign.

This was made still more manifest by their vote respecting the state of the nation, which was much more decisive than that of the English Convention. The Scots Whigs had no Tories to consult with and satisfy by a scrupulous choice of expressions, and of course gave themselves no trouble in choosing between the terms abdication or forfeiture. They openly declared that James had assumed the throne without taking the oaths appointed by law; that he had proceeded to innovate upon the constitution of the kingdom, with the purpose of converting a limited monarchy into one of despotic authority; they added that he had employed the power thus illegally assumed, for violating the laws and liberties, and altering the religion of Scotland; and in doing so, had FOR-FEITED his right to the crown, and the throne had thereby become vacant.

The forfeiture, in strict law, would have extended to all James's immediate issue, as in the case of treason in a subject; but as this would have injured the right of the Princess of Orange, the effects of the declaration were limited to King James's infant son, and to his future children. In imitation of England, the crown of Scotland was settled upon the Prince and Princess of Orange, and the survivor of them, after whose decease, and failing heirs of their body, the Princess Anne and her heirs were called to the succession.

When the crown was thus settled, the Convention entered into a long declaration, called the Claim of Rights, by which the dispensing powers were pronounced illegal; the various modes of oppression practised during the last two reigns were censured as offences against liberty, and Prelacy was pronounced an insupportable grievance.

These resolutions being approved of by the new sovereigns, they began to assume the regal power, and fixed an administration. The

Duke of Hamilton was named High Commissioner, in reward of his services as President of the Convention; Lord Melville was made Secretary of State, and the Earl of Crawford President of the Council. Some offices were put into commission, to serve as objects of ambition to those great men who were yet unprovided for; others were filled up by such as had given proofs of attachment to the Revolution. In general, the choice of the Ministry was approved of; but the King and his advisers were censured for bestowing too much confidence on Dalrymple, lately created Viscount Stair, and Sir John Dalrymple, his son, called Master of Stair. A vacancy occurred for the promotion of the Earl of Stair in a singular manner.

Sir George Lockhart, an excellent lawyer, who had been crown counsel in Cromwell's time, was, at the period of the Revolution, President of the Court of Session, or first judge in civil affairs. He had agreed to act as an arbiter in some disputes which occurred between a gentleman named Chiesley, of Dalry, and his wife. The President, in deciding this matter, had assigned a larger provision to Mrs. Chiesley than, in her husband's opinion, was just or necessary; at which Dalry, a man headlong in his passions, was desperately offended, and publicly threatened the President's life. He was cautioned by a friend to forbear such imprudent language, and to dread the just vengeance of Heaven. "I have much to reckon for with Heaven," said the desperate man, "and we will reckon for this amongst the rest." In pursuance of his dreadful threat, Chiesley, armed for the purpose of assassination, followed his victim to the Greyfriars Church, in which Sir George usually heard divine service; but feeling some reluctance to do the deed within the sacred walls, he dogged him home, till he turned into the entry to his own house in what is still called the President's Close. Here Chiesley shot the judge dead; and disdaining to save his life by flight, he calmly walked about in the neighbourhood of the place till he was apprehended. He was afterwards tried and executed.

The office of the murdered President (a most important one, being the head of the supreme civil court) was conferred upon Lord Stair, and that of King's advocate, equivalent to the situation of Attorney-General in England, was given to his son, Sir John Dalrymple, who was afterwards associated with Lord Melville in the still more important situation of Secretary of State. Both father and son were men of high talent, but of doubtful integrity, and odious to the Presbyterians for compliances with the late Government.

Besides his immediate and official counsellors, King William gave, in private, much of his confidence to a clergyman named Carstairs, who was one of his chaplains. This gentleman had given strong proof of his fidelity and fortitude; for, being arrested in Charles II.'s time, on account of his connection with the conspiracy called Jerviswood's Plot, he underwent the cruel torture of the thumbikins, which, as I before told you, were screws, that almost crushed the thumbs to pieces. After the success of the Revolution, the Magistrates of Edinburgh complimented Carstairs, then a man of importance, with a present of the instrument of torture by which be had suffered. The King, it is said, heard of this and desired to see the thumbikins. They were produced. He placed his thumbs in the engine, and desired Carstairs to turn the screw. "I should wish to judge of your fortitude," said the King, "by experiencing the pain which you endured." Carstairs obeyed, but turned the screws with a polite degree of attention not to injure the Royal thumbs. "This is unpleasant," said the King, "yet it might be endured. But you are trifling with me. Turn the engine so that I may really feel a share of the pain inflicted on you." Carstairs, on this reiterated command, and jealous of his own reputation, turned the screws so sharply, that William cried for mercy, and owned he must have confessed anything, true or false, rather than have endured the pain an instant longer. This gentleman became a particular confidant of the King, and more trusted than many who filled high and ostensible situations in the state. He was generally allowed to be a man of sagacity and political talent, but his countrymen accused him of duplicity and dissimulation; and from that character he was generally distinguished by the nickname of Cardinal Carstairs.[1]

But while King William was thus considering the mode and selecting the council by which he proposed to govern Scotland, an insurrection took place, by means of which the sceptre of that kingdom was well-nigh wrested from his grip. This was brought about by the exertions of the Viscount Dundee, one of those extraordinary persons by whose energies great national revolutions are sometimes wrought with the assistance of very small means.

---

[1] Mr. Carstairs became Principal of the University of Edinburgh, and died in 1715, much regretted on the score of his benevolence and charity to individuals of whatever sect. His Letters, State Papers, etc., with an account of his Life, appeared in a 4to volume in 1774.

LVI

Contending for the Throne

1689

WHEN the Viscount of Dundee retired, as I told you, from the city of Edinburgh, the Convention, in consequence of the intercourse which he had held, contrary to their order, with the Duke of Gordon, an intercommuned Catholic, sent him a summons to appear before them, and answer to an accusation to that effect. But Dundee excused himself on account of his lady's dangerous illness, and his own personal danger from the Cameronians.

In the meantime King James, with forces furnished him by the French king, had arrived in Ireland, and, welcomed by the numerous Catholics, had made himself master of that fine kingdom, excepting only the province of Ulster, where the Protestants of English and Scottish descent offered a gallant and desperate resistance. But in spite of such partial opposition as the north of Ireland could make, James felt so confident that, by his Secretary Melfort, he wrote letters to the Viscount Dundee, and to the Earl of Balcarras, Dundee's intimate friend, and a steady adherent of the exiled monarch, encouraging them to gather together his faithful subjects, and make a stand for his interest, and promising them the support of a considerable body of forces from Ireland, with a supply of arms and ammunition. So high were the hopes entertained by Lord Melfort that, in letters addressed to some of his friends, he expressed, in the most imprudent manner, his purpose of improving to the uttermost the triumph which he did not doubt to obtain. "We dealt too leniently with our enemies," he said, "when we were in power, and possessed means of crushing them. But now, when they shall be once more conquered by us, and subjected once more to our authority, we will reduce them to hewers of wood and drawers of water."

These letters falling into the hands of the Convention, excited the utmost indignation. The Duke of Hamilton and others, who conceived themselves particularly aimed at, became more decided than ever to support King William's government, since they had no mercy to expect from King James and his vindictive counsellors. A military force was despatched to arrest Balcarras and Dundee. They succeeded in seizing the first of these noblemen; but Dundee being surrounded by a strong bodyguard, and residing in a country where many of the gentlemen were Jacobites, the party sent to arrest him were afraid to attempt the execution of their commission. He remained, therefore, at his own castle of Dudhope, near Dundee, where he had an opportunity of corresponding with the Highland chiefs, and with the northern gentlemen, who were generally disposed to Episcopacy, and favourable to the cause of King James.

Of the same name with the great Marquis of Montrose, boasting the same devoted loyalty, and a character as enterprising, with judgment superior to that of his illustrious prototype, Dundee is said to have replied to those who, on the day of his memorable retreat, asked him whither he went,—"That he was going wherever the spirit of Montrose should conduct him." His whole mind was now bent upon realising this chivalrous boast. His habits were naturally prudent and economical; but while others kept their wealth as far as possible out of the reach of the revolutionary storm, Dundee liberally expended for the cause of his old master the treasures which he had amassed in his service. His arguments, his largesses, the high influence of his character among the Highland chiefs, whose admiration of *Ian Dhu Cean,* or Black John the Warrior, was no way diminished by the merciless exploits which had procured him in the Low country the name of the Bloody Clavers, united with their own predilection in favour of James and their habitual love of war, to dispose them to a general insurrection. Some of the clans, however, had, as usual, existing feuds amongst themselves, which Dundee was obliged to assist in composing before he could unite them all in the cause of the dethroned monarch.

I will give you an account of one of those feuds, which, I believe, led to the last considerable clan-battle fought in the Highlands.

There had been, for a great many years, much debate, and some skirmishing, betwixt MacIntosh of Moy, the chief of that ancient sur-name, and a tribe of MacDonalds, called MacDonalds of Keppoch. The MacIntoshes had claims of an ancient date upon the district of Glen Roy (now famous for the phenomenon called the Parallel Roads),[1] and the neighbouring valley of Glen Spean. MacIntosh had his right to these lands expressed in written grants from the crown, but Keppoch was in actual possession of the property. When asked upon what char-ters he founded his claim, MacDonald replied, that he held his lands, not by a sheep's skin, but by the sword; and his clan, an uncommonly bold and hardy race, were ready to support his boast. Several proposals having been in vain made to accommodate this matter, MacIntosh resolved to proceed to open force and possess himself of the disputed territory. He therefore displayed the yellow banner, which was the badge of his family, raised his clan and marched towards Keppoch, being assisted by an independent company of soldiers, raised for the service of Government, and commanded by Captain MacKenzie of Suddie. It does not appear by what interest this formidable auxiliary force was procured, but probably by an order from the Privy Council.

On their arrival at Keppoch, MacIntosh found his rival's house deserted, and imagining himself in possession of victory, even without a combat, he employed many workmen whom he had brought with him for that purpose to construct a castle, or fort, on a precipitous bank overhanging the river Roy, where the vestiges of his operations are still

---

[1] Glen Roy, in Lochaber, Inverness-shire. "The glen of itself," says Pennant, "is extremely narrow, and the hills on each side very high, and generally not rocky. In the face of these hills, both sides of the glen, there are three roads at small distances from each other, and directly opposite on each side. These roads have been measured in the completest parts of them, and found to be 26 paces of a man, five feet ten inches high. The two highest are pretty near each other, about 50 yards, and the lowest double that distance from the nearest to it. They are carried along the sides of the glen with the utmost regularity (extending eight miles), nearly as exact as drawn with a rule and compass."—*Tour,* vol. iii. p. 394.—Various theories have been employed to account for this extraordinary formation, and perhaps the most probable is that these three *roads* must have been the successive margins of a lake which had subsided under successive convulsions of nature.

to be seen. The work was speedily interrupted by tidings that the Mac-Donalds of Keppoch, assisted by their kindred tribes of Glengarry and Glencoe, had assembled, and that they were lying on their arms, in great numbers, in a narrow glen behind the ridge of hills which rises to the northeast of Keppoch, the sloping declivity of which is called Mull-roy. Their purpose was to attack MacIntosh at daybreak; but that chief determined to anticipate their design, and assembling his clan, marched towards his enemy before the first peep of dawn. The rival clan, with their chief, Coll of Keppoch, were equally ready for the conflict; and, in the gray light of the morning, when the MacIntoshes had nearly surmounted the heights of Mullroy, the MacDonalds appeared in possession of the upper ridge, and a battle instantly commenced.

A lad who had lately run away from his master, a tobacco-spinner in Inverness, and had enlisted in Suddie's independent company, gives the following account of the action. "The MacDonalds came down the hill upon us, without either shoe, stocking, or bonnet on their heads; they gave a shout, and then the fire began on both sides, and continued a hot dispute for an hour (which made me wish I had been spinning tobacco). Then they broke in upon us with sword and target, and Lochaber-axes, which obliged us to give way. Seeing my captain severely wounded, and a great many men lying with heads cloven on every side, and having never witnessed the like before, I was sadly affrighted. At length a Highlandman attacked me with sword and target, and cut my wooden-handled bayonet out of the muzzle of my gun. I then clubbed my gun and gave him a stroke with it, which made the butt-end to fly off, and seeing the Highlandmen come fast down upon me, I took to my heels and ran thirty miles before I looked behind me, taking every person whom I saw or met for my enemy." Many, better used to such scenes, fled as far and fast as Donald MacBane, the tobacco-spinner's apprentice. The gentleman who bore MacIntosh's standard, being a special object of pursuit, saved himself and the sacred deposit by a wonderful exertion. At a place where the river Roy flows between two precipitous rocks, which approach each other over the torrent, he hazarded a desperate leap where no enemy dared follow him, and bore off his charge in safety.

It is said by tradition, that the MacIntoshes fought with much bravery, and that the contest was decided by the desperation of a half-crazed man called "the redhaired Bo-man," or cowherd, whom Keppoch had not summoned to the fight but who came thither, uncalled, with a club on his shoulder. This man, being wounded by a shot, was so much incensed with the pain, that he darted forward into the thickest of the MacIntoshes, calling out, "They fly, they fly! upon them, upon them!" The boldness he displayed, and the strokes he dealt with his unusual weapon, caused the first impression on the array of the enemies of his chief.

MacDonald was very unwilling to injure any of the Government soldiers, yet Suddie, their commander, received his death wound. He was brave, and well armed with carabine, pistols, and a halbert or half-pike. This officer came in front of a cadet of Keppoch, called MacDonald of Tullich, and by a shot aimed at him, killed one of his brothers, and then rushed on with his pike. Notwithstanding this deep provocation, Tullich, sensible of the pretext which the death of a captain under Government would give against his clan, called out more than once, "Avoid me—avoid me."—"The MacDonald was never born that I would shun," replied the MacKenzie, pressing on with his pike. On which Tullich hurled at his head a pistol, which he had before discharged. The blow took effect, the skull was fractured, and MacKenzie died shortly after, as his soldiers were carrying him to Inverness.

MacIntosh himself was taken by his rival, who, in his esteem, was only an insurgent vassal. When the captive heard the MacDonalds greeting their chieftain with shouts of "Lord of Keppoch! Lord of Keppoch!" he addressed him boldly, saying, "You are as far from being lord of the lands of Keppoch at this moment, as you have been all your life."—"Never mind," answered the victorious chieftain, with much good humour, "we'll enjoy the good weather while it lasts." Accordingly, the victory of his tribe is still recorded in the pipe-tune called, "MacDonald took the brae on them."

Some turn of fortune seemed about to take place immediately after the battle; for before the MacDonalds had collected their scattered forces, the war-pipes were again heard, and a fresh body of Highlanders appeared advancing towards Keppoch, in the direction of Garvamoor. This unexpected apparition was owing to one of those sudden changes of sentiment by which men in the earlier stages of society are often influenced. The advancing party was the clan of MacPherson, members, like the MacIntoshes, of the confederacy called the Clan Chattan, but who, disputing with them the precedence in that body, were alternately their friends or enemies, as the recollection of former kindnesses, or ancient quarrels, prevailed. On this occasion the MacPhersons had not accompanied MacIntosh to the field, there being some discord betwixt the tribes at the time; but when they heard of MacIntosh's defeat, they could not reconcile it with their honour to suffer so important a member of the Clan Chattan to remain captive with the MacDonalds. They advanced, therefore, in order of battle, and sent Keppoch a flag of truce, to demand that MacIntosh should be delivered to them.

The chief of Keppoch, though victorious, was in no condition for a fresh contest, and therefore surrendered his prisoner, who was much more mortified by finding himself in the hands of the MacPhersons than rejoiced in escaping from those of his conqueror Keppoch. So predominant was his sense of humiliation, that when the MacPhersons proposed to conduct him to Cluny the seat of their chief, he resisted at first in fair terms, and when the visit was urged upon him, he threatened to pierce his bosom with his own dirk if they should persevere in compelling him to visit Cluny in his present situation. The MacPhersons were generous, and escorted him to his own estates.

The issue of the conflict at Mullroy, so mortifying to the conquered chief, was also followed with disastrous consequences to the victor.

The resistance offered to the Royal troops, and the death of MacKenzie of Suddie, who commanded them, together with the defeat of MacIntosh, who had the forms at least of the law on his side, gave effect to his complaint to the Privy Council. Letters of fire and sword, as they were called, that is, a commission to burn and destroy the country and lands of an offending chieftain, or district, were issued against Coll MacDonald of Keppoch. Sixty dragoons, and two hundred of the foot guards were detached into Glen Roy and Glen Spean, with orders to destroy man, woman, and child, and lay waste Keppoch's estates. Keppoch himself was for a time obliged to fly, but a wealthy kinsman purchased his peace by a large *erick*, or fine. We shall presently find him engaged in a conflict where the destiny, not of two barren glens, but of a fair kingdom, seemed to depend upon the issue.

This brings us back to Dundee, who, in spring 1689, received intelligence that General MacKay, an officer entrusted by King William with the command of the forces in Scotland, was marching against him at the head of an army of regular troops. MacKay was a man of courage, sense, and experience, but rather entitled to the praise of a good officer than an able general, and better qualified to obey the orders of an intelligent commander, than penetrate into, encounter, and defeat, the schemes of such an active spirit as Dundee.

Of this there was an instance in the very beginning of the conflict, when MacKay advanced towards Dudhope Castle, with the hope of coming upon his antagonist at unawares; but Dundee was not to be taken by surprise. Marching with a hundred and fifty horse to the town of Inverness, he found MacDonald of Keppoch at the head of several hundred Highlanders, blockading the place, on account of the citizens having taken part with MacIntosh against his clan. Dundee offered his mediation, and persuaded the magistrates to gratify Keppoch with the sum of two thousand dollars, for payment of which he granted his own bond in security. He manifested his influence over the minds of the mountain chiefs still more by prevailing on Keppoch, though smarting under the injuries he had sustained, by the letters of fire and sword issued against him by King James's government, to join him with his clan, for the purpose of restoring that monarch to the throne.

Thus reinforced, but still far inferior in numbers to his opponent MacKay, Dundee, by a rapid movement, surprised the town of Perth. He seized what public treasure he found in the hands of the receiver of taxes, saying that he would plunder no private person, but thought it was fair to take the King's money for the King's service. He dispersed, at the same time, two troops of horse, newly raised by Government, seized their horses and accoutrements, and made prisoners their commanding officers, the Lairds of Pollock and of Blair.

After this exploit, Dundee retreated into the Highlands to recruit his little army, to wait for a body of three thousand men, whom he expected from Ireland, and to seek a suitable time for forwarding the explosion of a conspiracy which had been formed in a regiment of dragoons now serving in MacKay's army, but which he had himself commanded before the Revolution. Both the officers and men of this regiment were willing to return to the command of their old leader, and the allegiance of their former King. Creichton, an officer in the regiment, the same whose attack on a conventicle I formerly told you of, was the chief conductor of this conspiracy. It was discovered by MacKay just when it was on the point of taking effect, and when the event, with such an enemy as Dundee in his vicinity, must have been destruction to his army. MacKay cautiously disguised his knowledge of the plot, until he was joined by strong reinforcements, which enabled him to seize upon the principal conspirators and disarm and disband their inferior accomplices.

The Privy Council had a great inclination to make an example, which should discourage such practices in future; and Captain Creichton, being the chief agent, a stranger, and without friends or intercessors, was selected for the purpose of being hanged as a warning to others. But Dundee did not desert his old comrade. He sent a message to the Lords of the Privy Council, saying that if they hurt a hair of Creichton's head, he would in the way of reprisal cut his prisoners, the lairds of Pollock and Blair, joint from joint, and send them to Edinburgh, packed up in hampers. The Council were alarmed on receiving this intimation. The Duke of Hamilton reminded them that they all knew Dundee so well that they could not doubt his being as good as his word, and that the gentlemen in his hands were too nearly allied to several of the Council to be endangered on account of Creichton. These remonstrances saved Creichton's life.

A good deal of marching, countermarching, and occasional skirmishing ensued between Dundee and MacKay, during which an incident is said to have occurred strongly indicative of the character of the former. A young man had joined Dundee's army, the son of one of his old and intimate friends. He was employed upon some reconnoitring service, in which, a skirmish taking place, the new recruit's heart failed him, and he fairly fled out of the fray. Dundee covered his dishonour by pretending that he himself had despatched him to the rear upon a message of importance. He then sent for the youth to speak with him in private. "Young man," he said, "I have saved your honour; but I must needs tell you, that you have chosen a trade for which you are constitutionally unfit. It is not perhaps your fault, but rather your misfortune, that you do not possess the strength of nerves necessary to encounter the dangers of battle. Return to your father—I will find an excuse for your doing so with honour—and I will besides put you in the way of doing King James's cause effectual service, without personally engaging in the war."

The young gentleman, penetrated with a sense of the deepest shame, threw himself at his general's feet and protested that his failure in duty was only the effect of a momentary weakness, the recollection of which should be effaced by his future conduct, and entreated Dundee, for the love he bore his father, to give him at least a chance of regaining his reputation. Dundee still endeavoured to dissuade him from remaining with the army, but as he continued urgent to be admitted to a second trial, he reluctantly gave way to his request. "But remember," he said, "that if your heart fails you a second time, you must die. The cause I am engaged in is a desperate one, and I can permit no man to serve under me who is not prepared to fight to the last. My own life, and those of all others who serve under me, are unsparingly devoted to the cause of King James; and death must be his lot who shows an example of cowardice."

The unfortunate young man embraced, with seeming eagerness, this stern proposal. But in the next skirmish in which he was engaged, his constitutional timidity again prevailed. He turned his horse to fly, when Dundee, coming up to him, only said, "The son of your father is too good a man to be consigned to the provost-marshal;" and without another word, he shot him through the head with his pistol, with a sternness and inflexibility of purpose resembling the stoicism of the ancient Romans.

Circumstances began now to render Dundee desirous of trying the chance of battle, which he had hitherto avoided. The Marquis of Athole, who had vacillated more than once during the progress of the Revolution, now abandoned entirely the cause of King James, and sent his son, Lord Murray, into Athole to raise the clans of that country, Stewarts, Robertsons, Fergussons, and others, who were accustomed to follow the family of Athole in war, from respect to the Marquis's rank and power, though they were not his patriarchal subjects or clansmen. One of these gentlemen, Stewart of Boquhan, although dependent on the Marquis, was resolved not to obey him through his versatile changes of politics. Having been placed in possession of the strong castle of Blair, a fortress belonging to the Marquis, which commands the most important pass into the Northern Highlands, Stewart refused to surrender it to Lord Murray, and declared he held it for King James by order of the Viscount of Dundee. Lord Murray, finding his father's own house thus defended against him, sent the tidings to General MacKay, who assembled about three thousand foot, and two troops of horse, and advanced with all haste into Athole, determined to besiege Blair, and to fight Dundee, should he march to its relief.

At this critical period Lord Murray had assembled about eight hundred Athole Highlanders, of the clans already named, who were brought together under pretence of preserving the peace of the country. Many of them, however, began to suspect the purpose of Lord Murray to join MacKay; and recollecting that it was under Montrose's command, and in the cause of the Stewarts, that their fathers had gained their fame, they resolved they would not be diverted from the same course of loyalty, as they esteemed it. They, therefore, let Lord

Murray know that if it was his intention to join Dundee, they would all follow him to the death; but if he proposed to embrace the side of King William, they would presently leave him. Lord Murray answered with threats of that vengeance which a feudal lord could take upon disobedient vassals, when his men, setting his threats at defiance, ran to the river, and filling their bonnets with water, drank King James's health, and left the standard of the Marquis to a man—a singular defection among the Highlanders of that period, who usually followed to the field their immediate superior, with much indifference concerning the side of politics which he was pleased to embrace.

These tidings came to Dundee, with the information that MacKay had reached Dunkeld, with the purpose of reducing Blair, and punishing the Athole gentlemen for their desertion of the standard of their chief. About the same time General Cannon joined the Viscount with the reinforcement so long expected from Ireland; but they amounted to only three hundred men, instead of as many thousands, and were totally destitute of money and provisions, both of which were to have been sent with them. Nevertheless, Dundee resolved to preserve the castle of Blair, so important as a key to the Northern Highlands, and marched to protect it with a body of about two thousand Highlanders with whom he occupied the upper and northern extremity of the pass between Dunkeld and Blair.

In this celebrated defile, called the Pass of Killiecrankie, the road runs for several miles along the banks of a furious river, called the Garry, which rages below, amongst cataracts and waterfalls which the eye can scarcely discern, while a series of precipices and wooded mountains rise on the other hand; the road itself is the only mode of access through the glen, and along the valley which lies at its northern extremity. The path was then much more inaccessible than at the present day, as it ran close to the bed of the river, and was narrower and more rudely formed.

A defile of such difficulty was capable of being defended to the last extremity by a small number against a considerable army; and considering how well adapted his followers were for such mountain warfare, many of the Highland chiefs were of opinion that Dundee ought to content himself with guarding the pass against MacKay's superior army, until a rendezvous, which they had appointed, should assemble a stronger force of their countrymen. But Dundee was of a different opinion, and resolved to suffer MacKay to march through the pass without opposition, and then to fight him in the open valley, at the northern extremity. He chose this bold measure, both because it promised a decisive result to the combat which his ardent temper desired; and also because he preferred fighting MacKay before that General was joined by a considerable body of English horse who were expected, and of whom the Highlanders had at that time some dread.

On the 17th June 1689 General MacKay with his troops entered the pass, which, to their astonishment, they found unoccupied by the enemy. His forces were partly English and Dutch regiments, who, with many of the Lowland Scots themselves, were struck with awe, and even fear, at finding themselves introduced by such a magnificent, and, at the same time, formidable avenue, to the presence of their enemies, the inhabitants of these tremendous mountains, into whose recesses they were penetrating. But besides the effect produced on their minds by the magnificence of natural scenery, to which they were wholly unaccustomed, the consideration must have hung heavy on them that if a general of Dundee's talents suffered them to march unopposed through a pass so difficult, it must be because he was conscious of possessing strength sufficient to attack and destroy them at the farther extremity, when their only retreat would lie through the narrow and perilous path by which they were now advancing.

Mid-day was past ere MacKay's men were extricated from the defile, when their general drew them up in one line three deep, without any reserve, along the southern extremity of the narrow valley into which the pass opens. A hill on the north side of the valley, covered with dwarf trees and bushes, formed the position of Dundee's army, which, divided into columns, formed by the different clans, was greatly outflanked by MacKay's troops.

The armies shouted when they came in sight of each other, but the enthusiasm of MacKay's soldiers being damped by the circumstances we have observed, their military shout made but a dull and sullen sound compared to the yell of the Highlanders, which rang far and shrill from all the hills around them. Sir Evan Cameron of Lochiel, of whom I formerly gave you some anecdotes, called on those around them to attend to this circumstance, saying, that in all his battles he observed victory had ever been on the side of those whose shout before joining seemed most sprightly and confident. It was accounted a less favourable augury by some of the old Highlanders, that Dundee at this moment, to render his person less distinguishable, put on a sad-coloured buff-coat above the scarlet cassock and bright cuirass, in which he had hitherto appeared.

It was some time ere Dundee had completed his preparations for the assault which he meditated, and only a few dropping shots were exchanged, while, in order to prevent the risk of being outflanked, he increased the intervals between the columns with which he designed to charge, insomuch that he had scarce men enough left in the centre. About an hour before sunset, he sent word to MacKay that he was about to attack him, and gave the signal to charge.

The Highlanders stripped themselves to their shirts and doublets, threw away everything that could impede the fury of their onset, and then put themselves in motion, accompanying with a dreadful yell the discordant sound of their war-pipes. As they advanced, the clansmen fired their pieces, each column thus pouring in a well-aimed though irregular volley, when throwing down their fusees, without waiting to reload, they drew their swords, and, increasing their pace to the utmost speed, pierced through and broke the thin line which was opposed to them, and profited by their superior activity and the nature of their weapons to make a great havoc among the regular troops. When thus mingled with each other, hand to hand, the advantages of superior discipline on the part of the Lowland soldier were lost. Agility and strength were on the side of the mountaineers. Some accounts of the battle give a terrific account of the blows struck by the Highlanders, which cleft heads down to the breast, cut steel headpieces asunder as night-caps, and slashed through pikes like willows. Two of MacKay's English regiments in the centre stood fast, the interval between the attacking columns being so great that none were placed opposite to them. The rest of King William's army were totally routed and driven headlong into the river.

Dundee himself, contrary to the advice of the Highland chiefs, was in front of the battle, and fatally conspicuous. By a desperate attack he possessed himself of MacKay's artillery, and then led his handful of cavalry, about fifty men, against two troops of horse, which fled without fighting. Observing the stand made by the two English regiments already mentioned, he galloped towards the clan of Mac-Donald, and was in the act of bringing them to the charge, with his

---

[1] "Claverhouse's sword, a straight cut-and-thrust blade, is in the possession of Lord Woodhouselee, and the buff coat which he wore at the battle of Killiecrankie, having the fatal shot-hole under the arm-pit of it, is preserved in Pennycuick House, the seat of Sir George Clerk, Bart."—*Border Minstrelsy*, vol. ii. p. 245.

right arm elevated, as if pointing the way to victory, when he was struck by a bullet beneath the arm-pit, where he was unprotected by his cuirass.[1] He tried to ride on, but being unable to keep the saddle, fell mortally wounded, and died in the course of the night.

It was impossible for a victory to be more complete than that gained by the Highlanders at Killiecrankie. The cannon, baggage, and stores of MacKay's army fell into their hands. The two regiments which kept their ground suffered so much in their attempt to retreat through the pass, now occupied by the Athole-men in their rear, that they might be considered as destroyed. Two thousand of MacKay's army were killed or taken, and the general himself escaped with difficulty to Stirling, at the head of a few horse. The Highlanders, whose dense columns, as they came down to the attack, underwent three successive volleys from MacKay's line, had eight hundred men slain.

But all other losses were unimportant compared to that of Dundee, with whom were forfeited all the fruits of that bloody victory. MacKay, when he found himself free from pursuit, declared his conviction that his opponent had fallen in the battle. And such was the opinion of Dundee's talents and courage, and the general sense of the peculiar crisis at which his death took place, that the common people of the low country cannot, even now, be persuaded that he died an ordinary death. They say that a servant of his own, shocked at the severities which, if triumphant, his master was likely to accomplish against the Presbyterians, and giving way to the popular prejudice of his having a charm against the effect of lead balls, shot him, in the tumult of the battle, with a silver button taken from his livery coat. The Jacobites, and Episcopal party, on the other hand, lamented the deceased victor as the last of the Scots, the last of the Grahams, and the last of all that was great in his native country.

LVII

De Facto and De Jure

1689-1690

THE Viscount of Dundee was one of those gifted persons upon whose single fate that of nations is sometimes dependent. His own party believed that, had he lived to improve the decisive victory which he had so bravely won, he would have soon recovered Scotland to King James's allegiance. It is certain a great many of the nobility only waited a gleam of success to return to the Jacobite side; nor were the revolutionary party so united amongst themselves as to have offered a very firm resistance. The battle of Killiecrankie, duly improved, would, unquestionably, have delivered the whole of Scotland north of the Forth into the power of Dundee, and rendered even Stirling and Edinburgh insecure. Such a flame kindled in Scotland must have broken many of King William's measures, rendered it impossible for him to go to Ireland, where his presence was of the last necessity, and have been, to say the least, of the highest prejudice to his affairs.

But all the advantages of the victory were lost in the death of the conquering general. Cannon, who succeeded to the chief command on Dundee's decease, was a stranger to Highland manners, and quite inadequate to the management of such an army as that which chance placed under his command. It was in vain that the fame of the victory, and the love of plunder and of war, which made part of the Highland character, brought around him, from the remote recesses of that warlike country, a more numerous body of the mountaineers than Montrose had ever commanded. By the timidity and indecision of his opponent, MacKay gained time enough to collect, which he did with celerity, a body of troops sufficient to coop up the Jacobite general within his mountains, and to maintain an indecisive war of posts and skirmishes, which wearied out the patience of the quick-spirited Highlanders.

Cannon attempted only one piece of service worthy of mention, and in that he was foiled. In the extremity of the alarm which followed the defeat of Killiecrankie, the Earl of Angus's newly raised regiment of Cameronians had been despatched to the Highlands. They had advanced as far as Dunkeld, when Cannon for once showed some activity, and avoiding MacKay by a rapid and secret march, he at once surrounded, in the village and castle of Dunkeld, about twelve hundred of this regiment, with more than double their numbers. Their situation seemed so desperate that a party of horse who were with them retired, and left the Cameronians to their fate.

But the newly acquired discipline of these hardy enthusiasts prevented their experiencing the fate of their predecessors at Bothwell and Pentland. They were judiciously posted in the Marquis of Athole's house and neighbouring enclosures, as also in the churchyard and the old cathedral; and with the advantage of this position they beat off repeatedly the fierce attacks of the Highlanders. This success restored the spirits of the King's troops and diminished considerably that of the Highlanders, who, according to their custom, began to disperse and return home.

The Cameronian regiment lost in this action their gallant lieutenant-colonel, Cleland, and many men. But they were victorious, and that was a sufficient consolation.

You may have some curiosity to know the future fate of this singular regiment. The peculiar and narrow-minded ideas of the sect led many of them to entertain doubts of the lawfulness of the part they had taken. The Presbyterian worship had indeed been established as the national church since the Revolution, but it was far from having attained that despotic authority claimed for it by the Cameronians, and therefore, although, at the first landing of the Prince of Orange, they had felt it matter of duty to espouse his cause, yet they were utterly disgusted with the mode in which he had settled the state, and especially the Church of Scotland.

What they in their enthusiasm imputed to King William as matter of censure, ought in reality to be considered as most meritorious. That wise and prudent monarch saw the impossibility of bringing the country to a state of quiet settlement if he kept alive the old feuds by which it had been recently divided, or if he permitted the oppressed Presbyterians to avenge themselves as they desired upon their former persecutors. He admitted all persons alike to serve the state, whatever had been their former principles and practice; and thus many were reconciled to his government, who, if they had felt themselves endangered in person and property, or even deprived of the hope of Royal patronage and official situation, would have thrown a heavy weight into the Jacobite scale. William, upon these principles, employed several persons who had been active enforcers of King James's rigorous measures, and whom the Cameronians accounted God's enemies and their own, and deemed more deserving of severe punishment and retaliation than of encouragement and employment.

In church affairs, King William's measures were still less likely to be pleasing to these fierce enthusiasts than in those which concerned the state. He was contented that there should be in Scotland, as in Holland, a national church, and that the form should be Presbyterian, as the model most generally approved by his friends in that kingdom. But the King was decided in opinion that this church should have no power either over the persons or consciences of those who were of different communions, to whom he extended a general toleration, from which the Catholics alone were excluded, owing to the terror inspired by their late strides towards predominant superiority during the reign of James II. The wisest, the most prudent, and the most learned of the Presbyterian ministers, those chiefly who, having fled from Scotland and resided in the Netherlands, had been enlightened on this subject of toleration, were willingly disposed to accommodate themselves to the King's inclination, and rest satisfied with the share of authority which he was willing to concede to the national church.

But wise and moderate opinions had no effect on the more stubborn Presbyterians, who, irritated at the kirk's being curbed of her supreme power, and themselves checked in the course of their vengeance upon their oppressors, accounted the model of King William's ecclesiastical government an Erastian establishment, in which the dignity of the Church was rendered subordinate to that of the state. There were many divines, even within the pale of the Church, whose opinions tended to this point, and who formed a powerful party in the General Assembly. But the Cameronians in particular, elated with the part, both in suffering and acting, which they had performed during the late times, considered the results of the Revolution as totally unworthy of the struggle which they had maintained. The ministers who were willing to acquiesce in a model of church government so mutilated in power and beauty as that conceded by King William, they termed a hive of lukewarm, indifferent shepherds, who had either deserted their flocks and fled to save themselves during the rage of persecution, or who, remaining in Scotland, had truckled to the enemy, and exercised their ministry in virtue of a niggardly indulgence from the tyrant, whilst they themselves endured want and misery, and the extremities of the sword and gallows, rather than renounce one iota of the doctrine held by the Presbyterian Kirk of Scotland in the time of her highest power in 1640. They considered the General Assembly held under the authority of King William as an association in which the black hand of defection was extended to the red hand of persecution, and where apostates and oppressors, leagued together, made common cause against pure Presbyterian government and discipline.

Feeling thus indisposed towards the existing Government, it followed as a matter of course, that the Cameronians, if they did not esteem themselves actually called upon to resist King William's authority, from which they were withheld by some glimmering of common sense,— which suggested, as the necessary consequence, the return of their old enemy James,—neither did they feel at liberty to own themselves his subjects, to take oaths of allegiance to his person and that of his queen, or to submit themselves, by any mark of homage, to a sovereign who had not subscribed and sworn to the Solemn League and Covenant.

Although, therefore, this extreme party differed among themselves to what extent they should disclaim the King and the Government, yet the general sense of their united societies became more and more scrupulous concerning the lawfulness of serving in the Earl of Angus's regiment; and while they continued to own these soldiers as brethren, and hold correspondence with them, we observe that they hint at the introduction of some of the errors of the time, even into this select regiment. Card-playing, dice, and other scandalous games, but in particular the celebration of King William's birthday, by rejoicing and drinking of healths, greatly afflicted the spirit of the general meeting of the more rigorous of the party, who held such practices as an abomination. It is probable, therefore, that the regiment of Cameronians received from this time few recruits out of the bosom of the party whose name they bore.

They were afterwards sent to serve on the Continent and behaved courageously at the bloody battle of Steinkirk, in 1692, where they lost many men, and amongst others their colonel, the Earl of Angus, who fell fighting bravely at their head. During these campaigns the regiment became gradually more indifferent to their religious duties. At last, we learn that their chaplain and they became heartily weary of each other, and that while the preacher upbraided his military flock with departing from the strictness of their religious professions, the others are said to have cursed him to his face, for having been instrumental in inducing them to enter into the service. In later times this regiment, which is still called the 26th, or Cameronian regiment, seems to have differed very little in its composition from other marching regiments, excepting that it was chiefly recruited in Scotland, and that, in memory of the original principles of the sect out of which it was raised, each soldier was, and perhaps is still, obliged to show himself possessed of a Bible when his necessaries are inspected.

During the course of the winter 1689–90, King James made an effort to reanimate the war in the Highlands, which had almost died away, after the repulse of the Highlanders at Dunkeld. He sent over General Buchan, an officer of reputation, and who was supposed to understand the Highland character and Highland warfare. The clans again assembled with renewed hopes; but Buchan proved as incapable as Cannon had shown himself the year before of profiting by the ardour of the Highlanders.

With singular want of caution, the Jacobite general descended the Spey as far as a level plain by the river-side, called Cromdale, where he quartered his army, about eighteen hundred men, in the hamlets in the vicinity.[1] Sir Thomas Livingstone, an excellent old officer, who commanded on the part of King William, assembled a large force of cavalry, some infantry, and a body of the Clan Grant, who had embraced William's interest. The general's guide on this night's march

---

[1] On the south side of the low valley of the Spey, near the old church of Cromdale, about three miles to the east of the position where Grantown now stands.

was Grant of Elchies, who conducted him from Forres, down the hill above Castle Grant, and through the valley of Auchinarrow, to the side of the Spey, opposite to the haugh of Cromdale. Elchies then, with the advanced guard of Grant, forded the broad and rapid river. He next killed with his own hand two of the Highlanders, outposts or sentinels, and led his own party, with Sir Thomas Livingstone and his cavalry, through a thicket of beech-trees, and thus surprised Buchan and his army asleep in their quarters. They fought gallantly, notwithstanding, with their swords and targets, but were at length compelled to take to flight. The pursuit was not so destructive to the defeated party as it would have been to the soldiers of any other nation, if pursued by the cavalry of a successful enemy. Light of foot, and well acquainted with their own mountains, the Highlanders escaped up the hills, and amongst the mists, with such an appearance of ease and agility that a spectator observed, they looked more like men received into the clouds than fugitives escaping from a victorious enemy.

But the skirmish of Cromdale, and the ruin of King James's affairs in Ireland, precluded all hopes on the part of the Jacobites, of bringing the war in the Highlands to a successful termination. A fort near Inverlochy, originally erected by Cromwell, was again repaired by Livingstone, received the name of Fort-William, and was strongly garrisoned, to bridle the Camerons, MacDonalds, and other Jacobite clans. The chiefs saw they would be reduced to maintain a defensive war in their own fastnesses, and that against the whole regular force of Scotland. They became desirous, therefore, of submitting for the present, and reserving their efforts in behalf of the exiled family for some more favourable time. King William was equally desirous to see this smouldering fire, which the appearance of such a general as Montrose or Dundee might soon have blown into a destructive flame, totally extinguished. For this purpose he had recourse to a measure which, had it been duly executed, was one of deep policy.

The Earl of Breadalbane, a man of great power in the Highlands, and head of a numerous clan of the Campbells, was entrusted with a sum of money, which some authors call twenty, and some twelve thousand pounds, to be distributed among the chieftains, on the condition of their submission to the existing Government, and keeping on foot, each chief in proportion to his means, a military force to act on behalf of Government, at home or abroad, as they should be called upon. This scheme, had it succeeded, would probably have rendered the

Highland clans a resource, instead of a terror, to the Government of King William. Their love of war, and their want of money, would by degrees have weaned them from their attachment to the exiled King, which would gradually have been transferred to a Prince who led them to battle, and paid them for following him.

But many of the chiefs were jealous of the conduct of the Earl of Breadalbane in distributing the funds entrusted to his care. Part of this treasure the wily Earl bestowed among the most leading men; when these were bought off, he intimidated those of less power into submission by threatening them with military execution; and it has always been said that he retained a very considerable portion of the gratuity in his own hands. The Highland chiefs complained to Government of Breadalbane's conduct, and, to prejudice the Earl, in the minds of the Ministry, they alleged that he had played a double part, and advised them only to submit to King William for the present, until an opportunity should occur of doing King James effectual service. They also charged Breadalbane with retaining, for his own purposes, a considerable part of the money deposited in his hands, to be distributed in the Highlands.

Government, it is said, attended to this information, so far as to demand, through the Secretary of State, a regular account of the manner in which the sum of money placed in his hands had been distributed. But Breadalbane, too powerful to be called in question, and too audacious to care for having incurred suspicion of what he judged Government dared not resent, is traditionally said to have answered the demand in the following cavalier manner:—"My dear Lord, the money you mention was given to purchase the peace of the Highlands. The money is spent—the Highlands are quiet, and this is the only way of accompting among friends."

We shall find afterwards that the selfish avarice and resentment of this unprincipled nobleman gave rise to one of the most bloody, treacherous, and cruel actions which dishonour the seventeenth century. Of this we shall speak hereafter; at present it is enough to repeat that Breadalbane bribed, soothed, or threatened into submission to the Government, all the chiefs who had hitherto embraced the interest of King James, and the Highland war might be considered as nearly, if not entirely ended. But the proposed measure of taking the clans into the pay of Government, calculated to attach them inalienably to the cause of King William, was totally disconcerted, and the Highlanders continued as much Jacobites at heart as before the pacification.

There remained, however, after the Highlands were thus partially settled, some necessity of providing for the numerous Lowland officers who had joined the standard of Dundee, and who afterwards remained with his less able successors in command. These individuals were entitled to consideration and compassion. They amounted to nearly a hundred and fifty gentlemen, who sacrificing their fortune to their honour, preferred following their old master into exile, to changing his service for that of another. It was stipulated by the treaty that they should have two ships to carry them to France, where they were received with the same liberal hospitality which Louis XIV. showed in whatever concerned the affairs of King James, and where, accordingly, they received for some time pay and subsistence, in proportion to the rank which they had severally enjoyed in the exiled King's service.

But when the battle of La Hogue had commenced, the train of misfortunes which France afterwards experienced, and put a period to all hopes of invading England, it could not be expected that Louis should continue the expense of supporting this body of Scottish officers, whom there was now so little prospect of providing for in their own country. They themselves being sensible of this, petitioned King James to permit them to reduce themselves to a company of private soldiers, with the dress, pay, and appointments of that rank, assuring his Majesty that they would esteem it a pleasure to continue in his service, even under the meanest circumstances, and the greatest hardships.

James reluctantly accepted of this generous offer, and, with tears in his eyes, reviewed this body of devoted loyalists, as stripped of the advantages of birth, fortune, and education, they prepared to take upon them the duties of the lowest rank in their profession. The unhappy Prince gave every man his hand to kiss,—promised never to forget their loyalty, and wrote the name of each individual in his pocket-book, as a pledge that when his own fortune permitted, he would not be unmindful of their fidelity.

Being in French pay, this company of gentlemen were of course engaged in the French service; and wherever they came, they gained respect by their propriety of behaviour, and sympathy from knowledge of their circumstances. But their allowance being only threepence a day, with a pound and a half of bread, was totally inadequate not only for procuring their accustomed comforts, but even for maintaining them in the most ordinary manner. For a time they found a resource in the sale of watches, rings, and such superfluous trinkets as had any value. It was not unusual to see individuals among them laying aside some little token of remembrance, which had been the gift of parental affection, of love, or of friendship, and to hear them protest that with this at least they would never part. But stern necessity brought all these relics to the market at last, and this little fund of support was entirely exhausted.

After its first formation this company served under Marshal Noailles, at the siege of Rosas, in Catalonia, and distinguished themselves by their courage on so many occasions, that their general called them his children; and pointing out their determined courage to others, used to say that the real gentleman was ever the same, whether in necessity or in danger.

In a subsequent campaign in Alsace, they distinguished themselves by their voluntary attempt to storm a fortified island on the Rhine, defended by five hundred Germans. They advanced to the shore of that broad river under shelter of the night, waded into the stream, with their ammunition secured about their necks for fear of its being wetted, and linked arm-in-arm, according to the Highland fashion, advanced into the middle of the current. Here the water was up to their breasts, but as soon as it grew more shallow, they untied their cartouch-boxes, and marching ashore with their muskets shouldered, poured a deadly volley upon the Germans, who, seized with a panic, and endeavouring to escape, broke down their own bridges, and suffered a severe loss, leaving the island in possession of the brave assailants. When the French general heard of the success of what he had esteemed a desperate bravado, he signed himself with the cross in astonishment, and declared that it was the boldest action that ever had been performed, and that the whole honour of contrivance and execution belonged to the company of officers. The place was long called *L'Ile d'Ecossais,* the Scotsmen's Island, and perhaps yet retains the name.

In these and similar undertakings, many of this little band fell by the sword; but the fate of such was enviable compared with that of the far greater part who died under the influence of fatigue, privations, and contagious diseases, which fell with deadly severity on men once accustomed to the decencies and accommodations of social life, and now reduced to rags, filth, and famine. When, at the peace of Ryswick, this little company was disbanded, there remained but sixteen men out of their original number; and only four of these ever again saw their native country, whose fame had been sustained and extended by their fidelity and courage.

At length the last faint embers of civil war died away throughout Scotland. The last place which held out for King James was the strong island and castle in the Firth of Forth, called the Bass. This singular rock rises perpendicularly out of the sea. The surface is pasture land sloping to the brink of a tremendous precipice, which on all sides sinks sheer down into the stormy ocean. There is no anchorage ground on any point near the rock; and although it is possible in the present state of the island to go ashore (not without danger, however), and to ascend by a steep path to the table-land on the top of the crag, yet at the time of the Revolution a strong castle defended the landing-place, and the boats belonging to the garrison were lowered into the sea, or heaved up into the castle, by means of the engine called a crane. Access was thus difficult to friends, and impossible to enemies.

This sequestered and inaccessible spot, the natural shelter and abode of gannets, gulls, and sea-fowl of all descriptions, had been, as I have before noticed, converted into a state prison during the reigns of Charles II. and James II.; and was often the melancholy abode of the nonconformists, who were prisoners to Government. When the Revolution took place, the Governor of the Bass held out from 1688 to 1690, when he surrendered the island and castle to King William. They were shortly after recovered for King James by some Jacobite officers, who, sent thither as prisoners, contrived to surprise and overpower the garrison, and again bade defiance to the new Government. They received supplies of provisions from their Jacobite friends on shore, and exercised, by means of their boats, a sort of privateering warfare on such merchant vessels as entered the firth. A squadron of English ships of war was sent to reduce the place, which, in their attempt to batter the castle, did so little damage, and received so much, that the siege was given up, or rather converted into a strict blockade. The punishment of death was denounced by the Scottish Government against all who should attempt to supply the island with provisions; and a gentleman named Trotter, having been convicted of such an attempt, was condemned to death, and a gallows erected opposite to the Bass, that the garrison might witness his fate. The execution was interrupted for the time by a cannon-shot from the island, to the great terror of the assistants, amongst whom the bullet lighted; but no advantage accrued to Trotter, who was put to death elsewhere. The intercourse between the island and the shore was in this manner entirely cut off. Shortly afterwards the garrison became so weak for want of provisions that they were unable to man the crane by which they launched out and got in their boats. They were thus obliged finally to surrender, but not till reduced to an allowance of two ounces of rusk to each man per day. They were admitted to honourable terms, with the testimony of having done their duty like brave men.

We must now return to the state of civil affairs in Scotland, which was far from being settled. The arrangements of King William had not included in his administration Sir James Montgomery and some other leading Presbyterians, who conceived their services entitled them to such distinction. This was bitterly resented; for Montgomery and his friends fell into an error very common to agents in great changes, who often conceive themselves to have been the authors of those events, in which they were only the subordinate and casual actors. Montgomery had conducted the debates concerning the forfeiture of the crown at the Revolution, and therefore believed himself adequate to the purpose of dethroning King William, who, he thought, owed his crown to him, and of replacing King James. This monarch, so lately deprived of his realm on account of his barefaced attempts to bring in Popery, was now supported by a party of Presbyterians who proposed to render him the nursing father of that model of church government, which he had so often endeavoured to stifle in the blood of its adherents. As extremes approach to each other, the most violent Jacobites began to hold inter- course with the most violent Presbyterians, and both parties voted together in Parliament, from hatred to the administration of King William. The alliance, however, was too unnatural to continue; and King William was only so far alarmed by its progress as to hasten a redress of several of those grievances which had been pointed out in the Declaration of Rights. He also deemed it prudent to concede some- thing to the Presbyterians, disappointed as many of them were with the result of the Revolution in ecclesiastical matters.

I have told you already that King William had not hesitated to declare that the National Church of Scotland should be Presbyterian; but, with the love of toleration, which was a vital principle in the King's mind, he was desirous of permitting the Episcopalian incumbents, as well as the forms of worship, to remain in the churches of such parishes as preferred that communion. Moreover, he did not deem it equitable to take from such proprietors as were possessed of it, the right of patronage, that is, of presenting to the Presbytery a candidate for a vacant charge; when, unless found unfit for such a charge, upon his life and doctrine being inquired into by formal trial, the person thus presented was of course admitted to the office.

A great part of the Presbyterians were much discontented at a privilege which threw the right of electing a clergyman for the whole congregation into the hands of one man, whilst all the rest might be dissatisfied with his talents, or with his character. They argued also that very many of these presentations being in the hands of gentry of the Episcopal persuasion, to continue the right of patronage was to afford such patrons the means of introducing clergymen of their own tenets, and thus to maintain a perpetual schism in the bosom of the Church. To this it was replied by the defenders of patronage that, as the stipends of the clergy were paid by the landholders, the nomination of the minister ought to be left in their hands; and that it had accordingly been the ancient law of Scotland that the advowson, or title to bestow the Church living, was a right of private property. The tendency towards Episcopacy, continued these reasoners, might indeed balance, but could not overthrow, the supremacy of the Presbyterian establishment, since every clergyman who was in possession of a living was bound to subscribe the Confession of Faith, as established by the Assembly of Divines at Westminster, and to acknowledge that the General Assembly was invested with the full government of the Church. They further argued, that in practice it was best this law of patronage should remain unaltered. The Presbyterian Church being already formed upon a model strictly republican, they contended that to vest the right of nominating the established clergy in the hearers was to give additional features of democracy to a system which was already sufficiently independent both of the crown and the aristocracy. They urged that to permit the flocks the choice of their own shepherd was to encourage the candidates for church preferment rather to render themselves popular by preaching to soothe the humours of the congregation, than to exercise the wholesome but unpleasing duties of instructing their ignorance and reproving their faults; and that thus assentation and flattery would be heard from the pulpit, the very place where they were most unbecoming, and were likely to be most mischievous.

Such arguments in favour of lay patronage had much influence with the King; but the necessity of doing something which might please the Presbyterian party induced his Scottish ministers,—not, it is said, with William's entire approbation,—to renew a law of Cromwell's time, which placed the nomination of a minister, with some slight restrictions, in the hands of the congregation. These, upon a vacancy, exercised a right of popular election, gratifying unquestionably to the pride of human nature, but tending to excite, in the case of disagreement, debates and strife, which were not always managed with the decency and moderation that the subject required.

King William equally failed in his attempt to secure toleration for such of the Episcopal clergy as were disposed to retain their livings under a Presbyterian supremacy. To have gained these divines would have greatly influenced all that part of Scotland which lies north of the Forth; but in affording them protection, William was desirous to be secured of their allegiance, which in general they conceived to be due to the exiled sovereign. Many of them had indeed adopted a convenient political creed, which permitted them to submit to William as King *de facto,* that is, as being actually in possession of the Royal power, whilst they internally reserved and acknowledged the superior claims of James as King *de jure,* that is, who had the right to the crown, although he did not enjoy it.

It was William's interest to destroy this sophistical species of reasoning, by which, in truth, he was only recognised as a successful usurper, and obeyed for no other reason but because he had the power to enforce obedience. An oath, therefore, was framed, called the Assurance, which, being put to all persons holding offices of trust, was calculated to exclude those temporisers who had contrived to reconcile their immediate obedience to King William with a reserved acknowledgment that James possessed the real title to the crown. The Assurance bore, in language studiously explicit, that King William was acknowledged, by the person taking the oath, not only as King in fact, but also as King in law and by just title. This oath made a barrier against most of the Episcopal preachers who had any tendency to Jacobitism; but there were some who regarded their own patrimonial advantages more than political questions concerning the rights of monarchs, and in spite of the intolerance of the Presbyterian clergy (which, considering their previous sufferings, is not to be wondered at), about a hundred Episcopal divines took the oaths to the new Government, retained their livings, and were exempted from the jurisdiction of the courts of Presbytery.

LVIII

The Massacre of Glencoe

1691-1692

I AM now to call your attention to an action of the Scottish Government, which leaves a great stain on the memory of King William, although probably that Prince was not aware of the full extent of the baseness, treachery, and cruelty for which his commission was made a cover.

I have formerly mentioned that some disputes arose concerning the distribution of a large sum of money, with which the Earl of Breadalbane was entrusted to procure, or rather to purchase, a peace in the Highlands. Lord Breadalbane and those with whom he negotiated disagreed, and the English Government, becoming suspicious of the intentions of the Highland chiefs to play fast and loose on the occasion, sent forth a proclamation in the month of August 1691, requiring all and each of them to submit to Government before the first day of January 1692. After this period, it was announced in the same proclamation that those who had not submitted themselves should be subjected to the extremities of fire and sword.

This proclamation was framed by the Privy Council, under the influence of Sir John Dalrymple (Master of Stair, as he was called), whom I have already mentioned as holding the place of Lord Advocate, and who had in 1690 been raised to be Secretary of State, in conjunction with

Lord Melville. The Master of Stair was at this time an intimate friend of Breadalbane, and it seems that he shared with that nobleman the warm hope and expectation of carrying into execution a plan of retaining a Highland army in the pay of Government, and accomplishing a complete transference of the allegiance of the chiefs to the person of King William from that of King James. This could not have failed to be a most acceptable piece of service, upon which, if it could be accomplished, the Secretary might justly reckon as a title to his master's further confidence and favour.

But when Breadalbane commenced his treaty, he was mortified to find that though the Highland chiefs expressed no dislike to King William's money, yet they retained their secret fidelity to King James too strongly to make it safe to assemble them in a military body, as had been proposed. Many chiefs, especially those of the MacDonalds, stood out also for terms, which the Earl of Breadalbane and the Master of Stair considered as extravagant; and the result of the whole was the breaking off the treaty, and the publishing of the severe proclamation already mentioned.

Breadalbane and Stair were greatly disappointed and irritated against those chiefs and tribes, who, being refractory on this occasion, had caused a breach of their favourite scheme. Their thoughts were now turned to revenge; and it appears from Stair's correspondence that he nourished and dwelt upon the secret hope that several of the most stubborn chiefs would hold out beyond the term appointed for submission, in which case it was determined that the punishment inflicted should be of the most severe and awful description. That all might be prepared for the meditated operations, a considerable body of troops were kept in readiness at Inverlochy and elsewhere. These were destined to act against the refractory clans, and the campaign was to take place in the midst of winter, when it was supposed that the season and weather would prevent the Highlanders from expecting an attack.

But the chiefs received information of these hostile intentions, and one by one submitted to Government within the appointed period, thus taking away all pretence of acting against them. It is said that they did so by secret orders from King James, who, having penetrated the designs of Stair, directed the chiefs to comply with the proclamation rather than incur an attack which they had no means of resisting.

The indemnity, which protected so many victims, and excluded both lawyers and soldiers from a profitable job, seems to have created great disturbance in the mind of the Secretary of State. As chief after chief took the oath of allegiance to King William, and by doing so put themselves one by one out of danger, the greater became the anxiety of the Master of Stair to find some legal flaw for excluding some of the Lochaber clans from the benefit of the indemnity. But no opportunity occurred for exercising these kind intentions, excepting in the memorable, but fortunately the solitary instance, of the clan of the MacDonalds of Glencoe.

This clan inhabited a valley formed by the river Coe, or Cona,[1] which falls into Lochleven, not far from the head of Loch Etive. It is distinguished, even in that wild country, by the sublimity of the mountains, rocks, and precipices in which it lies buried.[2] The minds of men are formed by their habitations. The MacDonalds of the Glen were not very numerous, seldom mustering above two hundred armed men; but they were bold and daring to a proverb, confident in the strength of their country, and in the protection and support of their kindred tribes, the MacDonalds of Clanranald, Glengarry, Keppoch, Ardnamurchan, and others of that powerful name. They also lay near the possessions of the Campbells, to whom, owing to the predatory habits to which they were especially addicted, they were very bad neighbours, so that blood had at different times been spilt between them.

MacIan of Glencoe (this was the patronymic title of the chief of this clan) was a man of a stately and venerable person and aspect. He possessed both courage and sagacity, and was accustomed to be listened to by the neighbouring chieftains, and to take a lead in their deliberations. MacIan had been deeply engaged both in the campaign of Killiecrankie and in that which followed under General Buchan; and when the insurgent Highland chiefs held a meeting with the Earl of

---

[1] This is the *Cona* of Ossian's poems.

[2] "The scenery of this valley is far the most picturesque of any in the Highlands, being so wild and uncommon as never fails to attract the eye of every stranger of the least degree of taste or sensibility. The entrance to it is strongly marked by the craggy mountain of *Brachal-ety,* a little west of King's House. All the other mountains of Glencoe resemble it, and are evidently but naked and solid rocks, rising on each side perpendicularly to a great height from a flat narrow bottom, so that in many places they seem to hang over, and make approaches, as they aspire, towards each other. The tops of the ridge of hills on one side are irregularly serrated for three or four miles, and shoot in places into spires, which forms the most magnificent part of the scenery above Lochleven."—Pennant.

Breadalbane, at a place called Auchallader, in the month of July 1691, for the purpose of arranging an armistice, MacIan was present with the rest, and, it is said, taxed Breadalbane with the design of retaining a part of the money lodged in his hands for the pacification of the Highlands. The Earl retorted with vehemence, and charged MacIan with a theft of cattle, committed upon some of his lands by a party from Glencoe. Other causes of offence took place, in which old feuds were called to recollection; and MacIan was repeatedly heard to say, he dreaded mischief from no man so much as from the Earl of Breadalbane. Yet this unhappy chief was rash enough to stand out to the last moment and decline to take advantage of King William's indemnity till the time appointed by the proclamation was wellnigh expired.

The displeasure of the Earl of Breadalbane seems speedily to have communicated itself to the Master of Stair, who, in his correspondence with Lieutenant-Colonel Hamilton, then commanding in the Highlands, expresses the greatest resentment against MacIan of Glencoe, for having, by his interference, marred the bargain between Breadalbane and the Highland chiefs. Accordingly, in a letter of 3d December, the Secretary intimated that Government was determined to destroy utterly some of the clans, in order to terrify the others and he hoped that, by standing out and refusing to submit under the indemnity, the MacDonalds of Glencoe would fall into the net,—which meant that they would afford a pretext for their extirpation. This letter is dated a month before the time limited by the indemnity; so long did these bloody thoughts occupy the mind of this unprincipled statesman.

Ere the term of mercy expired, however, MacIan's own apprehensions, or the advice of friends, dictated to him the necessity of submitting to the same conditions which others had embraced, and he went with his principal followers to take the oath of allegiance to King William. This was a very brief space before the 1st of January, when, by the terms of the proclamation, the opportunity of claiming the indemnity was to expire. MacIan was, therefore, much alarmed to find that Colonel Hill, the Governor of Fort-William, to whom he tendered his oath of allegiance, had no power to receive it, being a military, and not a civil officer. Colonel Hill, however, sympathised with the distress and even tears of the old chieftain, and gave him a letter to Sir Colin Campbell of Ardkinglas, Sheriff of Argyleshire, requesting him to receive the "lost sheep," and administer the oath to him, that he might have the advantage of the indemnity, though so late in claiming it.

MacIan hastened from Fort-William to Inverary, without even turning aside to his own house, though he passed within a mile of it. But the roads, always very bad, were now rendered almost impassable by a storm of snow; so that, with all the speed the unfortunate chieftain could exert, the fatal first of January was past before he reached Inverary.

The Sheriff, however, seeing that MacIan had complied with the spirit of the statute, in tendering his submission within the given period, under the sincere, though mistaken belief, that he was applying to the person ordered to receive it; and considering also, that, but for the tempestuous weather, it would after all have been offered in presence of the proper law-officer, did not hesitate to administer the oath of allegiance, and sent off an express to the Privy Council, containing an attestation of MacIan's having taken the oaths, and a full explanation of the circumstances which had delayed his doing so until the lapse of the appointed period. The Sheriff also wrote to Colonel Hill what he had done, and requested that he would take care that Glencoe should not be annoyed by any military parties until the pleasure of the Council should be known, which he could not doubt would be favourable.

MacIan, therefore, returned to his own house and resided there, as he supposed in safety, under the protection of the Government to which he had sworn allegiance. That he might merit this protection, he convoked his clan, acquainted them with his submission, and commanded them to live peaceably, and give no cause of offence, under pain of his displeasure.

In the meantime, the vindictive Secretary of State had procured orders from his sovereign respecting the measures to be followed with such of the chiefs as should not have taken the oaths within the term prescribed. The first of these orders, dated 11th January, contained peremptory directions for military execution, by fire and sword, against all who should not have made their submission within the time appointed. It was, however, provided, in order to avoid driving them to desperation, that there was still to remain a power of granting mercy to those clans who, even after the time was past, should still come in and submit themselves. Such were the terms of the first Royal warrant, in which Glencoe was not expressly named.

It seems afterwards to have occurred to Stair, that Glencoe and his tribe would be sheltered under this mitigation of the intended severities, since he had already come in and tendered his allegiance, without waiting for the menace of military force. A second set of instructions were therefore made out on the 16th January. These held out the same indulgence to other clans who should submit themselves at the very last hour (a hypocritical pretext, for there existed none which stood in such a predicament), but they closed the gate of mercy against the devoted MacIan, who had already done all that was required of others. The words are remarkable:—"As for MacIan of Glencoe and that tribe, if they can be well distinguished from the rest of the Highlanders, it will be proper for the vindication of public justice, to extirpate that set of thieves."

You will remark the hypocritical clemency and real cruelty of these instructions, which profess a readiness to extend mercy to those who needed it not (for all the other Highlanders had submitted within the limited time), and deny it to Glencoe, the only man who had not been able literally to comply with the proclamation, though in all fair construction, he had done what it required.

Under what pretence or colouring King William's authority was obtained for such cruel instructions, it would be in vain to inquire. The Sheriff of Argyle's letter had never been produced before the Council; and the certificate of MacIan's having taken the oath was blotted out, and, in the Scottish phrase, deleted from the books of the Privy Council. It seems probable therefore that the fact of that chief's submission was altogether concealed from the King, and that he was held out in the light of a desperate and incorrigible leader of banditti, who was the main obstacle to the peace of the Highlands; but if we admit that William acted under such misrepresentations, deep blame will still attach to him for rashly issuing orders of an import so dreadful. It is remarkable that these fatal instructions are both superscribed and subscribed by the King himself, whereas, in most state papers the sovereign only superscribes, and they are countersigned by the Secretary of State, who is answerable for their tenor; a responsibility which Stair, on that occasion, was not probably ambitious of claiming.

The Secretary's letters to the military officers, directing the mode of executing the King's orders, betray the deep and savage interest which he took personally in their tenor, and his desire that the bloody measure should be as general as possible. He dwelt in these letters upon the proper time and season for cutting off the devoted tribe. "The winter," he said, "is the only season in which the Highlanders cannot elude us, or carry their wives, children, and cattle, to the mountains. They cannot escape you; for what human constitution can then endure to be long out of house? This is the proper season to maul them, in the long dark nights." He could not suppress his joy that Glencoe had not come in within the term prescribed; and expresses his hearty wishes that others had followed the same course. He assured the soldiers that their powers should be ample; and he exacted from them proportional exertions. He entreated that the thieving tribe of Glencoe might be *rooted out* in earnest; and he was at pains to explain a phrase which is in itself terribly significant. He gave directions for securing every pass by which the victims could escape, and warned the soldiers that it were better to leave the thing unattempted than fail to do it to purpose. "To plunder their lands, or drive off their cattle, would," say his letters, "be only to render them desperate; they must be all slaughtered, and the manner of execution must be sure, secret, and effectual."

These instructions, such as have been rarely penned in a Christian country, were sent to Colonel Hill, the Governor of Fort-William, who, greatly surprised and grieved at their tenor, endeavoured for some time to evade the execution of them. At length, obliged by his situation to render obedience to the King's commands, he transmitted the orders to Lieutenant-Colonel Hamilton, directing him to take four hundred men of a Highland regiment belonging to the Earl of Argyle, and fulfil the Royal mandate. Thus, to make what was intended yet worse, if possible, than it was in its whole tenor, the perpetration of this cruelty was committed to soldiers who were not only the countrymen of the prescribed, but the near neighbours, and some of them the close connections, of the MacDonalds of Glencoe. This is the more necessary to be remembered, because the massacre has unjustly been said to have been committed by English troops. The course of the bloody deed was as follows.

Before the end of January, a party of the Earl of Argyle's regiment, commanded by Captain Campbell of Glenlyon, approached Glencoe. MacIan's sons went out to meet them with a body of men, to demand whether they came as friends or foes. The officer replied that they came as friends, being sent to take up their quarters for a short time in Glencoe, in order to relieve the garrison of Fort-William, which was crowded with soldiers. On this they were welcomed with all the hospitality which the chief and his followers had the means of extending to them, and they resided for fifteen days amongst the unsuspecting Mac-Donalds, in the exchange of every species of kindness and civility. That the laws of domestic affection might be violated at the same time with those of humanity and hospitality, you are to understand that Alaster MacDonald, one of the sons of MacIan, was married to a niece of Glenlyon, who commanded the party of soldiers. It appears also, that the intended cruelty was to be exercised upon defenceless men; for the MacDonalds, though afraid of no other ill-treatment from their military guests, had supposed it possible the soldiers might have a commission to disarm them, and therefore had sent their weapons to a distance, where they might be out of reach of seizure.

Glenlyon's party had remained in Glencoe for fourteen or fifteen days, when he received orders from his commanding officer, Major Duncanson, expressed in a manner which shows him to have been the worthy agent of the cruel Secretary. They were sent in conformity with orders of the same date, transmitted to Duncanson by Hamilton, directing that all the MacDonalds, under seventy years of age, were to be cut off, and that the *Government was not to be troubled with prisoners.* Duncanson's orders to Glenlyon were as follows:—

"You are hereby ordered to fall upon the rebels, and put all to the sword under seventy. You are to have especial care that the old fox and his cubs do on no account escape your hands; you are to secure all the avenues, that no man escape. This you are to put in execution at four in the morning precisely, and by that time, or very shortly after, I will strive to be at you with a stronger party. But if I do not come to you at four, you are not to tarry for me, but fall on. This is by the King's special command, for the good and safety of the country, that these miscreants be cut off root and branch. See that this be put into execution without either fear or favour, else you may expect to be treated as not true to the King or Government, nor a man fit to carry a commission in the King's service. Expecting that you will not fail in the fulfilling, hereof, as you love yourself, I subscribe these with my hand,

"Robert Duncanson."

This order was dated 12th February, and addressed, "For their Majesties' service, to Captain Robert Campbell of Glenlyon."

This letter reached Glenlyon soon after it was written; and he lost no time in carrying the dreadful mandate into execution. In the interval, he did not abstain from any of those acts of familiarity which had lulled asleep the suspicions of his victims. He took his morning draught, as had been his practice every day since he came to the glen, at the house of Alaster MacDonald, MacIan's second son, who was married to his (Glenlyon's) niece. He, and two of his officers named

Lindsay, accepted an invitation to dinner from MacIan himself, for the following day, on which they had determined he should never see the sun rise. To complete the sum of treachery, Glenlyon played at cards, in his own quarters, with the sons of MacIan, John and Alaster, both of whom were also destined for slaughter.

About four o'clock in the morning of 13th February the scene of blood began. A party, commanded by one of the Lindsays, came to MacIan's house and knocked for admittance, which was at once given. Lindsay, one of the expected guests at the family meal of the day, commanded this party, who instantly shot MacIan dead by his own bedside, as he was in the act of dressing himself, and giving orders for refreshments to be provided for his fatal visitors. His aged wife was stripped by the savage soldiery, who, at the same time, drew off the gold rings from her fingers with their teeth. She died the next day, distracted with grief, and the brutal treatment she had received. Several domestics and clansmen were killed at the same place.

The two sons of the aged chieftain had not been altogether so confident as their father respecting the peaceful and friendly purpose of their guests. They observed, on the evening preceding the massacre, that the sentinels were doubled, and the mainguard strengthened. John, the elder brother, had even overheard the soldiers muttering amongst themselves that they cared not about fighting the men of the glen fairly but did not like the nature of the service they were engaged in; while others consoled themselves with the military logic that their officers must be answerable for the orders given, they having no choice save to obey them. Alarmed with what had been thus observed and heard, the young men hastened to Glenlyon's quarters, where they found that officer and his men preparing their arms. On questioning him about these suspicious appearances, Glenlyon accounted for them by a story that he was bound on an expedition against some of Glengarry's men; and alluding to the circumstance of their alliance, which made his own cruelty more detestable, he added, "If anything evil had been intended, would I not have told Alaster and my niece?"

Reassured by this communication, the young men retired to rest, but were speedily awakened by an old domestic, who called on the two brothers to rise and fly for their lives. "Is it time for you," he said, "to be sleeping, when your father is murdered on his own hearth?" Thus roused, they hurried out in great terror, and heard throughout the glen, wherever there was a place of human habitation, the shouts of the murderers, the report of the muskets, the screams of the wounded, and the groans of the dying. By their perfect knowledge of the scarce accessible cliffs amongst which they dwelt, they were enabled to escape observation, and fled to the southern access of the glen.

Meantime, the work of death proceeded with as little remorse as Stair himself could have desired. Even the slight mitigation of their orders respecting those above seventy years was disregarded by the soldiery in their indiscriminate thirst for blood, and several very aged and bedridden persons were slain amongst others. At the hamlet where Glenlyon had his own quarters, nine men, including his landlord, were bound and shot like felons; and one of them, MacDonald of Auchintriaten, had General Hill's passport in his pocket at the time. A fine lad of twenty had, by some glimpse of compassion on the part of the soldiers, been spared, when one Captain Drummond came up, and demanding why the orders were transgressed in that particular, caused him instantly to be put to death. A boy, of five or six years old, clung to Glenlyon's knees, entreating for mercy and offering to become his servant for life if he would spare him. Glenlyon was moved; but the same Drummond stabbed the child with his dirk, while he was in this agony of supplication.

At a place called Auchnaion, one Barber, a sergeant, with a party of soldiers, fired on a group of nine MacDonalds, as they were assembled round their morning fire, and killed four of them. The owner of the house, a brother of the slain Auchintriaten, escaped unhurt, and expressed a wish to be put to death rather in the open air than within the house. "For your bread which I have eaten," answered Barber, "I will grant the request." MacDonald was dragged to the door accordingly; but he was an active man, and when the soldiers were presenting their firelocks to shoot him, he cast his plaid over their faces, and taking advantage of the confusion, broke from them, and escaped up the glen.

The alarm being now general, many other persons, male and female, attempted their escape in the same manner as the two sons of MacIan and the person last mentioned. Flying from their burning huts, and from their murderous visitors, the half-naked fugitives committed themselves to a winter morning of darkness, snow, and storm, amidst a wilderness the most savage in the West Highlands, having a bloody death behind them, and before them tempest, famine, and desolation. Bewildered in the snow-wreaths, several sank to rise no more. But the severities of the storm were tender mercies compared to the cruelty of their persecutors.[1] The great fall of snow, which proved fatal to several of the fugitives, was the means of saving the remnant that escaped. Major Duncanson, agreeably to the plan expressed in his orders to Glenlyon, had not failed to put himself in motion, with four hundred men, on the evening preceding the slaughter; and had he reached the eastern passes out of Glencoe by four in the morning, as he calculated, he must have intercepted and destroyed all those who took that only way of escape from Glenlyon and his followers. But as this reinforcement arrived so late as eleven in the forenoon, they found no MacDonald alive in Glencoe, save an old man of eighty whom they slew; and after burning such houses as were yet unconsumed, they collected the property of the tribe, consisting of twelve hundred head of cattle and horses, besides goats and sheep, and drove them off to the garrison of Fort-William.

Thus ended this horrible deed of massacre. The number of persons murdered was thirty-eight; those who escaped might amount to a hundred and fifty males, who, with the women and children of the tribe, had to fly more than twelve miles through rocks and wildernesses, ere they could reach any place of safety or shelter.

This detestable butchery excited general horror and disgust, not only throughout Scotland, but in foreign countries, and did King William, whose orders, signed and superscribed by himself, were the warrant of the action, incredible evil both in popularity and character.

---

[1] "The hand that mingled in the meal,
 At midnight drew the felon steel,
 And gave the host's kind breast to feel
   Meed for his hospitality!
 The friendly hearth which warm'd that hand,
 At midnight arm'd it with the brand,
 That bade destruction's flames expand,
   Their red and fearful blazonry.

"Then woman's shriek was heard in vain,
 Nor infancy's unpitied pain,
 More than the warrior's groan could gain
   Respite from ruthless butchery!
 The winter wind that whistled shrill,
 The snows that night that cloaked the hill,
 Though wild and pitiless, had still
   Far more than Southron clemency."

Poetical Works.

Stair, however, seemed undaunted and had the infamy to write to Colonel Hill, while public indignation was at the highest, that all that could be said of the matter was, that the execution was not so complete as it might have been. There was besides a pamphlet published in his defence, offering a bungled vindication of his conduct; which, indeed, amounts only to this, that a man of the Master of Stair's high place and eminent accomplishments, who had performed such great services to the public, of which a laboured account was given; one also who, it is particularly insisted upon, performed the duty of family worship regularly in his household, ought not to be over-severely questioned for the death of a few Highland Papists, whose morals were no better than those of English highwaymen.

No public notice was taken of this abominable deed until 1695, three years after it had been committed, when, late and reluctantly, a Royal Commission, loudly demanded by the Scottish nation, was granted to inquire into the particulars of the transaction, and to report the issue of their investigations to Parliament.

The members of the Commission, though selected as favourable to King William, proved of a different opinion from the apologist of the Secretary of State, and reported that the letters and instructions of Stair to Colonel Hill and others were the sole cause of the murder. They slurred over the King's share of the guilt by reporting, that the Secretary's instructions went beyond the warrant which William had signed and superscribed. The Royal mandate, they stated, only ordered the tribe of Glencoe to be subjected to military execution, *in case* there could be any mode found of separating them from the other Highlanders. Having thus found a screen, though a very flimsy one, for William's share in the transaction, the report of the Commission let the whole weight of the charge fall on Secretary the Master of Stair, whose letters, they state, intimated no mode of separating the Glencoe men from the rest, as directed by the warrant; but, on the contrary did, under, a pretext of public duty, appoint them, without inquiry or distinction, to be cut off and rooted out in earnest and to purpose, and that "suddenly, secretly, and quietly." They reported, that these instructions of Stair had been the warrant for the slaughter; that it was unauthorised by his Majesty's orders, and, in fact, deserved no name save that of a most barbarous murder. Finally, the report named the Master of Stair as the deviser, and the various military officers employed as the perpetrators, of the same, and suggested with great moderation that Parliament should address his Majesty to send home Glenlyon and the other murderers to be tried, or should do otherwise as his Majesty pleased.

The Secretary, being by this unintelligible mode of reasoning thus exposed to the whole severity of the storm, and overwhelmed at the same time by the King's displeasure, on account of the Darien affair (to be presently mentioned), was deprived of his office, and obliged to retire from public affairs. General indignation banished him so entirely from public life that, having about this period succeeded to his father's title of Viscount Stair, he dared not take his seat in Parliament as such, on account of the threat of the Lord Justice-Clerk that if he did so, he would move that the address and report upon the Glencoe Massacre should be produced and inquired into. It was the year 1700 before the Earl of Stair found the affair so much forgotten that he ventured to assume the place in Parliament to which his rank entitled him; and he died in 1707, on the very day when the treaty of Union was signed, not without suspicion of suicide.

Of the direct agents in the massacre, Hamilton absconded and afterwards joined King William's army in Flanders, where Glenlyon, and the officers and soldiers connected with the murder, were then serving. The King, availing himself of the option left to him in the address of the Scottish Parliament, did *not* order them home for trial; nor does it appear that any of them were dismissed the service or punished for their crime otherwise than by the general hatred of the age in which they lived, and the universal execration of posterity.

Although it is here a little misplaced, I cannot refrain from telling you an anecdote connected with the preceding events, which befell so late as the year 1745–46, during the romantic attempt of Charles Edward, grandson of James II., to regain the throne of his fathers. He marched through the Lowlands, at the head of an army consisting of the Highland clans, and obtained for a time considerable advantages. Amongst other Highlanders, the descendant of the murdered MacIan of Glencoe joined his standard with a hundred and fifty men. The route of the Highland army brought them near to a beautiful seat built by the Earl of Stair, so often mentioned in the preceding narrative, and the principal mansion of his family. An alarm arose in the councils of Prince Charles, lest the MacDonalds of Glencoe should seize this opportunity of marking their recollection of the injustice done to their ancestors by burning or plundering the house of the descendant of their persecutor; and, as such an act of violence might have done the

Prince great prejudice in the eyes of the people of the Lowlands, it was agreed that a guard should be posted to protect the house of Lord Stair.

MacDonald of Glencoe heard the resolution, and deemed his honour and that of his clan concerned. He demanded an audience of Charles Edward, and admitting the propriety of placing a guard on a house so obnoxious to the feelings of the Highland army, and to those of his own clan in particular, he demanded, as a matter of right rather than favour, that the protecting guard should be supplied by the MacDonalds of Glencoe. If this request were not granted, he announced his purpose to return home with his people, and prosecute the enterprise no farther. "The MacDonalds of Glencoe," he said, "would be dishonoured by remaining in a service where others than their own men were employed to restrain them, under whatsoever circumstances of provocation, within the line of their military duty." The Royal adventurer granted the request of the high-spirited chieftain, and the MacDonalds of Glencoe guarded from the slightest injury the house of the cruel and crafty statesman who had devised and directed the massacre of their ancestors. Considering how natural the thirst of vengeance becomes to men in a primitive state of society, and how closely it was interwoven with the character of the Scottish Highlander, Glencoe's conduct on this occasion is a noble instance of a high and heroic preference of duty to the gratification of revenge.

We must now turn from this terrible story to one, which, though it does not seize on the imagination with the same force in the narrative, yet embraces a far wider and more extensive field of death and disaster.

LIX

Darien and Anne

1692-1702

HUMAN character, whether national or individual, presents often to our calm consideration the strangest inconsistencies; but there are few more striking than that which the Scots exhibit in their private conduct, contrasted with their views when united together for any general or national purpose. In his own personal affairs the Scotsman is remarked as cautious, frugal, and prudent, in an extreme degree, not generally aiming at enjoyment or relaxation till he has realised the means of indulgence, and studiously avoiding those temptations of pleasure to which men of other countries most readily give way. But when a number of the natives of Scotland associate for any speculative project, it would seem that their natural caution becomes thawed and dissolved by the union of their joint hopes, and that their imaginations are liable in a peculiar degree to be heated and influenced by any splendid prospect held out to them. They appear, in particular, to lose the power of calculating and adapting their means to the end which they desire to accomplish, and are readily induced to aim at objects magnificent in themselves, but which they have not, unhappily, the wealth or strength necessary to attain. Thus the Scots are often found to attempt splendid designs, which, shipwrecked for want of the necessary expenditure, give foreigners occasion to smile at the great error and equally great misfortune of the nation,—I mean their pride and their poverty. There is no greater instance of this tendency to daring speculation, which rests at the bottom of the coldness and caution of the Scottish character, than the disastrous history of the Darien colony.

Paterson, a man of comprehensive views and great sagacity, was the parent and inventor of this memorable scheme. In youth he had been an adventurer in the West Indies, and it was said a *bucanier,* that is, one of a species of adventurers nearly allied to pirates, who, consisting of different nations, and divided into various bands, made war on the Spanish commerce and settlements in the South Seas, and among the West Indian islands. In this roving course of life, Paterson had made himself intimately acquainted with the geography of South America, the produce of the country, the nature of its commerce, and the manner in which the Spaniards governed that extensive region.

On his return to Europe, however, the schemes which he had formed respecting the New World were laid aside for another project, fraught with the most mighty and important consequences. This was the plan of that great national establishment the Bank of England, of which he had the honour to suggest the first idea. For a time he was admitted a director of that institution; but it befell Paterson as often happens to the first projectors of great schemes. Other persons possessed of wealth and influence interposed, and, taking advantage of the ideas of the obscure and unprotected stranger, made them their own by alterations or improvements more or less trivial, and finally elbowed the inventor out of all concern in the institution, the foundation of which he had laid.

Thus expelled from the Bank of England, Paterson turned his thoughts to the plan of settling a colony in America, and in a part of that country so favoured in point of situation that it seemed to him formed to be the site of the most flourishing commercial capital in the universe.

The two great continents of North and South America are joined together by an isthmus, or narrow tract of land, called Darien. This neck of land is not above a day's journey in breadth, and as it is washed by the Atlantic Ocean on the eastern side, and the great Pacific Ocean on the west, the isthmus seemed designed by nature as a common centre for the commerce of the world. Paterson ascertained, or at least alleged that he had ascertained, that the isthmus had never been the property of Spain, but was still possessed by the original natives, a tribe of fierce and warlike Indians, who made war on the Spaniards. According to the law of nations, therefore, any state had a right of forming a settlement in Darien, providing the consent of the Indians was first obtained; nor could their doing so be justly made subject of challenge even by Spain, so extravagantly jealous of all interference with her South American provinces. This plan of a settlement, with so many advantages to recommend it, was proposed by Paterson to the merchants of Hamburg, to the Dutch, and even to the Elector of Brandenburg; but it was coldly received by all these states.

The scheme was at length offered to the merchants of London, the only traders probably in the world who, their great wealth being seconded by the protection of the British navy, had the means of realising the splendid visions of Paterson. But when the projector was in London, endeavouring to solicit attention to his plan, he became intimate with the celebrated Fletcher of Saltoun. This gentleman, one of the most accomplished men, and best patriots, whom Scotland has produced in any age, had, nevertheless, some notions of her interests which were more fanciful than real, and in his anxiety to render his country service, did not sufficiently consider the adequacy of the means by which her welfare was to be obtained. He was dazzled by the vision of opulence and grandeur which Paterson unfolded, and thought of nothing less than securing, for the benefit of Scotland alone, a scheme which promised to the state which should adopt it the keys, as it were, of the New World. The projector was easily persuaded to give his own country the benefit of his scheme of colonisation, and went to Scotland along with Fletcher. Here the plan found general acceptation, and particularly with the Scottish administration, who were greatly embarrassed at the time by the warm prosecution of the affair of Glencoe, and who easily persuaded King William that some freedom and facilities of trade granted to the Scots would divert the public attention from the investigation of a matter not very creditable to his Majesty's reputation any more than to their own. Stair, in particular, a party deeply interested, gave the Darien scheme the full support of his eloquence and interest, in the hope to regain a part of his lost popularity.

The Scottish ministers obtained permission, accordingly, to grant such privileges of trade to their country as might not be prejudicial to that of England. In June 1695 these influential persons obtained a statute from Parliament, and afterwards a charter from the crown, for creating a corporate body, or stock company, by name of the Company of Scotland trading to Africa and the Indies, with power to plant colonies and build forts in places not possessed by other European nations, the consent always of the inhabitants of the places where they settled being obtained.

The hopes entertained of the profits to arise from this speculation were in the last degree sanguine; not even the Solemn League and Covenant was signed with more eager enthusiasm. Almost every one who had, or could command, any sum of ready money, embarked it in the Indian and African Company; many subscribed their all; maidens threw in their portions, and widows whatever sums they could raise upon their dower, to be repaid an hundredfold by the golden shower which was to descend upon the subscribers. Some sold estates to vest the money in the Company's funds, and so eager was the spirit of speculation that when eight hundred thousand pounds formed the whole circulating capital of Scotland, half of that sum was vested in the Darien stock.

That everything might be ready for their extensive operations, the Darien Company proceeded to build a large tenement near Bristo Port, Edinburgh, to serve as an office for transacting their business, with a large range of buildings behind it, designed as warehouses, to be filled with the richest commodities of the eastern and western world. But, sad event of human hopes and wishes! the office is now occupied as a receptacle for paupers, and the extensive warehouses as a lunatic asylum.

But it was not the Scots alone whose hopes were excited by the rich prospects held out to them. An offer being made by the managers of the Company, to share the expected advantages of the scheme with English and foreign merchants, it was so eagerly grasped at that three hundred thousand pounds of stock was subscribed for in London within nine days after opening the books. The merchants of Hamburg and of Holland subscribed two hundred thousand pounds.

Such was the hopeful state of the new Company's affairs, when the English jealousy of trade interfered to crush an adventure which seemed so promising. The idea which then and long afterwards prevailed in England was, that all profit was lost to the British empire which did not arise out of commerce exclusively English. The increase of trade in Scotland or Ireland they considered, not as an addition to the general prosperity of the united nations, but as a positive loss to

England. The commerce of Ireland they had long laid under severe shackles, to secure their own predominance; but it was not so easy to deal with Scotland, which, totally unlike Ireland, was governed by its own independent legislature, and acknowledged no subordination or fealty to England, being in all respects, a separate and independent country, though governed by the same King.

This new species of rivalry on the part of an old enemy, was both irritating and alarming. The English had hitherto thought of the Scots as a poor and fierce nation, who, in spite of fewer numbers and far inferior resources, was always ready to engage in war with her powerful neighbour; and now that these wars were over, it was embarrassing and provoking to find the same nation display, in spite of its proverbial caution, a hardy and ambitious spirit of emulating them in the paths of commerce.

These narrow-minded, unjust, and ungenerous apprehensions prevailed so widely throughout the English nation, that both Houses of Parliament joined in an address to the King, stating that the advantages given to the newly-erected Scottish Indian and African Company would ensure that Kingdom so great a superiority over the English East India Company that a great part of the stock and shipping of England would be transported to the north, and Scotland would become a free port for all East Indian commodities, which they would be able to furnish at a much cheaper rate than the English. By this means it was said England would lose all the advantages of an exclusive trade in the eastern commodities, which had always been a great article in her foreign commerce, and sustain infinite detriment in the sale of her domestic manufactures. The King, in his gracious reply to this address, acknowledged the justice of its statements, though as void of just policy as of grounds in public law. His royal answer bore, "That the King had been ill served in Scotland, but hoped some remedies might still be found to prevent the evils apprehended." To show that his resentment was serious against his Scottish ministers, King William, as we have already mentioned, deprived the Master of Stair of his office as Secretary of State. Thus a statesman, who had retained his place in spite of the bloody deed of Glencoe, was disgraced for attempting to serve his country in the most innocent and laudable manner, by extending her trade and national importance.

The English Parliament persisted in the attempt to find remedies for the evils which they were pleased to apprehend from the Darien scheme, by appointing a committee of inquiry, with directions to summon before them such persons as had, by subscribing to the Company, given encouragement to the progress of an undertaking, so fraught, as they alleged, with danger to the trade of England. These persons, being called before Parliament and menaced with impeachment, were compelled to renounce their connection with the undertaking, which was thus deprived of the aid of English subscriptions, to the amount, as already mentioned, of three hundred thousand pounds. Nay, so eager did the English Parliament show themselves in this matter, that they even extended their menace of impeachment to some native-born Scotsmen, who had offended the House by subscribing their own money to a Company formed in their own country, and according to their own laws.

That this mode of destroying the funds of the concern might be yet more effectual, the weight of the King's influence with foreign states was employed to diminish the credit of the undertaking, and to intercept the subscriptions which had been obtained for the Company abroad. For this purpose, the English envoy at Hamburg was directed to transmit to the Senate of that commercial city a remonstrance on the part of King William, accusing them of having encouraged the commissioners of the Darien Company; requesting them to desist from doing so; intimating that the plan, said to be fraught with many evils, had not the support of his Majesty; and protesting that the refusal of the Senate to withdraw their countenance from the scheme would threaten an interruption to the friendship which his Majesty desired to cultivate with the good city of Hamburg. The Senate returned to this application a spirited answer—"The city of Hamburg," they said, "considered it as strange that the King of England should dictate to them, a free people, with whom they were to engage in commercial arrangements; and were yet more astonished to find themselves blamed for having entered into such engagements with a body of his own Scottish subjects, incorporated under a special act of Parliament." But as the menace of the envoy showed that the Darien Company must be thwarted in all its proceedings by the superior power of England, the prudent Hamburgers, ceasing to consider it as a hopeful speculation, finally withdrew their subscriptions. The Dutch, to whom William could more decidedly dictate, from his authority as Stadtholder, and who were jealous, besides, of the interference of the Scots with their own East Indian trade, adopted a similar course without remonstrance.

Thus, the projected Company, deserted both by foreign and English associates, were crippled in their undertaking, and left to their own limited resources.

The managers of the scheme, supported by the general sense of the people of Scotland, made warm remonstrances to King William on the hostile interference of his Hamburg envoy, and demanded redress for so gross a wrong. In William's answer, he was forced meanly to evade what he was resolved not to grant and yet could not in equity refuse. "The King," it was promised, "would send instructions to his envoy not to make use of his Majesty's name or authority for obstructing their engagements with the city of Hamburg." The Hamburgers, on the other hand, declared themselves ready to make good their subscriptions if they should receive any distinct assurance from the King of England, that in so doing they would be safe from his threatened resentment. But, in spite of repeated promises, the envoy received no power to make such declaration. Thus the Darien Company lost the advantage of support, to the extent of two hundred thousand pounds, subscribed in Hamburg and Holland, and that by the personal and hostile interference of their own monarch under whose charter they were embodied.

Scotland, left to her unassisted resources, would have acted with less spirit but more wisdom in renouncing her ambitious plan of colonisation, sure as it now was to be thwarted by the hostile interference of her unfriendly but powerful neighbour and rival. But those engaged in the scheme, comprising great part of the nation, could not be expected easily to renounce hopes which had been so highly excited, and enough remained of the proud and obstinate spirit with which their ancestors had maintained their independence to induce the Scots, even when thrown back on their own limited means, to determine upon the establishment of their favourite settlement at Darien, in spite of the desertion of their English and foreign subscribers, and in defiance of the invidious opposition of their powerful neighbours. They caught the spirit of their ancestors, who, after losing so many dreadful battles, were always found ready, with sword in hand, to dispute the next campaign.

The contributors to the enterprise were encouraged in this stubborn resolution by the flattering account which was given of the country to be colonised, in which every class of Scotsmen found something to flatter their hopes, and to captivate their imaginations. The description given of Darien by Paterson was partly derived from his own knowledge, partly from the report of bucaniers and adventurers, and the whole was exaggerated by the eloquence of an able man, pleading in behalf of a favourite project.

The climate was represented as healthy and cool, the tropical heats being, it was said, mitigated by the height of the country, and by the shade of extensive forests, which yet presented neither thicket nor underwood, but would admit a horseman to gallop through them unimpeded. Those acquainted with trade were assured of the benefits of a safe and beautiful harbour, where the advantage of free commerce and universal toleration would attract traders from all the world; while the produce of China, Japan, the Spice Islands, and Eastern India, brought to the bay of Panama in the Pacific Ocean, might be transferred by a safe and easy route across the isthmus to the new settlement, and exchanged for all the commodities of Europe. "Trade," said the commercial enthusiast, "will beget trade—money will beget money—the commercial world will no longer want work for their hands, but will rather want hands for their work. This door of the seas, and key of the universe, will enable its possessors to become the legislators of both worlds, and the arbitrators of commerce. The settlers at Darien will acquire a nobler empire than Alexander or Caesar, without fatigue, expense, or danger, as well as without incurring the guilt and bloodshed of conquerors." To those more vulgar minds who cannot separate the idea of wealth from the precious metals, the projector held out the prospect of golden mines. The hardy Highlanders, many of whom embarked in the undertaking, were to exchange their barren moors for extensive savannahs of the richest pasture, with some latent hopes of a creagh (or foray) upon Spaniards or Indians. The Lowland laird was to barter his meagre heritage, and oppressive feudal tenure, for the free possession of unlimited tracts of ground, where the rich soil, three or four feet deep, would return the richest produce for the slightest cultivation. Allured by these hopes, many proprietors actually abandoned their inheritances, and many more sent their sons and near relations to realise their golden hopes, while the poor labourers, who desired no more than bread and freedom of conscience, shouldered their mattocks and followed their masters in the path of emigration.

Twelve hundred men, three hundred of whom were youths of the best Scottish families, embarked on board of five frigates, purchased at Hamburg for the service of the expedition; for the King refused the Company even the trifling accommodation of a ship of war, which lay idle at Burntisland. They sailed (26th July 1698) from Leith Roads, reached their destination in safety, and disembarked at a place called Acta, where, by cutting through a peninsula, they obtained a safe and insulated situation for a town, called New Edinburgh, and a fort named St. Andrew. With the same fond remembrance of their native land, the colony itself was called Caledonia. They were favourably received by the native princes, from whom they purchased the land they required. The harbour, which was excellent, was proclaimed a free port; and in the outset the happiest results were expected from the settlement.[1]

The arrival of the colonists took place in winter when the air was cool and temperate; but with the summer returned the heat, and with the heat came the diseases of a tropical climate. Those who had reported so favourably of the climate of Darien, had probably been persons who had only visited the coast during the healthy season, or mariners, who, being chiefly on shipboard, find many situations healthy which prove pestilential to Europeans residing on shore. The health of the settlers, accustomed to a cold and mountainous country, gave way fast under the constant exhalations of the sultry climate, and even a more pressing danger than disease itself arose from the scarcity of food. The provisions which the colonists had brought from Scotland were expended, and the country afforded them only such supplies as could be procured by the precarious success of fishing and the chase.

This must have been foreseen; but it was never doubted that ample supplies would be procured from the English provinces in North America, which afforded great superabundance of provisions, and from the West India colonies, which always possessed superfluities. It was here that the enmity of the King and the English nation met the unfortunate settlers most unexpectedly, and most severely. In North America, and in the West India islands, the most savage pirates and bucaniers, men who might be termed enemies to the human race and had done deeds which seemed to exclude them from intercourse with mankind had nevertheless found repeated refuge,—had been permit-

---

[1] "The news of their settlement in the isthmus of Darien arrived at Edinburgh on the 25th March 1699, and was celebrated with the most extravagant rejoicings. Thanks were publicly offered up to God in all the churches of the city. At a public graduation of students, at which the magistrates in their formalities attended, the Professor of Philosophy pronounced a harangue in favour of that settlement, the legality of which, against all other pretenders, was maintained in their printed theses; and it seems even to have been a common subject of declamation from the pulpit."—ARNOT.

ted to refit their squadrons, and, supplied with every means of keeping the sea, had set sail in a condition to commit new murders and piracies. But no such relief was extended to the Scottish colonists at Darien, though acting under a charter from their sovereign, and establishing a peaceful colony according to the law of nations, and for the universal benefit of mankind.

The governors of Jamaica, Barbadoes, and New York, published proclamations, setting forth, that whereas it had been signified to them (the governors) by the English Secretary of State, that his Majesty was unacquainted with the purpose and design of the Scottish settlers at Darien (which was a positive falsehood), and that it was contrary to the peace entered into with his Majesty's allies (no European power having complained of it), and that the governors of the said colonies had been commanded not to afford them any assistance; therefore, they did strictly charge the colonists over whom they presided, to hold no correspondence with the said Scots, and to give them no assistance of arms, ammunition, provisions, or any other necessary whatsoever, either by themselves or any others for them; as those transgressing the tenor of the proclamation would answer the breach of his Majesty's commands at their highest peril.

These proclamations were strictly obeyed; and every species of relief, not only that which countrymen may claim of their fellow-subjects, and Christians of their fellow-Christians, but such as the vilest criminal has a right to demand, because still holding the same human shape with the community whose laws he has offended—the mere supply, namely, of sustenance, the meanest boon granted to the meanest beggar,—was denied to the colonists of Darien.

Famine aided the diseases which swept them off in large numbers; and undoubtedly they, who thus perished for want of the provisions for which they were willing to pay, were as much murdered by King William's Government as if they had been shot in the snows of Glencoe. The various miseries of the colony became altogether intolerable, and after waiting for assistance eight months, by far the greater part of the adventurers having died, the miserable remainder abandoned the settlement.

Shortly after the departure of the first colony, another body of thirteen hundred men, who had been sent out from Scotland, arrived at Darien, under the hope of finding their friends in health, and the settlement prosperous. This reinforcement suffered by a bad passage, in which one of their ships was lost and several of their number died. They took possession of the deserted settlement with sad anticipations, and were not long in experiencing the same miseries which had destroyed and dispersed their predecessors. Two months after, they were joined by Campbell of Finab, with a third body of three hundred men, chiefly from his own Highland estate, many of whom had served under him in Flanders, where he had acquired an honourable military reputation. It was time the colony should receive such military support, for in addition to their other difficulties, they were now threatened by the Spaniards.

Two years had elapsed since the colonisation of Darien had become matter of public discussion, and notwithstanding their feverish jealousy of their South American settlements, the Spaniards had not made any remonstrance against it. Nay, so close and intimate was the King of Spain's friendship with King William, that it seems possible he might never have done so, unless the colonists had been disowned by their sovereign, as if they had been vagabonds and outlaws. But finding the Scottish colony so treated by their Prince, the Spaniards felt themselves invited in a manner to attack it, and not only lodged a remonstrance against the settlement with the English Cabinet, but seized one of the vessels wrecked on the coast, confiscated the ship, and made the crew prisoners. The Darien Company sent an address to the King by the hands of Lord Basil Hamilton, remonstrating against this injury; but William, who studied every means to discountenance the unfortunate scheme, refused, under the most frivolous pretexts, to receive the petition. This became so obvious that the young nobleman determined that the address should reach the Royal hands in season or out of season, and taking a public opportunity to approach the King as he was leaving the saloon of audience, he obtruded himself and the petition upon his notice, with more bluntness than ceremony. "That young man is too bold," said William; but, doing justice to Lord Basil's motive, he presently added,—"if a man can be too bold in the cause of his country."

The fate of the colony now came to a crisis. The Spaniards had brought from the Pacific a force of sixteen hundred men, who were stationed at a place called Tubucantee, waiting the arrival of an armament of eleven ships, with troops on board, destined to attack fort St. Andrew. Captain Campbell, who, by the unanimous consent of the settlers, was chosen to the supreme military command, marched against them with two hundred men, surprised and stormed their camp, and dispersed their army, with considerable slaughter. But in returning from his successful expedition he had the mortification to learn that the Spanish ships had arrived before the harbour, disembarked their troops, and invested the place. A desperate defence was maintained for six weeks; until loss of men, want of ammunition, and the approach of famine, compelled the colonists to an honourable surrender. The survivors of this unhappy settlement were so few, and so much exhausted, that they were unable to weigh the anchor of the vessel, called the *Rising Sun,* in which they were to leave the fatal shore, without assistance from the conquering Spaniards.

Thus ended the attempt of Darien, an enterprise splendid in itself, but injudicious, because far beyond the force of the adventurous little nation by which it was undertaken. Paterson survived the disaster, and, even when all was over, endeavoured to revive the scheme by allowing the English three-fourths in a new Stock Company. But national animosities were too high to suffer his proposal to be listened to. He died at an advanced age, poor and neglected.

The failure of this favourite project, deep sorrow for the numbers who had fallen, many of whom were men of birth and blood, the regret for pecuniary losses which threatened national bankruptcy, and indignation at the manner in which their charter had been disregarded, all at once agitated from one end to the other a kingdom which is, to a proverb, proud, poor, and warm in their domestic attachments. Nothing could be heard throughout Scotland but the language of grief and of resentment. Indemnification, redress, revenge, were demanded by every mouth, and each hand seemed ready to vouch for the justice of the claim. For many years no such universal feeling had occupied the Scottish nation.

King William remained indifferent to all complaints of hardship and petitions of redress, unless when he showed himself irritated by the importunity of the supplicants, and hurt at being obliged to evade what it was impossible for him, with the least semblance of justice, to refuse. The motives of a Prince, naturally just and equitable, and who, himself the President of a great trading nation, knew well the injustice which he was committing, seem to have been, first, a reluctance to disoblige the King of Spain, but, secondly, and in a much greater degree, what William might esteem the political necessity of sacrificing the interests of Scotland to the jealousy of England, a jealousy equally unworthy and impolitic. But what is unjust can never be in a true sense necessary, and the sacrifice of principle to circumstances will, in every sense, and in all cases, be found as unwise as it is unworthy.

It is, however, only justice to William to state, that though in the Darien affair he refused the Scots the justice which was unquestionably their due, he was nevertheless the only person in either kingdom who proposed, and was anxious to have carried into execution, an union between the kingdoms, as the only effectual means of preventing in future such subjects of jealousy and contention. But the prejudices of England as well as Scotland, rendered more inveterate by this unhappy quarrel, disappointed the King's wise and sagacious overture.

Notwithstanding the interest in her welfare which King William evinced, by desiring the accomplishment of a union, the people of Scotland could not forget the wrongs which they had received concerning the Darien project; and their sullen resentment showed itself in every manner, excepting open rebellion, during the remainder of his reign.

In this humour Scotland became a useless possession to the King. William could not wring from that kingdom one penny for the public service, or, what he would have valued more, one recruit to carry on his continental campaigns. These hostile feelings subsisted to a late period.

William died in 1702, having for six years and upwards survived his beloved consort Queen Mary. This great King's memory was, and is, justly honoured in England, as their deliverer from slavery, civil and religious, and is almost canonised by the Protestants of Ireland, whom he rescued from subjugation, and elevated to supremacy. But in Scotland, his services to church and state, though at least equal to those which he rendered to the sister countries, were in a considerable degree obliterated by the infringement of her national rights on several occasions. Many persons, as well as your grandfather, may recollect that on the 5th of November 1788, when a full century had elapsed after the Revolution, some friends to constitutional liberty proposed that the return of the day should be solemnised by an agreement to erect a monument to the memory of King William, and the services which he had rendered to the British kingdoms. At this period an anonymous letter appeared in one of the Edinburgh newspapers, ironically applauding the undertaking, and proposing as two subjects of the entablature, for the base of the projected column, the massacre of Glencoe, and the distresses of the Scottish colonists at Darien. The proposal was abandoned as soon as this insinuation was made public.[1] You may observe from this how cautious a monarch should be of committing wrong or injustice, however strongly recommended by what may seem political necessity; since the recollection of such actions cancels the sense of the most important national services, as in Scripture it is said, "that a dead fly will pollute a rich and costly unguent."

James II. died only four months before his son-in-law William. The King of France proclaimed James's son, that unfortunate Prince of Wales, born in the very storm of the Revolution, as William's successor in the kingdoms of England, Scotland, and Ireland; a step which greatly irritated the three nations, to whom Louis seemed by this act disposed to nominate a sovereign. Anne, the sister of the late Queen Mary, ascended the throne of these kingdoms, according to the provision made at the Revolution by the legislature of both nations.

---

[1] See a copy of this *jeu d'esprit* in the *Scots Magazine* of November 1788.

LX

Acts of Succession and Union

1702-1707

AT the period of Queen Anne's accession, Scotland was divided into three parties. These were, first, the Whigs, staunch favourers of the Revolution, in the former reign called Williamites; secondly, the Tories, or Jacobites, attached to the late King; and thirdly, a party sprung up in consequence of the general complaints arising out of the Darien adventure, who associated themselves for asserting the rights and independence of Scotland.

This latter association comprehended several men of talent, among whom Fletcher of Saltoun, already mentioned, was the most distinguished. They professed that, providing the claims and rights of the country were ascertained and secured against the encroaching influence of England, they did not care whether Anne or her brother, the titular Prince of Wales, was called to the throne. These statesmen called themselves the Country Party, as embracing exclusively for their object the interests of Scotland alone. This party, formed upon a plan and principle of political conduct hitherto unknown in the Scottish Parliament, was numerous, bold, active, and eloquent; and as a critical period had arrived in which the measures to be taken in Scotland must necessarily greatly affect the united empire, her claims could no longer be treated with indifference or neglect, and the voice of her patriots disregarded.

The conjuncture which gave Scotland new consequence was as follows:—When Queen Anne was named to succeed to the English throne, on the death of her sister Mary and brother-in-law William III., she had a family. But the young Duke of Gloucester, the last of her children, had died before her accession to the crown, and there were no hopes of her having more; it became, therefore, necessary to make provision for the succession to the crown when the new Queen should die. The titular Prince of Wales, son of the abdicated James, was undoubtedly the next heir; but he was a Catholic, bred up in the court of France, inheriting all the extravagant claims, and probably the arbitrary sentiments, of his father; and to call him to the throne would be in all likelihood to undo the settlement between king and people which had taken place at the Revolution. The English legislature, therefore, turned their eyes to another descendant of King James VI, namely Sophia, the Electress Dowager of Hanover, grand-daughter of James the First of England and Sixth of Scotland, by the marriage of his daughter, Elizabeth, with the Prince Palatine. This Princess was the nearest Protestant heir in blood to Queen Anne, supposing the claims of the son of James II. were to be passed over. She was a Protestant and would necessarily, by accepting the crown, become bound to maintain the civil and religious rights of the nation, as settled at the Revolution, upon which her own right would be dependent. For these weighty reasons the English Parliament passed an Act of Succession, settling the crown, on the failure of Queen Anne and her issue, upon the Princess Sophia, Electress Dowager of Hanover, and her descendants. This act, most important in its purport and consequences, was passed in June 1700.

It became of the very last importance to Queen Anne's administration to induce, if possible, the legislation of Scotland to settle the crown of that kingdom on the same series of heirs to which that of England was destined. If, after the death of Queen Anne, the Scottish nation, instead of uniting in choosing the Electress Sophia, should call to the crown the titular Prince of Wales, the two kingdoms would again be separated, after having been under the same sway for a century, and all the evils of mutual hostilities betwixt the two extremities of the island, encouraged by the alliance and assistance of France, must again distract Great Britain. It became necessary, therefore to try every species of persuasion to prevent a consequence fraught with so much mischief.

But Scotland was not in a humour to be either threatened or soothed into the views of England on this important occasion. The whole party of Anti-Revolutionists, Jacobites, or, as they called themselves, Cavaliers, although they thought it prudent for the present to submit to Queen Anne, entertained strong hopes that she herself was favourable to the succession of her brother after her own death; while their principles dictated to them that the wrong, as they termed it, done to James II., ought as speedily as possible to be atoned for by the restoration of his son. They were of course directly and violently hostile to the proposed Act of Succession in favour of the Electress Sophia.

The Country Party, headed by the Duke of Hamilton and the Marquis of Tweeddale, opposed this Act for different reasons. They resolved to take this favourable opportunity to diminish or destroy the ascendency which had been exercised by England respecting the affairs of Scotland, and which, in the case of Darien, had been so unjustly and unworthily employed to thwart and disappoint a national scheme. They determined to obtain for Scotland a share in the plantation trade of England, and a freedom from the restrictions imposed by the English Navigation Act, and other regulations enacted to secure a monopoly of trade to the English nation. Until these points were determined in favour of Scotland, they resolved they would not agree to pass the Act of Succession, boldly alleging, that unless the rights and privileges of Scotland were to be respected, it was of little consequence whether she chose a king from Hanover or Saint Germains.

The whole people of Scotland, excepting those actually engaged in the administration, or expecting favours from the court, resolutely adopted the same sentiments and seemed resolved to abide all the consequences of a separation of the two kingdoms, nay, of a war with England, rather than name the Electress Sophia successor to the crown, till the country was admitted to an equitable portion of those commercial privileges which England retained with a tenacious grasp. The crisis seemed an opportunity of Heaven's sending to give Scotland consequence enough to insist on her rights.

With this determined purpose, the country party in the Scottish Parliament, instead of adopting, as the English ministers eagerly desired, the Protestant Act of Succession, proposed a measure called an Act of Security. By this it was provided that in case of Queen Anne's death without children, the whole power of the crown should, for the time, be lodged in the Scottish Parliament, who were directed to choose a successor of the Royal line and Protestant religion. But the choice was to be made with this special reservation, that the person so chosen should take the throne only under such conditions of government as should secure, from English or foreign influence, the honour and independence of the Scottish crown and nation. It was further stipulated that the same person should be incapable of holding the crowns of both kingdoms, unless the Scottish people were admitted to share with the English the full benefits of trade and navigation. That the nation might assume an appearance of strength necessary to support such lofty pretensions, it was provided by the same statute that the whole men in Scotland capable of bearing arms should be trained to the use of them by monthly drills; and that the influence of England might expire at the same time with the life of the Queen, it was provided that all commissions of the officers of state, as well as those of the military employed by them, should cease and lose effect so soon as Anne's death took place.

This formidable act, which in fact hurled the gauntlet of defiance at the far stronger kingdom of England, was debated in the Scottish Parliament, clause by clause, and article by article, with the utmost fierceness and tumult. "We were often," says an eyewitness, "in the form of a Polish Diet, with our swords in our hands, or at least our hands on our swords."

The Act of Security was carried in Parliament by a decided majority, but the Queen's commissioner refused the Royal assent to so violent a statute. The Parliament, on their part, would grant no supplies, and when such were requested by the members of administration, the hall rung with the shouts of "Liberty before subsidy!" The Parliament was adjourned amidst the mutual discontent of both Ministers and Opposition.

The dispute betwixt the two nations was embroiled during the recess of Parliament by intrigues. Simon Fraser of Beaufort, afterwards Lord Lovat, had undertaken to be the agent of France in a Jacobite conspiracy, which he afterwards discovered to Government, involving in his accusation the Duke of Hamilton and other noblemen. The persons accused defended themselves by alleging that the plot was a mere pretext, devised by the Duke of Queensberry, to whom it had been discovered by Fraser. The English House of Peers, in allusion to this genuine or pretended discovery, passed a vote that a dangerous plot had existed in Scotland, and that it had its origin in the desire to overthrow the Protestant succession in that nation. This resolution was highly resented by the Scots, being considered as an unauthorised interference, on the part of the English peers, with the concerns of another kingdom. Everything seemed tending to a positive rupture between the sister kingdoms; and yet, my dear child, it was from this state of things that the healing measure of an incorporating Union finally took its rise.

In the very difficult and critical conduct which the Queen had to observe betwixt two high-spirited nations, whose true interest it was to enter into the strictest friendship and alliance, but whose irritated passions for the present breathed nothing but animosity, Anne had the good fortune to be assisted by the Wise counsels of Godolphin, one of the most sagacious and profound ministers who ever advised a crowned head. By his recommendation, the Queen proceeded upon a plan which, while at first sight it seemed to widen the breach between the two nations, was in the end to prove the means of compelling both to lay aside their mutual prejudices and animosities. The scheme of a Union was to be proceeded upon, like that of breaking two spirited horses to join in drawing the same yoke, when it is of importance to teach them, that by moving in unison, and at an equal pace, the task will be easy to them both. Godolphin's first advice to the Queen, was to suffer the Scottish Act of Security to pass. The English in their superior wealth and importance had for many years looked with great contempt on the Scottish nation, as compared with themselves, and were prejudiced against the Union, as a man of wealth and importance might be against a match with a female in an inferior rank of society. It was necessary to change this feeling, and to show plainly to the English people that if the Scots were not allied with them in intimate friendship, they might prove dangerous enemies.

The Act of Security finally passed in 1704, having, according to Godolphin's advice, received the Queen's assent; and the Scottish Parliament, as the provisions of the statute bore, immediately began to train their countrymen, who have always been attached to the use of arms, and easily submit to military discipline.

The effect of these formidable preparations was, to arouse the English from their indifference to Scottish affairs. Scotland might be poor, but her numerous levies, under sanction of the Act of Security, were not the less formidable. A sudden inroad on Newcastle, as in the great Civil War, would distress London by interrupting the coal trade; and whatever might be the event, the prospect of a civil war, as it might be termed, after such a duration of peace, was doubtful and dangerous.

The English Parliament, therefore, showed a mixture of resentment tempered with a desire of conciliation. They enacted regulations against the Scottish trade, and ordered the Border towns of Newcastle, Berwick, and Carlisle to be fortified and garrisoned; but they declined, at the same time, the proposed measure of inquiring concerning the person who advised the Queen to consent to the Act of Security. In abstaining from this, they paid respect to Scottish independence, and at the same time, by empowering the Queen to nominate Commissioners for a Union, they seemed to hold out the olive branch to the sister kingdom.

While this lowering hurricane appeared to be gathering darker and darker betwixt the two nations, an incident took place which greatly inflamed their mutual resentment.

A Scottish ship,[1] equipped for a voyage to India, had been seized and detained in the Thames, at the instance of the English East India Company. The Scots were not in a humour to endure this; and by way of reprisal, they took possession of a large English vessel trading to India, called the *Worcester,* which had been forced into the Firth of Forth by unfavourable weather. There was something suspicious about this vessel. Her men were numerous, and had the air of pirates. She was better provided with guns and ammunition than is usual for vessels fitted out merely for objects of trade. A cipher was found among her papers, for corresponding with the owners, as if upon secret and dangerous business. All these mysterious circumstances seemed to intimate that the *Worcester,* as was not uncommon, under the semblance of a trader, had been equipped for the purpose of exercising, when in remote Indian latitudes, the profession of a bucanier or pirate.

One of the seamen belonging to this ship, named Haines, having been ashore with some company, and drinking rather freely, fell into a fit of melancholy, an effect which liquor produces on some constitutions, and in that humour told those who were present that it is a wonder his captain and crew were not lost at sea, considering the wickedness which had been done aboard that ship which was lying in the roadstead. Upon these and similar hints of something doubtful or illegal, the Scottish authorities imprisoned the officers and sailors of the *Worcester,* and examined them rigorously in order to discover what the expressions of their shipmate referred to.

---

[1] The *Annandale,* belonging to the African Company.

Among other persons interrogated, a black slave of the captain (surely a most suspicious witness) told a story, that the *Worcester,* during their late voyage, had, upon the Coromandel coast, near Calicut, engaged, and finally boarded and captured a vessel bearing a red flag, and manned with English, or Scotch, or at least with people speaking the English language; that they had thrown the crew overboard, and disposed of the vessel and the cargo to a native merchant. This account was in some degree countenanced by the surgeon of the *Worcester,* who, in confirmation of the slave's story, said that being on shore in a harbour on the coast of Malabar, he heard the discharge of great guns at sea; and saw the *Worcester,* which had been out on a cruise, come in next morning with another vessel under her stern, which he understood was afterwards sold to a native merchant. Four days afterwards he went on board the *Worcester,* and finding her decks lumbered with goods, made some inquiry of the crew how they had come by them, but was checked for doing so by the mate, and desired to confine himself to his own business. Further, the surgeon stated, that he was called to dress the wounds of several of the men, but the captain and mate forbade him to ask, or the patients to answer, how they came by their hurts.

Another black servant, or slave, besides the one before mentioned, had not himself seen the capture of the supposed ship, or the death of the crew, but had been told of it by the first informer shortly after it had happened. Lastly, a Scottish witness declared that Green, the captain of the vessel, had shown him a seal bearing the arms of the Scottish African and Indian Company.

This story was greatly too vague to have been admitted to credit on any occasion when men's minds were cool and their judgments unprejudiced. But the Scottish nation was almost frantic with resentment on the subject of Darien. One of the vessels belonging to that unfortunate Company, called the *Rising Sun,* and commanded by Captain Robert Drummond, had been missing for some time; and it was received as indisputable truth that this must have been the vessel taken by the Worcester, and that her master and men had been murdered, according to the black slave's declaration.

Under this cloud of prejudice, Green, with his mate and crew, fifteen men in all, were brought to trial for their lives. Three of these unfortunate men, Linstead, the supercargo's mate, Bruckley, the cooper of the *Worcester,* and Haines, whose gloomy hints gave the first suspicion, are said to have uttered declarations before trial, confirming the truth of the charge, and admitting that the vessel so seized upon was the *Rising Sun,* and that Captain Robert Drummond and his crew were the persons murdered in the course of that act of piracy. But Haines seems to have laboured under attacks of hypochondria, which sometimes induce men to suppose themselves spectators and accomplices in crimes which have no real existence. Linstead, like the surgeon May, only spoke to a hearsay story, and that of Bruckley was far from being clear. It will hereafter be shown, that if any ship was actually taken by Green and his crew, it could not be that of Captain Drummond, which met a different fate. This makes it probable that these confessions were made by the prisoners only in the hope of saving their own lives, endangered by the fury of the Scottish people. And it is certain that none of these declarations were read or produced as evidence in court, nor were those stated to have made them examined as witnesses.

The trial of Green and his crew took place before the High Court of Admiralty; and a jury, upon the sole evidence of the black slave,— for the rest was made up of suggestions, insinuations, and reports, taken from hearsay,—brought in a verdict of guilty against Green and all his crew. The Government were disposed to have obtained a reprieve from the crown for the prisoners, whose guilt was so very doubtful; but the mob of Edinburgh, at all times a fierce and intractable multitude, arose in great numbers and demanded their lives with such an appearance of uncontrollable fury, that the authorities became intimidated and yielded. Captain Green himself, Madder his first mate, and Simpson the gunner, were dragged to Leith, loaded by the way with curses and execrations, and even struck at and pelted by the furious populace; and finally executed in terms of their sentence, denying with their last breath the crime which they were accused of.

The ferment in Scotland was somewhat appeased by this act of vengeance, for it has no title to be called a deed of justice. The remainder of Green's crew were dismissed after a long imprisonment, during the course of which cooler reflection induced doubts of the validity of the sentence. At a much later period it appeared that, if the *Worcester* had committed an act of piracy upon any vessel, it could not at least have been on the *Rising Sun,* which ship had been cast away on the island of Madagascar, when the crew were cut off by the natives, excepting Captain Drummond himself, whom Drury, an English seaman in similar circumstances, found alive upon the island.[1]

This unhappy affair, in which the Scots, by their precipitate and unjust procedure, gave the deepest offence to the English nation, tended greatly to increase the mutual prejudices and animosity of the people of both countries against each other. But the very extremity of their mutual enmity inclined wise men of both nations to be more disposed to submit to a Union, with all the inconveniences and difficulties which must attend the progress of such a measure, rather than that the two divisions of the same island should again engage in intestine war.

The principal obstacle to a Union, so far as England was concerned, lay in a narrow-minded view of the commercial interests of the nation, and a fear of the loss which might accrue by admitting the Scots to a share of their plantation trade and other privileges. But it was not difficult to show, even to the persons most interested, that public credit and private property would suffer immeasurably more by a war with Scotland than by sacrificing to peace and unity some share in the general commerce. It is true, the opulence of England, the command of men, the many victorious troops which she then had in the field, under the best commanders in Europe, seemed to ensure final victory, if the two nations should come to open war. But a war with Scotland was always more easily begun than ended; and wise men saw it would be better to secure the friendship of that kingdom by an agreement on the basis of mutual advantage than to incur the risk of invading, and the final necessity of securing it as a conquered country, by means of forts and garrisons. In the one case, Scotland would become an integral part of the empire; and, improving in the arts of peaceful industry, must necessarily contribute to the prosperity of England. In the case supposed she must long remain a discontented and disaffected province in which the exiled family of James II. and his allies the French would always find friends and correspondents. English statesmen were therefore desirous of a union. But they stipulated that it should be of the most intimate kind; such as should free England from the great inconvenience arising from the Scottish nation possessing a separate legislature and constitution of her own; and in order to blend her interests indelibly with those of England, they demanded that the supreme power of the state should be

---

[1] This, however, supposes Drury's Adventures in Madagascar to be a genuine production, of which there may be doubts.

reposed in a Parliament of the united countries, to which Scotland might send a certain proportion of members, but which should meet in the English capital, and be of course more immediately under the influence of English counsels and interests.

The Scottish nation, on the other hand, which had of late become very sensible of the benefits of foreign trade, were extremely desirous of a federative union, which should admit them to the commercial advantages which they coveted. But while they grasped at a share in the English trade, they desired that Scotland should retain her rights as a separate kingdom, making as heretofore her own laws, and adopting her own public measures, uncontrolled by the domination of England. Here, therefore, occurred a preliminary point of dispute, which was necessarily to be settled previous to the further progress of the treaty.

In order to adjust the character of the proposed Union-treaty in this and other particulars, commissioners for both kingdoms were appointed to make a preliminary inquiry, and report upon the articles which ought to be adopted as the foundation of the measure, and which report was afterwards to be subjected to the Legislatures of both kingdoms.

The English and Scottish commissioners being both chosen by the Queen, that is, by Godolphin and the Queen's ministers, were indeed taken from different parties, but carefully selected, so as to preserve a majority of those who could be reckoned upon as friendly to the treaty, and who would be sure to do their utmost to remove such obstacles as might arise in the discussion.

I will briefly tell you the result of these numerous and anxious debates. The Scottish commissioners, after a vain struggle, were compelled to submit to an incorporating Union, as that which alone would ensure the purposes of combining England and Scotland into one single nation, to be governed in its political measures by the same Parliament. It was agreed that in contributing to the support of the general expenses of the kingdom, Scotland should pay a certain proportion of taxes, which were adjusted by calculation. But in consideration that the Scots, whose revenue, though small, was unencumbered, must thereafter become liable for a share of the debt which England had incurred since the Revolution, a large sum of ready money was to be advanced to Scotland as an equivalent for that burden; which sum, however, was to be repaid to England gradually from the Scottish revenue. So far all went on pretty well between the two sets of commissioners. The English statesmen also consented, with no great scruple, that Scotland should retain her own national Presbyterian Church, her own system of civil and municipal laws, which is in many important respects totally different from that of England, and her own courts for the administration of justice. The only addition to her judicial establishment was the erection of the Court of Exchequer in Scotland, to decide in fiscal matters, and which follows the English forms.

But the treaty was nearly broken off when the English announced, that, in the Parliament of the United Kingdoms, Scotland should only enjoy a representation equal to one-thirteenth of the whole number. The proposal was received by the Scottish commissioners with a burst of surprise and indignation. It was loudly urged that a kingdom resigning her ancient independence should at least obtain in the great national council a representation bearing the same proportion the population of Scotland did to that of England, which was one to six. If this rule, which seems the fairest that could be found, had been adopted, Scotland would have sent sixty-six members to the united Parliament. But the English refused peremptorily to consent to the admission of more than forty-five at the very utmost; and the Scottish commissioners were bluntly and decisively informed that they must either acquiesce in this proposal or declare the treaty at an end. With more prudence, perhaps, than spirit the majority of the commissioners chose to yield the point rather than run the risk of frustrating the Union entirely.

The Scottish Peerage were to preserve all the other privileges of their rank; but their right of sitting in Parliament, and acting as hereditary legislators, was to be greatly limited. Only sixteen of their number were to enjoy seats in the British House of Lords, and these were to be chosen by election from the whole body. Such peers as were amongst the number of commissioners were induced to consent to this degradation of their order by the assurance that they themselves should be created British peers, so as to give them personally, by charter, the right which the sixteen could only acquire by election.

To smooth over the difficulties, and reconcile the Scottish commissioners to the conditions which appeared hard to them, and above all, to afford them some compensation for the odium which they were certain to incur, they were given to understand that a considerable sum out of the equivalent money would be secured for their especial use. We might have compassionated these statesmen, many of whom were able and eminent men, had they, from the sincere conviction that Scotland was under the necessity of submitting to the Union at all events, accepted the terms which the English commissioners dictated. But when they united with the degradation of their country the prospect of obtaining personal wealth and private emoluments, we cannot acquit them of the charge of having sold their own honour and that of Scotland. This point of the treaty was kept strictly secret; nor was it fixed how the rest of the equivalent was to be disposed of. There remained a disposable fund of about three hundred and sixty thousand pounds, which was to be bestowed on Scotland in indemnification for the losses of Darien, and other gratuities, upon which all those members of the Scottish Parliament who might be inclined to sell their votes, and whose interest was worth purchasing, might fix their hopes and expectations.

When the articles agreed upon by the commissioners as the basis of a Union were made public in Scotland, it became plain that few suffrages would be obtained in favour of the measure, save by menaces or bribery, unless perhaps from a very few, who, casting their eyes far beyond the present time, considered the uniting of the island of Britain as an object which could not be purchased too dearly. The people in general had awaited, in a state of feverish anxiety, the nature of the propositions on which this great national treaty was to rest; but even those who had expected the least favourable terms were not prepared for the rigour of the conditions which had been adopted, and the promulgation of the articles gave rise to the most general expressions, not only of discontent, but of rage and fury against the proposed Union.

There was indeed no party or body of men in Scotland who saw their hopes or wishes realised in the plan adopted by the commissioners. I will show you, in a few words, their several causes of dissatisfaction.

The Jacobites saw in the proposed Union an effectual bar to the restoration of the Stewart family. If the treaty was adopted, the two kingdoms must necessarily be governed by the English act, settling the succession of the crown on the Electress of Hanover. They were therefore resolved to oppose the Union to the utmost. The Episcopal clergy could hardly be said to have had a separate interest from the Jacobites, and, like them, dreaded the change of succession which must take place at the death of Queen Anne. The Highland chiefs also, the most zealous and formidable portion of the Jacobite interest, anticipated in the Union a decay of their own patriarchal power. They remembered the times of

Cromwell, who bridled the Highlands by garrisons filled with soldiers, and foresaw that when Scotland came to be only a part of the British nation, a large standing army, at the constant command of Government, must gradually suppress the warlike independence of the clans.

The Presbyterians of the Church of Scotland, both clergy and laity, were violently opposed to the Union, from the natural apprehension that so intimate an incorporation of two nations was likely to end in a uniformity of worship, and that the hierarchy of England would, in that case, be extended to the weaker and poorer country of Scotland, to the destruction of the present establishment. This fear seemed the better founded as the Bishops, or Lords Spiritual of the English House of Lords, formed a considerable portion of what was proposed to be the legislature of both kingdoms; so that Scotland, in the event of the Union taking place, must, to a certain extent, fall under the dominion of prelates. These apprehensions extended to the Cameronians themselves, who, though having so many reasons to dread the restoration of the Stewarts, and to favour the Protestant succession, looked, nevertheless, on the proposed Union as almost a worse evil, and a still further departure from the engagements of the Solemn League and Covenant, which, forgotten by all other parties in the nation, was still their professed rule of action.

The nobility and barons of the kingdom were alarmed, lest they should be deprived, after the example of England, of those territorial jurisdictions and privileges which preserved their feudal influence; while, at the same time, the transference of the seat of government to London must necessarily be accompanied with the abolition of many posts and places of honour and profit connected with the administration of Scotland as a separate kingdom, and which were naturally bestowed on her nobility and gentry. The Government, therefore, must have so much less to give away, the men of influence so much less to receive; and those who might have expected to hold situations of power and authority in their own country while independent, were likely to lose by the Union both power and patronage.

The persons who were interested in commerce complained that Scotland was only tantalised by a treaty which held out to the kingdom the prospect of a free trade, when, at the same time, it subjected them to all the English burdens and duties, raising the expenses of commerce to a height which Scotland afforded no capital to defray; so that the apprehension became general that the Scottish merchants would lose the separate trade which they now possessed without obtaining any beneficial share in that of England.

Again, the whole body of Scottish tradespeople, artisans, and the like, particularly those of the metropolis, foresaw that, in consequence of the Union, a large proportion of the nobility and gentry would be withdrawn from their native country, some to attend their duties in the British Parliament, others from the various motives of ambition, pleasure, or vanity, which induced persons of comparative wealth to frequent courts and reside in capitals. The consequences to be apprehended were, that the Scottish metropolis would be deserted by all that were wealthy and noble, and deprived at once of the consideration and advantages of a capital; and that the country must suffer in proportion by the larger proprietors ceasing to reside on their estates and going to spend their rents in England.

These were evils apprehended by particular classes of men. But the loss and disgrace to be sustained by the ancient kingdom, which had so long defended her liberty and independence against England, were common to all her children; and should Scotland at this crisis voluntarily surrender her rank among nations, for no immediate advantages that could be anticipated, excepting such as might be obtained by private individuals, who had votes to sell, and consciences that permitted them to traffic in such ware, each inhabitant of Scotland must have his share in the apprehended dishonour. Perhaps, too, those felt it most who, having no estates or wealth to lose, claimed yet a share, with the greatest and the richest, in the honour of their common country.

The feelings of national pride were inflamed by those of national prejudice and resentment. The Scottish people complained that they were not only required to surrender their public rights, but to yield them up to the very nation who had been most malevolent to them in all respects; who had been their constant enemies during a thousand years of almost continual war; and who, even since they were united under the same crown, had shown, in the massacre of Glencoe, and the disasters of Darien, at what a slight price they held the lives and rights of their northern neighbours. The hostile measures adopted by the English Parliament,—their declarations against the Scottish trade—their preparations for war on the Border,—were all circumstances which envenomed the animosity of the people of Scotland; while the general training which had taken place under the Act of Security made them confident in their own military strength and disposed to stand their ground at all hazards.

Moved by anxiety, doubt, and apprehension, an unprecedented confluence of people, of every rank, sex, and age, thronged to Edinburgh from all corners of Scotland, to attend the meeting of the Union Parliament, which met 3d October 1706.

The Parliament was divided, generally speaking, into three parties. The first was composed of the courtiers or followers of Government determined at all events to carry through the Union, on the terms proposed by the Commissioners. This party was led by the Duke of Queensberry, Lord High Commissioner, a person of talents and accomplishments, and great political address, who had filled the highest situations during the last reigns. He was assisted by the Earl of Mar, Secretary of State, who was suspected to be naturally much disposed to favour the exiled family of Stewart, but who, sacrificing his political principles to love of power or of emolument, was deeply concerned in the underhand and private management by which the Union was carrying through. But the most active agent in the treaty was the Viscount Stair, long left out of administration on account of his share in the scandalous massacre of Glencoe and the affair of Darien. He was raised to an earldom in 1703 and was highly trusted and employed by Lord Godolphin and the English administration. This celebrated statesman, now again trusted and employed, contributed greatly by his address, eloquence, and talents, to accomplish the Union, and gained on that account, from a great majority of his displeased countrymen, the popular nickname of the Curse of Scotland.

The party opposing the Union consisted of those who were attached to the Jacobite interest, joined with the Country Party, who, like Fletcher of Saltoun, resisted the treaty, not on the grounds of the succession to the crown, but as destructive of the national independence of the kingdom. They were headed by the Duke of Hamilton, the premier peer of Scotland, an excellent speaker, and admirably qualified to act as the head of a party in ordinary times, but possessed of such large estates as rendered him unwilling to take any decisive steps by which his property might be endangered. To this it seems to have been owing, that the more decided and effectual measures by which alone the Union treaty might have been defeated, though they often seemed to gain his approbation for a time, never had his hearty or effectual support in the end.

There was a third party, greatly smaller than either of the others, but which secured to themselves a degree of consequence by keeping together, and affecting to act independently of the rest, from which they were termed the Squadróne Volánte. They were headed by the Marquis of Tweeddale, and consisted of the members of an administration of which the Marquis had been the head, but which were turned out of office to make way for the Duke of Queensberry and the present ruling party. These discontented politicians were neither favourers of the Court which had dismissed them nor of the opposition party. To speak plainly, in a case where their country demanded of them a decisive opinion the Squadróne seemed to have waited to see what course of conduct would best serve their own interest. We shall presently see that they were at last decided to support the treaty by a reconciliation with the court.

The unpopularity of the proposed measure throughout Scotland in general was soon made evident by the temper of the people of Edinburgh. The citizens of the better class exclaimed against the favourers of the Union, as willing to surrender the sovereignty of Scotland to her ancient rival, whilst the populace stated the same idea in a manner more obvious to their gross capacities, and cried out that the Scottish crown, sceptre, and sword, were about to be transferred to England as they had been in the time of the usurper, Edward Longshanks.

On the 23d October the popular fury was at its height. The people crowded together in the High Street and Parliament Square, and greeted their representatives as friends or enemies to their country, according as they opposed or favoured the Union. The Commissioner was bitterly reviled and hooted, while, in the evening of the day, several hundred persons escorted the Duke of Hamilton to his lodgings, encouraging him by loud huzzas to stand by the cause of national independence. The rabble next assailed the house of the Lord Provost, destroyed the windows, and broke open the doors, and threatened him with instant death as a favourer of the obnoxious treaty.

Other acts of riot were committed, which were not ultimately for the advantage of the anti-Unionist, since they were assigned as reasons for introducing strong bodies of troops into the city. These mounted guard in the principal streets; and the Commissioner dared only pass to his coach through a lane of soldiers under arms, and was then driven to his lodgings in the Canongate amidst repeated volleys of stones and roars of execration. The Duke of Hamilton continued to have his escort of shouting apprentices, who attended him home every evening.

But the posting of the guards overawed opposition both within and without the Parliament; and notwithstanding the remonstrances of the opposition party, that it was an encroachment both on the privileges of the city of Edinburgh and of the Parliament itself, the hall of meeting continued to be surrounded by a military force.

The temper of the kingdom of Scotland at large was equally unfavourable to the treaty of Union with that of the capital. Addresses against the measure were poured into the House of Parliament from the several shires, counties, burghs, towns, and parishes. Men, otherwise the most opposed to each other, Whig and Tory, Jacobite and Williamite, Presbyterian, Episcopalian, and Cameronian, all agreed in expressing their detestation of the treaty, and imploring the Estates of Parliament to support and preserve entire the sovereignty and independence of the crown and kingdom, with the rights and privileges of Parliament, valiantly maintained through so many ages, so that the succeeding generations might receive them unimpaired; in which good sense the petitioners offered to concur with life and fortune. While addresses of this description loaded the table of the Parliament, the promoters of the Union could only procure from a few persons in the town of Ayr a single address in favour of the measure, which was more than overbalanced by one of an opposite tendency, signed by a very large majority of the inhabitants of the same burgh.

The Unionists, secure in their triumphant majorities, treated these addresses with scorn. The Duke of Argyle said they were only fit to be made kites of, while the Earl of Marchmont proposed to reject them as seditious, and, as he alleged, got up collusively, and expressing the sense of a party rather than of the nation. To this it was boldly answered by Sir James Foulis of Colinton, that, if the authenticity of the addresses were challenged, he had no doubt that the parties subscribing would attend the right honourable House in person, and enforce their petitions by their presence. This was an alarming suggestion, and ended the debate.

Amongst these addresses against the Union, there was one from the Commissioner of the General Assembly, which was supposed to speak the sentiments of most of the clergymen of the Church of Scotland, who saw great danger to the Presbyterian Church from the measure under deliberation. But much of the heat of the clergy's opposition was taken off by the Parliament's passing an act for the security of the Church of Scotland as by law established at the Revolution, and making this declaration an integral part of the treaty of Union. This cautionary measure seems to have been deemed sufficient; and although some presbyteries sent addresses against the Union, and many ministers continued to preach violently on the subject, yet the great body of the clergy ceased to vex themselves and others with the alarming tendency of the measure, so far as religion and church discipline were concerned.

The Cameronians, however, remained unsatisfied, and not having forgotten the impression which their arms had produced at the time of the Revolution, they conceived that a similar crisis of public affairs had again arrived, and required their active interference. Being actually embodied and possessed of arms, they wanted nothing save hardy and daring leaders to have engaged them in actual hostilities. They were indeed so earnest in opposing the Union, that several hundreds of them appeared in formal array, marched into Dumfries, and, drawing up in military order around the cross of the town, solemnly burnt the articles of Union, and published a testimony declaring that the Commissioners who adjusted them must have been either silly, ignorant, or treacherous, if not all three, and protesting, that if an attempt should be made to impose the treaty on the nation by force, the subscribers were determined that they and their companions would not become tributaries and bond slaves to their neighbours, without acquitting themselves as became men and Christians. After publishing this threatening manifesto the assembly dispersed.

This conduct of the Cameronians led to a formidable conspiracy. One Cunningham of Eckatt, a leading man of that sect at the time of the Revolution, afterwards a settler at Darien, offered his services to the heads of the opposition party, to lead to Edinburgh such an army of Cameronians as should disperse the Parliament and break off the treaty of Union. He was supported by money and promises and encouraged to collect the sense of the country on the subject of his proposal.

This agent found the west country ripe for revolt, and ready to join with any others who might take arms against the Government on the footing of resistance to the treaty of Union. Cunningham required that a body of the Athole Highlanders should secure the town of Stirling, in order to keep the communication open between the Jacobite chiefs and the army of western insurgents, whom he himself was in the first instance to command. And had this design taken effect, the party which had suffered so much during the late reigns of the Stewarts, and the mountaineers who had been found such ready agents in oppressing them, would have been seen united in a common cause, so strongly did the universal hatred to the Union overpower all other party feelings at this time.

A day was named for the proposed insurrection in the west, on which Cunningham affirmed he would be able to assemble at Hamilton, which was assigned as the place of rendezvous, seven or eight thousand men, all having guns and swords, several hundred with muskets and bayonets, and about a thousand on horseback; with which army he proposed to march instantly to Edinburgh, and disperse the Parliament. The Highlanders were to rise at the same time; and there can be little doubt that the country in general would have taken arms. Their first efforts would probably have been successful, but the final event must have been a bloody renewal of the wars between England and Scotland.

The Scottish Government were aware of the danger and employed among the Cameronians two or three agents of their own, particularly one Ker of Kersland, who possessed some hereditary influence among them. The persons so employed did not venture to cross the humour of the people, or argue in favour of the Union; but they endeavoured in various ways to turn the suspicion of the Cameronians upon the Jacobite nobility and gentry, to awaken hostile recollections of the persecutions they had undergone in which the Highlanders had been willing actors, and to start other causes of jealousy among people who were more influenced by the humour of the moment than any reasoning which could be addressed to them.

Notwithstanding the underhand practices of Kersland, and although Cunningham himself is said to have been gained over by the Government, the scheme of rising went forward, and the day of rendezvous was appointed; when the Duke of Hamilton, either reluctant to awaken the flames of civil war, or doubting the strength of Eckatt's party, and its leader's fidelity, sent messengers into the west country to countermand and postpone the intended insurrection; in which he so far succeeded, that only four hundred men appeared at the rendezvous, instead of twice as many thousands; and these, finding their purpose frustrated, dispersed peaceably.

Another danger which threatened the Government passed as easily over. An address against the Union had been proposed at Glasgow, where, as in every place of importance in Scotland, the treaty was highly unpopular. The magistrates, acting under the directions of the Lord Advocate, endeavoured to obstruct the proposed petition, or at least to resist its being expressed in the name of the city. At this feverish time there was a national fast appointed to be held, and a popular preacher made choice of a text from Ezra viii. 21, "Then I proclaimed a fast there, at the river of Ahava, that we might afflict ourselves before our God, to seek of him a right way for us and for our little ones, and for all our substance." Addressing himself to the people, who were already sufficiently irritated, the preacher told them that prayers would not do, addresses would not do—prayer was indeed a duty, but it must be seconded by exertions of a very different nature; "wherefore," he concluded, "up, and be valiant for the city of our God."

The populace of the city, taking this as a direct encouragement to insurrection, assembled in a state of uproar, attacked and dispersed the guards, plundered the houses of the citizens, and seized what arms they could find; in short, took possession of the town, and had everybody's life and goods at their mercy. No person of any consequence appeared at the head of these rioters; and after having put themselves under the command of a mechanic named Finlay, who had formerly been a serjeant, they sent small parties to the neighbouring towns to invite them to follow their example. In this they were unsuccessful; the proclamations of Parliament, and the adjournment of the rendezvous appointed by the Cameronians, having considerably checked the disposition to insurrection. In short, the Glasgow riot died away, and the insurgents prevented bloodshed by dispersing quietly; Finlay and another of their leaders were seized by a party of dragoons from Edinburgh, conveyed to that city, and lodged in the castle. And thus was extinguished a hasty fire which might otherwise have occasioned a great conflagration.

To prevent the repetition of such dangerous examples as the rendezvous at Hamilton and the tumults at Glasgow, the Parliament came to the resolution of suspending that clause of the Act of Security which appointed general military musters throughout Scotland; and enacted instead, that, in consideration of the tumults which had taken place, all assembling in arms without the Queen's special order should be punished as an act of high treason. This being made public by proclamation, put a stop to future attempts at rising.

The project of breaking off the treaty by violence being now wholly at an end, those who opposed the measure determined upon a more safe and moderate attempt to frustrate it. It was resolved that as many of the nobility, barons, and gentry of the realm as were hostile to the Union should assemble in Edinburgh, and join in a peaceful, but firm and personal remonstrance to the Lord Commissioner, praying that the obnoxious measure might be postponed until the subscribers should receive an answer to a national address which they designed to present to the Queen at this interesting crisis. It was supposed that the intended application to the Commissioner would be so strongly supported, that either the Scottish Government would not venture to favour a Union in the face of such general opposition, or that the English ministers themselves might take the alarm, and become doubtful of the efficacy or durability of a treaty to which the bulk of Scotland seemed so totally averse. About four hundred nobles and gentlemen of the first distinction assembled in Edinburgh for the purpose of attending the Commissioner with the proposed remonstrance; and an address was drawn up praying her Majesty to withdraw her countenance from the treaty, and to call a new Parliament.

When the day was appointed for executing the intended plan, it was interrupted by the Duke of Hamilton, who would on no terms agree to proceed with it unless a clause was inserted in the address expressive of the willingness of the subscribers to settle the succession on the House of Hanover. This proposal was totally at variance with the sentiments of the Jacobite part of those who supported the address, and occasioned great and animated discussions among them, and considerable delay. In the meanwhile the Commissioner, observing the city unusually crowded with persons of condition, and obtaining information of the purpose for which so many gentlemen had repaired to the capital, made an application to Parliament, setting forth that a convocation had been held in Edinburgh of various persons, under pretence of requiring personal answers to their addresses to Parliament, which was likely to endanger the public peace; and obtained a proclamation against any meetings under such pretexts during the sitting of Parliament, which he represented as both inexpedient and contrary to law.

While the Lord Commissioner was thus strengthening his party, the Anti-Unionists were at discord among themselves. The Dukes of Hamilton and Athole quarrelled on account of the interruption given by the former to the original plan of remonstrance; and the country gentlemen who had attended on their summons returned home mortified, disappointed, and, as many of them thought, deceived by their leaders.

Time was meanwhile flying fast, and Parliament, in discussing the separate articles of the Union, had reached the twenty-second, being that designed to fix the amount of the representation which Scotland was to possess in the British Parliament, and, on account of the inadequacy of such representation, the most obnoxious of the whole.

The Duke of Hamilton, who still was, or affected to be, firmly opposed to the treaty, now assembled the leaders of the opposition and entreated them to forget all former errors and mismanagement, and to concur in one common effort for the independence of Scotland. He then proposed that the Marquis of Annandale should open their proceedings, by renewing a motion formerly made for the succession of the crown in the House of Hanover, which was sure to be rejected if coupled with any measure interrupting the treaty of Union. Upon this the Duke proposed that all the opposers of the Union, after joining in a very strong protest, should publicly secede from the Parliament; in which case it was likely, either that the Government party would hesitate to proceed further in a matter which was to effect such total changes in the constitution of Scotland, or that the English might become of opinion that they could not safely carry on a national treaty of such consequence with a mere faction, or party of the Parliament, when deserted by so many persons of weight and influence.

The Jacobites objected to this course of proceeding on account of the preliminary motion, which implied a disposition to call the House of Hanover to the succession, provided the Union were departed from by the Government. The Duke of Hamilton replied that as the proposal was certain to be rejected, it would draw with it no obligation on those by whom it was made. He said, that such an offer would destroy the argument for forcing on the Union, which had so much weight in England, where it was believed that if the treaty did not take place, the kingdoms of England and Scotland would pass to different monarchs. He then declared frankly, that if the English should not discontinue pressing forward the Union after the formal protestation and secession which he proposed, he would join with the Jacobites for calling in the son of James II., and was willing to venture as far as any one for that measure.

It is difficult to suppose that the Duke of Hamilton was not serious in this proposal; and there seems to be little doubt that if the whole body opposing the Union had withdrawn in the manner proposed, the Commissioner would have given up the treaty and prorogued the Parliament. But the Duke lost courage, on its being intimated to him, as the story goes, by the Lord High Commissioner, in a private interview, that his Grace would be held personally responsible if the treaty of Union was interrupted by adoption of the advice which he had given, and that he should be made to suffer for it in his English property. Such at least is the general report; and such an interview could be managed without difficulty, as both these distinguished persons were lodged in the palace of Holyrood.

Whether acting from natural instability, whether intimidated by the threats of Queensberry, or dreading to encounter the difficulties when at hand, which he had despised when at a distance, it is certain that Hamilton was the first to abandon the course which he had himself recommended. On the morning appointed for the execution of their plan, when the members of opposition had mustered all their forces, and were about to go to Parliament, attended by great numbers of gentlemen and citizens prepared to assist them if there should be an attempt to arrest any of their number, they learned that the Duke of Hamilton was so much afflicted with the toothache that he could not attend the House that morning. His friends hastened to his chambers, and remonstrated with him so bitterly on this conduct that he at length came down to the House; but it was only to astonish them by asking whom they had pitched upon to present their protestation. They answered, with extreme surprise, that they had reckoned on his Grace, as the person of the first rank in Scotland, taking the lead in the measure which he had himself proposed. The Duke persisted, however, in refusing to expose himself to the displeasure of the court by being foremost in defeating their favourite measure, but offered to second any one whom the party might appoint to offer the protest. During this altercation the business of the day was so far advanced that the vote was put and carried on the disputed article respecting the representation, and the opportunity of carrying the scheme into effect was totally lost.

The members who had hitherto opposed the Union being thus three times disappointed in their measures by the unexpected conduct of the Duke of Hamilton, now felt themselves deserted and betrayed. Shortly afterwards, most of them retired altogether from their attendance on Parliament; and those who favoured the treaty were suffered to proceed in their own way, little encumbered either by remonstrance or opposition.

Almost the only remarkable change in the articles of the Union, besides that relating to church government, was made to quiet the minds of the common people, disturbed, as I have already mentioned, by rumours that the Scottish regalia were to be sent into England. A special article was inserted into the treaty declaring that they should on no occasion be removed from Scotland. At the same time, lest the sight of these symbols of national sovereignty should irritate the jealous feelings of the Scottish people, they were removed from the public view and secured in a strong chamber, called the Crown-room, in the castle of Edinburgh, where they remained so long in obscurity that their very existence was generally doubted. But his Majesty King George IV. having directed that a commission should be issued to search after these venerable relics, they were found (4th Feb. 1818) in safety in the place where they had been deposited, and are now made visible to the public under proper precautions.

It had been expected that the treaty of Union would have met with delays or alterations in the English Parliament. But it was approved of there, after very little debate, by a large majority; and the exemplification or copy was sent down to be registered by the Scottish Parliament. This was done on the 25th March; and on the 22d April the Parliament of Scotland adjourned for ever. Seafield, the Chancellor, on an occasion which every Scotsman ought to have considered as a melancholy one, behaved himself with a brutal levity, which in more patriotic times would have cost him his life on the spot, and said that "there was an end of an auld sang."

On the 1st of May 1707 the Union took place, amid the dejection and despair which attend on the downfall of an ancient state, and under a sullen expression of discontent that was far from promising the course of prosperity which the treaty finally produced.

And here I must point out to you at some length that, though there never could be a doubt that the Union in itself was a most desirable event, yet by the erroneous mode in which it was pushed on and opposed by all parties concerned, such obstacles were thrown in the way of the benefits it was calculated to produce as to interpose a longer interval of years betwixt the date of the treaty and the national advantages arising out of it, than the term spent by the Jews in the wilderness ere they attained the promised land. In both cases the frowardness and passions of men rejected the blessings which Providence held out to them.

To understand this, you must know that while the various plans for interrupting the treaty were agitated without doors, the debates in Parliament were of the most violent kind. "It resembled," said an eyewitness, "not the strife of tongues, but the clash of arms; and the hatred, rage, and reproach which we exhausted on each other seemed to be those of civil war rather than of political discussion." Much talent was displayed on both sides. The promoters of the Union founded their arguments not merely on the advantage, but the absolute necessity, of associating the independence of the two nations for their mutual honour and defence; arguing that otherwise they must renew the scenes of past ages, rendered dreadful by the recollection of three hundred and fourteen battles fought between two kindred nations, and more than a million of men slain on both sides. The imaginary sacrifice of independent sovereignty was represented as being in reality an escape from the petty tyranny of their own provincial aristocracy, and a most desirable opportunity of having the ill-defined and worse administered government of Scotland blended with that of a nation the most jealous of her rights and liberties which the world ever saw.

While the Unionists pointed out the general utility of the amalgamation of the two nations into one, the opposition dwelt on the immediate disgrace and degradation which the measure must instantly and certainly impose on Scotland, and the distant and doubtful nature of the advantages which she was to derive from it.

Lord Belhaven, in a celebrated speech, which made the strongest impression on the audience, declared that he saw, in prophetic vision, the peers of Scotland, whose ancestors had raised tribute in England, now walking in the Court of Requests like so many English attorneys, laying aside their swords lest self-defence should be called murder; he saw the Scottish barons with their lips padlocked, to avoid the penalties of unknown laws; he saw the Scottish lawyers struck mute and confounded at being subjected to the intricacies and technical jargon of an unknown jurisprudence; he saw the merchants excluded from trade by the English monopolies; the artisans ruined for want of custom; the gentry reduced to indigence; the lower ranks to starvation and beggary. "But, above all, my lord," continued the orator, "I think I see our ancient mother Caledonia, like Caesar, sitting in the midst of our senate, ruefully looking round her, covering herself with her Royal mantle, awaiting the fatal blow, and breathing out her last with the exclamation, 'And thou too, my son!'"

These prophetic sounds made the deepest impression on the House, until the effect was in some degree dispelled by Lord Marchmount, who, rising to reply, said he too had been much struck by the noble lord's vision, but that he conceived the exposition of it might be given in a few words. "I awoke, and behold it was a dream." But though Lord Belhaven's prophetic harangue might be termed in one sense a vision, it was one which continued to exist for many years; nor was it until half a century had passed away that the Union began to produce those advantages to Scotland which its promoters had fondly hoped, and the fruits of which the present generation has so fully reaped. We must seek in the temper of the various parties interested in carrying on and concluding this great treaty, the reasons which for so many years prevented the incalculable benefits which it was expected to bestow, and which have been since realised.

The first, and perhaps most fatal error, arose out of the conduct and feelings of the English, who were generally incensed at the conduct of the Scots respecting the Act of Security, and in the precipitate execution of Green and his companions, whom their countrymen, with some reason, regarded as men murdered on a vague accusation, merely because they were Englishmen. This, indeed, was partly true; but though the Scots acted cruelly, it should have been considered that they had received much provocation, and were in fact only revenging, though rashly and unjustly, the injuries of Darien and Glencoe. But the times were unfavourable to a temperate view of the subject in either country. The cry was general throughout England that Scotland should be conquered by force of arms, and secured by garrisons and forts, as in the days of Cromwell. Or, if she was to be admitted to a Union, there was a general desire on the part of the English to compel her to receive terms as indifferent as could be forced upon an inferior and humbled people.

These were not the sentiments of a profound statesman, and could not be those of Godolphin. He must have known that the mere fact of accomplishing a treaty could no more produce the cordial and intimate state of unity which was the point he aimed at, than the putting a pair of quarrelsome hounds into the same couples could reconcile the animals to each other. It may therefore be supposed that, left to himself, so great a politician would have tried, by the most gentle means, to reconcile Scotland to the projected measure; that he would have been studious to efface everything that appeared humiliating in the surrender of national independence; would have laboured to smooth those difficulties which prevented the Scots from engaging in the English trade; and have allowed her a more adequate representation in the national Parliament, which, if arranged according to her proportion of public expenses, would only have made the inconsiderable addition of fifteen members to the House of Commons. In fine, the English minister would probably have endeavoured to arrange the treaty on such terms of advantage for the poorer country as should, upon its being adopted, immediately prove to the Scots, by its effects, that it was a measure they ought for their own sakes to have desired and concurred in. In this manner the work of many years would have been, to a certain degree, anticipated, and the two nations would have felt themselves united in interest and in affection also, soon after they had become nominally one people. Whatever England might have sacrificed in this way would have been gained by Great Britain of which England must necessarily be the predominant part, and as such must always receive the greatest share of benefit by whatever promotes the good of the whole.

But though Godolphin's wisdom might have carried him to such conclusions, the passions and prejudices of the English nation would not have permitted him to act upon them. They saw, or thought they saw, a mode of bringing under subjection a nation which had been an old enemy and a troublesome friend; and they, very impolitically, were more desirous to subdue Scotland than to reconcile her. In this point the English statesmen committed a gross error, though rendered perhaps inevitable by the temper and prejudices of the nation.

The Scottish supporters of the Union might, on their part, have made a stand for better terms on behalf of their country. And it can scarcely be supposed that the English would have broken off a treaty of such importance either for the addition of a few members or for such advantages of commerce as Scotland might reasonably have demanded. But these Scottish commissioners, or a large part of them, had unhappily negotiated so well for themselves, that they had lost all right of interfering on the part of their country. We have already explained the nature of the equivalent, by which a sum of four hundred thousand pounds, or thereabouts, advanced at this time by England, but to be repaid out of the Scottish revenue within fifteen years, was to be distributed in the country, partly to repay the losses sustained by the Darien Company, partly to pay arrears of public salaries in Scotland, most of which were due to members of the Scottish Parliament: and finally, to satisfy such claims of damage arising out of the Union as might be brought forward by any one whose support was worth having.

The distribution of this money constituted the charm by which refractory Scottish members were reconciled to the Union. I have already mentioned the sum of thirty thousand pounds, which was peculiarly apportioned to the commissioners who originally laid the basis of the treaty. I may add there was another sum of twenty thousand pounds, employed to secure to the measures of the court the party called the Squadróne Volánte. The account of the mode in which this last sum was distributed has been published; and it may be doubted whether the descendants of the noble lords and honourable gentlemen who accepted this gratification would be more shocked at the general fact of their ancestors being corrupted, or scandalised at the paltry amount of the bribe. One noble lord accepted of so low a sum as eleven guineas; and the bargain was the more hard, as he threw his religion into the bargain, and from Catholic turned Protestant to make his vote a good one.

Other disgraceful gratuities might be mentioned, and there were many more which cannot be traced. The treasure for making good the equivalent was sent down in waggons from England, to be deposited in the castle of Edinburgh; and never surely was so valuable an importation received with such marks of popular indignation. The dragoons who guarded the wains were loaded with execrations, and the carters, nay, even their poor horses, were nearly pelted to death for being accessary in bringing to Edinburgh the price of the independence of the kingdom.

The public indignation was the more just, that this large sum of money in fact belonged to the Scottish nation, being the compensation to be paid to them for undertaking to pledge their revenue for a part of the English national debt. So that, in fact, the Parliament of Scotland was bribed with the public money belonging to their own country. In this way, Scotland herself was made to pay the price given to her legislators for the sacrifice of her independence.

The statesmen who accepted of these gratuities, under whatever name disguised, were marked by the hatred of the country and did not escape reproach even in the bosom of their own families. The advantage of their public services was lost by the general contempt which they had personally incurred. And here I may mention that while carrying on the intrigues which preceded the passing of the Union, those who favoured that measure were obliged to hold their meetings in secret and remote places of rendezvous, lest they should have been assaulted by the rabble. There was a subterranean apartment in the High Street (No. 177), called the Union Cellar,[1] from its being one of their haunts; and the pavilion in the gardens belonging to the Earl of Moray's House, in the Canongate, was distinguished by tradition as having been used for this purpose.

Men, of whom a majority had thus been bought and sold, forfeited every right to interfere in the terms which England insisted upon; and

---

[1] This was on the north side of the High Street, opposite Hunter Square, now occupied as business premises.

Scotland, therefore, lost that support which, had these statesmen been as upright and respectable as some of them were able and intelligent, could not have failed to be efficacious. But, despised by the English, and detested by their own country; fettered, as Lord Belhaven expressed it, by the golden chain of equivalents, the Unionists had lost all freedom of remonstrance, and had no alternative left save that of fulfilling the unworthy bargain they had made.

The Opposition party also had their share of error on this occasion. If they had employed a part of that zeal with which they vindicated the shadowy rights of Scotland's independence (which, after all, resolved itself into the title of being governed like a province, by a viceroy, and by English influence, not the less predominant that it was indirect), in order to obtain some improvement in the more unfavourable clauses of the treaty; if, in other words, they had tried to make a more advantageous agreement when the Union was under discussion, instead of attempting to break it off entirely, they might perhaps have gained considerable advantages for Scotland. But the greater part of the anti-Unionists were also Jacobites; and therefore, far from desiring to render the treaty more unexceptionable, it was their object that it should be as odious to the people of Scotland as possible, in order that the universal discontent excited by it might turn to the advantage of the exiled family.

Owing to all these adverse circumstances, the interests of Scotland were considerably neglected in the treaty of Union; and in consequence the nation, instead of regarding it as an identification of the interests of both kingdoms, considered it as a total surrender of their independence, by their false and corrupted statesmen, into the hand of their proud and powerful rival. The gentry of Scotland looked on themselves as robbed of their natural consequence, and disgraced in the eyes of the country; the merchants and tradesmen lost the direct commerce between Scotland and foreign countries, without being, for a length of time, able to procure a share in a more profitable trade with the English colonies, although ostensibly laid open to them. The populace in the towns, and the peasants throughout the kingdom, conceived the most implacable dislike to the treaty; factions, hitherto most bitterly opposed to each other, seemed ready to rise on the first opportunity which might occur for breaking it; and the cause of the Stewart family gained a host of new adherents, more from dislike to the Union than any partiality to the exiled prince.

A long train of dangers and difficulties was the consequence, which tore Scotland to pieces with civil discord, and exposed England also to much suffering. Three rebellions, two of which assumed a very alarming character, may, in a great measure, be set down to the unpopularity of this great national act; and the words, "Prosperity to Scotland, and no Union," is the favourite inscription to be found on Scottish sword blades betwixt 1707 and 1746.

But although the passions and prejudices of mankind could for a time delay and interrupt the advantages to be derived from this most important national measure, it was not the gracious will of Providence that, being thus deferred, they should be ultimately lost.

The unfortunate insurrection of 1745–46 entirely destroyed the hopes of the Scottish Jacobites, and occasioned the abolition of the hereditary jurisdictions and military tenures, which had been at once dangerous to the Government and a great source of oppression to the subject. This, though attended with much individual suffering, was the final means of at once removing the badges of feudal tyranny, extinguishing civil war, and assimilating Scotland to the sister-country. After this period, the advantages of the Union were gradually perceived and fully experienced.

It was not, however, till the accession of King George III.,[1] that the beneficial effects of this great national treaty were generally felt and recogonised. From that period there was awakened a spirit of industry formerly unknown in Scotland; and ever since, the two kingdoms of England and Scotland, incalculably to their mutual benefit, have been gradually forgetting former subjects of discord and uniting cordially, as one people, in the improvement and defence of the island which they inhabit.

This happy change from discord to friendship,—from war to peace, and from poverty and distress to national prosperity,—was not attained without much peril and hazard; and should I continue these volumes, from the period of the Union to that of the Accession of George the Third, I can promise you the addition will be neither the least interesting nor the least useful of your Grandfather's labours in your behalf.

---

[1] Acceded to the throne 1760.

LXI

Intrigues of the Jacobites

1701-1706

W E are now, my dear child, approaching a period more resembling our own than those through which I have hitherto conducted you. In England, and in the Lowlands of Scotland, men used the same language, possessed in a considerable degree the same habits of society, and lived under the same forms of government, which have existed in Britain down to the present day. The Highlanders, indeed, retained their ancient manners; and although, from the establishment of forts and garrisons in their country, the laws had much more power over them than formerly, so that they could no longer break out into the same excesses, they still remained, in their dress, customs, manners, and language, much more like the original Scots in the reign of Malcolm Canmore than the Lowlanders of the same period resembled their ancestors of the seventeenth century.

But though the English and Lowland Scots exhibited little distinction in their manners and habits, excepting that those of the latter people indicated less wealth or refinement of luxury, there was no sympathy of feeling between them, and the recent measure of the Union had only an effect resembling that of putting two quarrelsome dogs into the same couples, or two sullen horses into the same yoke. Habit may in course of time teach them to accommodate themselves to each other; but the first consequence of the compulsory tie which unites them is the feeling of aggravated hostility.

The predominant prejudices of the English represented the Scots, in the language of the celebrated Dean Swift, as a poor, ferocious, and haughty people, detesting their English neighbours and looking upon them as a species of Egyptians, whom it was not only lawful but commendable to plunder, whether by open robbery or secret address. The poverty of the North Britons, and the humble and patient labour by which individuals were frequently observed to emerge from it, made them the objects of contempt to the English; while, on the other hand, the irascible and turbulent spirit of the nation, and a habitual use of arms, exposed them to aversion and hatred. This peculiar characteristic was, at the time of the Union, very general in Scotland. The Highlanders, you must remember, always carried weapons, and if thought of at all by their southern neighbours, they must have been considered as absolute and irreclaimable savages. The Lowlanders were also used to arms at this period, for almost the whole Scottish nation had been trained under the Act of Security; the population was distributed into regiments, and kept ready for action; and in the gloomy and irritated state of mind in which the Scots had been placed by the management of the Union treaty, they spoke of nothing more loudly and willingly than of war with England. The English had their especial reasons for disliking the Union. They did not, in general, feel flattered by the intimate confederacy and identification of their own rich country and civilised inhabitants with the boreal region of the north, and its rude and savage tribes. They were afraid that the craft and patient endurance of labour of the Scots would give them more than their share of the colonial trade which they had hitherto monopolised to themselves.

Yet, though such was the opinion held by the English in general, the more enlightened part of the nation, remembering the bloody wars which had so long desolated Britain in its divided state, dated from the Union an era of peace and happiness to both countries; and looking far into futurity, foresaw a time when the national prejudices, which for the present ran so high, would die out or be eradicated like the weeds which deface the labours of the agriculturist, and give place to plenty and to peace. It was owing to the prevalence of such feelings that the Duke of Queensberry, the principal negotiator of the treaty of Union, when he left Scotland for London after the measure was perfected, was received with the greatest distinction in the English towns through which he passed. And when he approached the neighbourhood of London, many of the members of the two Houses came to meet and congratulate a statesman who, but for the guards that surrounded him, would, during the progress of the treaty, have been destroyed by his countrymen in the streets of Edinburgh!

In England, therefore, the Union had its friends and partisans. In Scotland it was regarded with an almost universal feeling of discontent and dishonour. The Jacobite party, who had entertained great hopes of eluding the act for settling the kingdom upon the family of Hanover, beheld them entirely blighted; the Whigs, or Presbyterians, found themselves forming part of a nation in which Prelacy was an institution of the state; the Country Party, who had nourished a vain but honourable idea of maintaining the independence of Scotland, now saw it, with all its symbols of ancient sovereignty, sunk and merged under the government of England. All the different professions and classes of men saw each something in the obnoxious treaty which affected their own interest.

The nobles of an ancient and proud land, which they were wont to manage at their pleasure, were now stripped of their legislative privilege, unless in as far as exercised, like the rights of a petty corporation, by a handful of delegates; the smaller barons and gentry shared their humiliation, their little band of representatives being too few, and their voices too feeble, to produce any weight in the British House of Commons, to which a small portion was admitted.

The clergy's apprehension for their own system of church discipline was sensitively awakened, and their frequent warnings from the pulpit kept the terror of innovation before their congregations.

The Scottish lawyers had equal reason for alarm. They witnessed what they considered as the degradation of their profession, and of the laws, to the exposition of which they had been bred up. They saw their supreme civil court, which had spurned at the idea of having their decrees reviewed even in the Parliament, now subjected to appeal to the British House of Peers; a body who could be expected to know little of law at all, and in which the Chancellor, who presided, was trained in the jurisprudence of another country. Besides, when the sceptre departed from Scotland, and the lawgiver no longer sat at her feet it was likely that her municipal regulations should be gradually assimilated to those of England, and that her lawyers should by degrees be laid aside and rendered useless by the introduction of the institutions of a foreign country which were strange to their studies.

The merchants and trading portion of Scotland also found grievances in the Union peculiar to themselves. The privileges which admitted the Scots into the colonial trade of England only represented the apples of Tantalus, so long as local prejudices, want of stock, and all the difficulties incident to forcing capital into a new channel, or line of business, obstructed their benefiting by them. On the other hand, they lost all the advantage of their foreign trade whenever their traffic became obstructed by the imposition of English duties. They lost, at the same time, a beneficial though illicit trade with England itself, which took place in consequence of foreign commodities being so much cheaper in Scotland. Lastly, the establishment of two Boards of Customs and Excise, with the introduction of a shoal of officers, all Englishmen, and, it was said, frequently men of indifferent and loose character, was severely felt by the commercial part of a nation whose poverty had hitherto kept them tolerably free from taxation.

The tradesmen and citizens were injured in the tenderest point, by the general emigration of families of rank and condition, who naturally went to reside in London, not only to attend their duties in Parliament, but to watch for those opportunities of receiving favours which are only to be obtained by being constantly near the source of preferment; not to mention numerous families of consequence who went to the metropolis merely for fashion's sake. This general emigration naturally drained Scotland of the income of the non-residents, who expended their fortunes among strangers, to the prejudice of those of their country folk who had formerly lived by supplying them with necessaries or luxuries.

The agricultural interest was equally affected by the scarcity of money, which the new laws, the money drawn by emigrants from their Scottish estates, to meet the unwonted expenses of London, the decay of external commerce and of internal trade, all contributed to produce.

Besides these peculiar grievances which affected certain classes or professions, the Scots felt generally the degradation, as they conceived it, of their country being rendered the subservient ally of the state, of which, though infinitely more powerful, they had resisted the efforts for the space of two thousand years. The poorest and meanest, as well as the richest and most noble, felt that he shared the national honour; and the former was even more deeply interested in preserving it untarnished than the latter, because he had no dignity or consideration due to him personally or individually beyond that which belonged to him as a native of Scotland.

There was, therefore, nothing save discontent and lamentation to be heard throughout Scotland, and men of every class vented their complaints against the Union the more loudly because their sense of personal grievances might be concealed and yet indulged under popular declamations concerning the dishonour done to the country.

To all these subjects of complaint there lay obvious answers grounded on the future benefits which the Union was calculated to produce, and the prospect of the advantages which have since arisen from it. But at the time immediately succeeding that treaty, these benefits were only the subject of distant and doubtful speculation, while the immediate evils which we have detailed were present, tangible, and certain. There was a want of advocates for the Union, as well as of arguments having immediate and direct cogency. A considerable number of the regular clergy, indeed, who did not share the feverish apprehensions of prelatic innovation, which was a bugbear to the majority of their order, concluded it was the sounder policy to adhere to the Union with England, under the sovereignty of a Protestant prince, than to bring back, under King James VII., the evils in church and state which had occasioned the downfall of his father. But by such arguments, the ministers who used them only lowered themselves in the eyes of the people, who petulantly replied to their pastors that none had been more loud than they against the Union until they had got their own manses,[1] glebes, and stipends[2] assured to them; although, that being done, they were now contented to yield up the civil rights of the Scottish monarchy, and endanger the stability of the Scottish Church. Their hearers abandoned the kirks, and refused to attend the religious ordinances of such clergymen as favoured the Union, and went in crowds to wait upon the doctrines of those who preached against the treaty with the same zeal with which they had formerly magnified the Covenant. Almost all the dissenting and Cameronian ministers were anti-Unionists, and some of the more enthusiastic were so peculiarly vehement that, long after the controversy had fallen asleep, I have heard my grandfather say (for your grandfather, Mr. Hugh Littlejohn, had a grandfather in his time), that he had heard an old clergyman confess he could

---

[1] *Anglice*—Parsonages.

[2] *Anglice*—Tithes.

never bring his sermon, upon whatever subject, to a conclusion, without having what he called a *blaud*, that is a slap, at the Union.

If the mouths of the clergymen who advocated the treaty were stopped by reproaches of personal interest, with far more justice were those reproaches applied to the greater part of the civil statesmen, by whom the measure had been carried through and completed. The people of Scotland would not hear these gentlemen so much as speak upon the great incorporating alliance, for the accomplishment of which they had laboured so effectually. Be the event of the Union what it would, the objection was personal to many of those statesmen by whom it was carried through, that they had pressed the destruction of Scottish independence, which it necessarily involved, for private and selfish reasons, resolving into the gratification of their own ambition or avarice. They were twitted with the meanness of their conduct even in the Parliament of Britain. A tax upon linen cloth, the staple commodity of Scotland, having been proposed in the House of Commons, was resisted by Mr. Baillie of Jerviswood, and other Scottish members, favourers of the Union, until Mr. Harley, who had been Secretary of State during the treaty, stood up and cut short the debate, by saying, "Have we not bought the Scots, and did we not acquire a right to tax them? or for what other purpose did we give the equivalent?" Lockhart of Carnwath arose in reply, and said he was glad to hear it plainly acknowledged that the Union had been a matter of bargain, and that Scotland had been bought and sold on that memorable occasion; but he was surprised to hear so great a manager in the traffic name the equivalents as the price, since the revenue of Scotland itself being burdened in relief of that sum, no price had been in fact paid, but what must ultimately be discharged by Scotland from her own funds.

The detestation of the treaty being for the present the ruling passion of the times, all other distinctions of party, and even of religious opinions in Scotland, were laid aside, and a singular coalition took place in which Episcopalians, Presbyterians, Cavaliers, and many friends of the Revolution drowned all former hostility in the predominant aversion to the Union. Even the Cameronians, who now formed a powerful body in the state, retained the same zeal against the Union, when established, which had induced them to rise in arms against it while it was in progress.

It was evident that the treaty of Union could not be abolished without a counter-revolution; and for a time almost all the inhabitants of

Scotland were disposed to join unanimously in the Restoration, as it was called, of James the Second's son to the throne of his fathers; and had his ally, the King of France, been hearty in his cause, or his Scottish partisans more united among themselves, or any leader amongst them possessed of distinguished talent, the Stewart family might have repossessed themselves of their ancient domain of Scotland and perhaps of England also. To understand the circumstances by which that hope was disappointed, it is necessary to look back on the history of James II., and to take some notice of the character and situation of his son.

The Chevalier de St. George, as he was called by a conventional name, which neither gave nor denied his Royal pretensions, was that unfortunate child of James II., whose birth, which ought in ordinary cases to have been the support of his father's throne, became by perverse chance the strongest incentive for pressing forward the Revolution. He lost his hopes of a kingdom, therefore, and was exiled from his native country, ere he knew what the words country or kingdom signified, and lived at the court of St. Germains, where Louis XIV. permitted his father to maintain a hollow pageant of Royalty. Thus the son of James II. was brought up in what is generally admitted to be the very worst way in which a prince can be educated; that is, he was surrounded by all the pomp and external ceremony of imaginary Royalty, without learning by experience any part of its real duties or actual business. Idle and discontented men, who formed the mimicry of a council, and played the part of ministers, were as deeply engaged in political intrigues for ideal offices and dignities at the court of St. Germains, as if actual rank or emolument had attended them—as reduced gamblers have been known to spend days and nights in play, although too poor to stake anything on the issue of the game.

It is no doubt true that the versatility of the statesmen of England, including some great names, offers a certain degree of apology for the cabinet of the dethroned prince, to an extent even to justify the hopes that a counter-revolution would soon take place, and realise the expectations of the St. Germains courtiers. It is a misfortune necessarily attending the success of any of those momentous changes of government, which, innovating upon the constitution of a country, are termed revolutions, that the new establishment of things cannot for some time attain that degree of respect and veneration which antiquity can alone impress. Evils are felt under the new government, as they must under every human institution, and men readily reconcile their minds to correct them, either by adopting further alterations or by returning to that order of things which they have so lately seen in existence. That which is new itself may, it is supposed, be subjected to further innovations without inconvenience; and if these are deemed essential and necessary, or even advantageous, there seems to ardent and turbulent spirits little reason to doubt that the force which has succeeded so lately in destroying the institutions which had the venerable sanction of antiquity, may be equally successful in altering or remodelling that which has been the work of the present generation, perhaps of the very statesmen who are now desirous of innovating upon it. With this disposition to change still further what has been recently the subject of alteration mingle other passions. There must always be many of those that have been active in a recent revolution, who have not derived the personal advantages which they were entitled, or, which is the same thing, thought themselves entitled, to expect. Such disappointed men are apt, in their resentment, to think that it depends only upon themselves to pull down what they have assisted to build, and to rebuild the structure in the destruction of which they have been so lately assistants. This was in the utmost extent evinced after the English Revolution. Not only subordinate agents who had been active in the Revolution, but some men of the highest and most distinguished talents were induced to enter into plots for the restoration of the Stewarts. Marlborough, Carmarthen, and Lord Russell, were implicated in a correspondence with France in 1692; and indeed, throughout the reigns of William III. and Queen Anne, many men of consequence, not willing explicitly to lend themselves to counter-revolutionary plots, were yet not reluctant to receive projects, letters, and promises from the ex-king, and return in exchange vague expressions of good-will for the cause of their old monarch, and respect for his person.

It is no wonder, therefore, that the Jacobite ministers at St. Germains were by such negotiations rendered confident that a counter-revolution was approaching, or that they intrigued for their share in the honours and power which they conceived would be very soon at their master's disposal. In this they might, indeed, have resembled the hunters in the fable, who sold the bear's hide before they had killed him; but, on the other hand, they were less like simpletons who spend their time in gambling for nothing, than eager gamesters who play for a stake, which, though they do not yet possess, they soon expect to have at their disposal.

Amid such petty and empty feuds, it was not likely that the son of James II. should greatly augment the strength of mind of which nature had given him but a small share, especially as his father had laid aside those habits of business with which he was once familiar, and resigning all hopes of his restoration, had abandoned himself entirely to the severities of ascetic devotion. From his advice and example, therefore, the Chevalier de St. George could derive no advantage; and Heaven had not granted him the talents which supply the place of instruction.

The heir of this ancient line was not, however, deficient in the external qualities which associate well with such distinguished claims. He was of tall stature, and possessed a nobly formed countenance, and courteous manners. He had made one or two campaigns with applause, and showed no deficiency of courage if he did not display much energy. He appears to have been good-humoured, kind, and tractable. In short, born on a throne, and with judicious ministers, he might have been a popular prince; but he had not the qualities necessary either to win or to regain a kingdom.

Immediately before the death of his unfortunate father, the Chevalier de St. George was consigned to the protection of Louis XIV., in an affecting manner. The French monarch came for the last time to bid adieu to his unfortunate ally when stretched on his deathbed. Affected by the pathos of the scene, and possessing in reality a portion of that Royal magnanimity by which he was so ambitious of being distinguished, Louis declared publicly his purpose to recognise the title of his friend's son, as heir to the throne of Britain, and take his family under his protection. The dying prince half raised himself from his bed and endeavoured to speak his gratitude; but his failing accents were drowned in a murmur of mingled grief and joy, which broke from his faithful followers. They were melted into tears, in which Louis himself joined. And thus was given, in a moment of enthusiasm, a promise of support which the French King had afterwards reason to repent of, as he could not gracefully shake off an engagement contracted under such circumstances of affecting solemnity, although in after periods of his reign he was little able to supply the Chevalier de St. George with such succours as his promise had entitled that prince to expect.

Louis was particularly embarrassed by the numerous plans and schemes for the invasion of Scotland and England, proposed either by real Jacobites eager to distinguish themselves by their zeal, or by adventurers, who, like the noted Captain Simon Fraser, assumed that character so as to be enabled either to forward the Chevalier de St. George's interest or betray his purpose to the English Ministry, whichever might best advance the interest of the emissary. This Captain Fraser (afterwards the celebrated Lord Lovat) was looked upon with coldness by the Chevalier and Lord Middleton, his secretary, but he gained the confidence of Mary of Esté, the widow of James II. Being at length, through her influence, despatched to Scotland, Fraser trafficked openly with both parties; and although, whilst travelling through the Highlands, he held the character and language of a high-flying Jacobite, and privately betrayed whatever he could worm out of them to the Duke of Queensberry, then the Royal commissioner and representative of Queen Anne, he had nevertheless the audacity to return to France and use the language of an injured and innocent man till he was thrown into the Bastille for his double dealing. It is probable that this interlude of Captain Fraser, which happened in 1703, contributed to give Louis a distrust of Scottish Jacobite agents, and inclined him, notwithstanding the general reports of disaffection to Queen Anne's government, to try the temper of the country by an agent of his own, before resolving to give any considerable assistance towards an invasion which his wars in Flanders and the victories of Marlborough rendered him ill able to undertake.

LXII

The Rising of the Chevalier

1707-1708

THERE are two reflections which arise from what we have stated in the former chapter, too natural to escape observation.

In the first place, we are led to conclude that all leagues or treaties between nations, which are designed to be permanent, should be grounded not only on equitable, but on liberal principles. Whatever advantages are assumed from the superior strength, or more insidiously attained by the superior cunning, of one party or the other, operate as so many principles of decay by which the security of the league is greatly endangered, if not actually destroyed. There can be no doubt that the open corruption and precipitate violence with which the Union was forced on retarded for two generations the benefits which would otherwise have arisen from it; and that resentment, not so much against the measure itself as against the disadvantageous terms granted to Scotland, gave rise to two, or, taking into account the battle of Glenshiel, to three civil wars, with all the peculiar miseries which attended them. The personal adherence of many individuals to the Stewart family might have preserved Jacobite sentiments for a generation, but would scarce have had intensity sufficient to kindle a general flame in the country had not the sense of the unjust and illiberal manner in which the Union was concluded come in aid of the zeal of the Jacobites, to create a general or formidable attack on the existing Government. As the case actually stood, we shall presently see how narrowly the Union itself escaped destruction, and the nation a counter-revolution.

This conducts us to the second remark, which I wish you to attend to, namely, how that, with all the facilities of intercourse afforded by the manners of modern nations, it nevertheless is extremely difficult for one government to obtain what they may consider as trustworthy information concerning the internal affairs and actual condition of another, either from the statements of partisans who profess themselves in league with the state which makes the inquiry, or from agents of their own sent on purpose to pursue the investigation. The first class of informants deceive their correspondents and themselves by the warm and sanguine view which they take of the strength and importance of their own party; the last are incapable of forming a correct judgment of what they see and hear for want of that habitual and familiar knowledge of the manners of a country which is necessary to enable them to judge what peculiar allowances ought to be made, and what special restrictions may be necessary, in interpreting the language of those with whom they communicate on the subject of their mission.

This was exemplified in the inquiries instituted by Louis XIV. for ascertaining the exact disposition of the people of Scotland towards the Chevalier de St. George. The agent employed by the French monarch was Lieutenant-Colonel Hooke, an Englishman of good family. This gentleman followed King James II. to France, and was there received into the service of Louis XIV. to which he seems to have become so much attached as to have been comparatively indifferent to that of the son of his former master. His instructions from the French King were to engage the Scots who might be disposed for an insurrection as deeply as possible to France, but to avoid precise promises, by which he might compromise France in any corresponding obligation respecting assistance or supplies. In a word, the Jacobite or anti-Unionist party were to have leave from Louis to attempt a rebellion against Queen Anne, at their own proper risk, providing the Grand Monarque, as he was generally termed, should be no further bound to aid them in the enterprise, or protect them in case of its failure, than he should think consistent with his magnanimity, and convenient for his affairs. This was no doubt a bargain by which nothing could be lost by France, but it had been made with too great anxiety to avoid hazard to be attended with much chance of gaining by it.

With these instructions Colonel Hooke departed for Scotland in the end of February or beginning of March 1707, where he found, as had been described by the correspondence kept up with the Scots, different classes of people eager to join in an insurrection, with the purpose of breaking the Union, and restoring the Stewart family to the throne. We must first mention the state in which he found the Jacobite party, with whom principally he came to communicate.

This party, which, as it now included *the Country* faction, and all others who favoured the dissolution of the Union, was much more universally extended than at any other period in Scottish history, either before or afterwards, was divided into two parties, having for their heads the Dukes of Hamilton and Athole, noblemen who stood in opposition to each other in claiming the title of the leader of the Jacobite interests. If these two great men were to be estimated according to their fidelity to the cause which they had espoused, their pretensions were tolerably equal, for neither of them could lay much claim to the honour due to political consistency. The conduct of Athole during the Revolution had been totally adverse to the Royal interest; and that of the Duke of Hamilton, though affecting to act as head of the opposition to the Union, was such as to induce some suspicion that be was in league with the Government; since, whenever a decisive stand was to be made, Hamilton was sure to find some reason, better or worse, to avoid coming to extremities with the opposite party. Notwithstanding such repeated acts of defection on the part of these great dukes, their rank, talents, and the reliance on their general sincerity in the Jacobite cause, occasioned men of that party to attach themselves as partisans to one or other of them. It was natural that, generally speaking, men should choose for their leader the most influential person in whose neighbourhood they themselves resided or had their property; and thus the Highland Jacobites beyond the Tay rallied under the Duke of Athole; those of the south and west under the Duke of Hamilton. From this it also followed, that the two divisions of the same faction, being of different provinces, and in different circumstances, held separate opinions as to the course to be pursued in the intended restoration.

The northern Jacobites, who had more power of raising men, and less of levying money than those of the south, were for rushing at once into war without any delay, or stipulation of foreign assistance; and without further aid than their own good hearts and ready swords, expressed themselves determined to place on the throne him whom they termed the lawful heir.

When Hooke entered into correspondence with this class of the Jacobite party, he found it easy to induce them to dispense with any special or precise stipulations concerning the amount of the succours to be furnished by France, whether in the shape of arms, money, or auxiliaries, so soon as he represented to them that any specific negotiation of this kind would be indelicate and unhandsome to the King of France, and probably diminish his inclination to serve the Chevalier de St. George. On this point of pretended delicacy were these poor gentlemen induced to pledge themselves to risks likely to prove fatal to themselves, their rank, and their posterity, without any of the reasonable precautions which were absolutely necessary to save them from destruction.

But when the Duke of Hamilton (by his Secretary), Lord Kilsythe, Lockhart of Carnwath, Cochrane of Kilmarnock, and other leaders among the Jacobites of the west, had a conference with Colonel Hooke, their answers were of a different tenor. They thought that to render the plan of insurrection at all feasible, there should be a distinct engagement on the part of the King of France to send over the Chevalier de St. George to Scotland, with an auxiliary army of ten, or, at the very least, eight thousand men. Colonel Hooke used very haughty language in answer to this demand, which he termed a "presuming to give advice to Louis XIV. how to manage his own affairs;" as if it had not been the business of the Jacobites themselves to learn to what extent they were to expect support before staking their lands and lives in so dangerous an enterprise.

The extent of Colonel Hooke's success was obtaining a memorial, signed by ten lords and chiefs, acting in the name, as they state, of the bulk of the nation, but particularly of thirty persons of distinction, from whom they had special mandates, in which paper they agreed that upon the arrival of the Chevalier de St. George, they would make him master of Scotland, which was entirely in his interest, and immediately thereafter proceed to raise an army of twenty-five thousand foot and five thousand horse. With this force they proposed to march into England, seize upon Newcastle, and distress the City of London by interrupting the coal trade. They stated their hope that the King would send with the Chevalier an auxiliary army of at least five thousand men, some officers, and a general of high rank, such as the Scottish nobles would not scruple to obey. The Duke of Berwick, a natural son of the late King, and a general of first-rate talent, was particularly fixed upon. They also complained of a want of field-pieces, battering-cannon, and arms of every kind, and stated their desire of a supply. And lastly, they dwelt upon the need they had of a subsidy of six hundred thousand livres to enable them to begin the war. But they stated these in the shape of humble requests rather than demands or conditions, and submitted themselves in the same memorial to any modification or alteration of the terms which might render them more acceptable to King Louis. Thus Hooke made good the important point in his instructions, which enjoined him to take the Scottish Jacobites bound as far as possible to the King of France, while he should on no account enter into any negotiations which might bind his Majesty to any counter-stipulations. Louis showed considerable address in playing this game, as it is vulgarly called, of Fast and Loose, giving every reason to conclude that his ministers, if not the sovereign himself, looked less upon the invasion of Scotland as the means of effecting a counter-revolution, than in the light of a diversion, which would oblige the British to withdraw a large proportion of the troops which they employed in Flanders, and thus obtain a superiority for France on the general theatre of War. With this purpose, and to take the chance, doubtless, of fortunate events, and the generally discontented state of Scotland, the French court received and discussed at their leisure the prodigal offer of the Scottish Jacobites.

At length, after many delays, the French monarch actually determined upon making an effort. It was resolved to send to Scotland the heir of the ancient kings of that country, with a body of about five or six thousand men, being the force thought necessary by the faction of Athole—that of Hamilton having demanded eight thousand men at the very least. It was agreed that the Chevalier de St. George should embark at Dunkirk with this little army, and that the fleet should be placed under the command of the Comte de Forbin, who had distinguished himself by several naval exploits.

When the plan was communicated by Monsieur de Chamillard, then minister for naval affairs, the commodore stated numerous objections to throwing so large a force ashore on the naked beach without being assured of possessing a single harbour, or fortified place, which might serve them for a defence against the troops which the English

Government would presently despatch against them. "If," pursued Forbin, "you have five thousand troops to throw away on a desperate expedition, give me the command of them; I will embark them in shallops and light vessels, and I will surprise Amsterdam, and, by destroying the commerce of the Dutch capital, take away all means and desire on the part of the United Provinces to continue the war."—"Let us have no more of this," replied the Minister; "you are called upon to execute the King's commands, not to discuss them. His Majesty has promised to the King and Queen Dowager of England (the Chevalier de St. George and Mary d'Esté) that he is to give them the stipulated assistance, and you are honoured with the task of fulfilling his Royal word." To hear was to obey, and the Comte de Forbin set himself about the execution of the design entrusted to him; but with a secret reluctance, which boded ill for the expedition, since, in bold undertakings, success is chiefly insured by the zeal, confidence, and hearty co-operation of those to whom the execution is committed. Forbin was so far from being satisfied with the commission assigned him that he started a thousand difficulties and obstacles, all of which he was about to repeat to the monarch himself in a private interview, when Louis, observing the turn of his conversation, cut his restive admiral short by telling him that he was busy at that moment, and wished him a good voyage.

The commander of the land forces was the Comte de Gassé who afterwards bore the title of Maréchal de Matignon. Twelve battalions were embarked on board of eight ships of the line and twenty-four frigates, besides transports and shallops for disembarkation. The King of France displayed his magnificence by supplying the Chevalier de St. George with a Royal wardrobe, services of gold and silver plate, rich liveries for his attendants, splendid uniforms for his guards, and all external appurtenances befitting the rank of a sovereign prince. At parting, Louis bestowed on his guest a sword, having its hilt set with diamonds, and, with that felicity of compliment which was natural to him above all other princes, expressed, as the best wish he could bestow upon his departing friend, his hope that they might never meet again. It was ominous that Louis used the same turn of courtesy in bidding adieu to the Chevalier's father, previous to the battle of La Hogue.

The Chevalier departed for Dunkirk, and embarked the troops; and thus far all had been conducted with such perfect secrecy that England was totally unaware of the attempt which was meditated. But an accident at the same time retarded the enterprise and made it public. This was the illness of the Chevalier de St. George, who was seized with the measles. It could then no longer remain a secret that he was lying sick in Dunkirk, with the purpose of heading an expedition, for which the troops were already embarked.

It was scarcely possible to imagine a country more unprepared for such an attack than England, unless it were Scotland. The great majority of the English army were then in Flanders. There only remained within the kingdom five thousand men, and these chiefly new levies. The situation of Scotland was still more defenceless. Edinburgh Castle was alike unfurnished with garrison, artillery, ammunition, and stores. There were not in the country above two thousand regular soldiers, and these were Scottish regiments whose fidelity was very little to be reckoned upon if there should, as was probable, be a general insurrection of their countrymen. The panic in London was great, at court, in camp, and in city; there was also an unprecedented run on the Bank, which, unless that great national institution had been supported by an association of wealthy British and foreign merchants, must have given a severe shock to public credit. The consternation was the more overwhelming that the great men in England were jealous of each other, and, not believing that the Chevalier would have ventured over upon the encouragement of the Scottish nation only, suspected the existence of some general conspiracy, the explosion of which would take place in England.

Amid the widespreading alarm, active measures were taken to avert the danger. The few regiments which were in South Britain were directed to march for Scotland in all haste. Advices were sent to Flanders to recall some of the British troops there for the more pressing service at home. General Cadogan, with ten battalions, took shipping in Holland, and actually sailed for Tynemouth. But even amongst these there were troops which could not be trusted. The Earl of Orkney's Highland regiment, and that which was called the Scots Fusiliers, are said to have declared they would never use their swords against their country in an English quarrel. It must be added that the arrival of this succour was remote and precarious. But England had a readier and more certain resource in the superiority of her navy.

With the most active exertions a fleet of forty sail of the line was assembled and put to sea, and, ere the French squadron commanded by Forbin had sailed, they beheld this mighty fleet before Dunkirk on the 28th of February 1708. The Comte de Forbin, upon this formidable apparition, despatched letters to Paris for instructions, having no doubt of receiving orders, in consequence, to disembark the troops, and postpone the expedition. Such an answer arrived accordingly; but while Forbin was preparing, on the 14th March, to carry it into execution, the English fleet was driven off the blockade by stress of weather; which news having soon reached the court, positive orders came that at all risks the invading squadron should proceed to sea.

They sailed accordingly on 17th March from the roads of Dunkirk; and now not a little depended on the accidental circumstance of wind and tide, as these should be favourable to the French or English fleets. The elements were adverse to the French. They had no sooner left Dunkirk roads than the wind became contrary, and the squadron was driven into the roadstead called Newport-pits, from which place they could not stir for the space of two days, when, the wind again changing, they set sail for Scotland with a favourable breeze. The Comte de Forbin and his squadron arrived in the entrance of the Firth of Forth, sailed as high up as the point of Crail, on the coast of Fife, and dropped anchor there, with the purpose of running up the Firth as far as the vicinity of Edinburgh on the next day and there disembarking the Chevalier de St. George, Maréchal Matignon, and his troops. In the meantime they showed signals, fired guns, and endeavoured to call the attention of their friends, whom they expected to welcome them ashore.

None of these signals were returned from the land; but they were answered from the sea in a manner as unexpected as it was unpleasing. The report of five cannon, heard in the direction of the mouth of the Firth gave notice of the approach of Sir George Byng and the English fleet, which had sailed the instant their admiral learned that the Comte de Forbin had put to sea; and though the French had considerably the start of them, the British admiral contrived to enter the Firth immediately after the French squadron.

The dawn of morning showed the far superior force of the English fleet advancing up the Firth and threatening to intercept the French squadron in the narrow inlet of the sea into which they had ventured. The Chevalier de St. George and his attendants demanded to be put on board a smaller vessel than that commanded by Monsieur de Forbin, with the purpose of disembarking at the ancient castle of Wemyss, on the Fife coast, belonging to the Earl of the same name, a constant adherent of the Stewart family. This was at once the wisest and most manly course which he could have followed. But the son of James II. was doomed to learn how little freewill can be exercised by the prince who has placed himself under the protection of a powerful auxiliary. Monsieur de Forbin, after evading his request for some time, at length decidedly said to him—"Sire, by the orders of my Royal master, I am directed to take the same precautions for the safety of your august person as for his Majesty's own. This must be my chief care. You are at present in safety, and I will never consent to your being exposed in a ruinous chateau in an open country where a few hours might put you in the hands of your enemies. I am entrusted with your person; I am answerable for your safety with my head; I beseech you, therefore, to repose your confidence in me entirely, and to listen to no one else. All those who dare give you advice different from mine are either traitors or cowards." Having thus settled the Chevalier's doubts in a manner savouring something of the roughness of his profession, the Comte de Forbin bore down on the English admiral as if determined to fight his way through the fleet. But Sir George Byng having made signal for collecting his ships to meet the enemy, the Frenchman went off on another tack, and, taking advantage of the delay thus occasioned, steered for the mouth of the Firth. The English ships having been long at sea, were rather heavy sailers, while those of Forbin had been carefully selected and careened for this particular service. This pursuit of Byng was therefore in vain, excepting that the *Elizabeth,* a slow-sailing vessel of the French fleet, fell into his hands.

Admirable Byng, when the French escaped him, proceeded to Edinburgh to assist in the defence of the capital, in case of any movement of the Jacobites which might have endangered it. The Comte de Forbin with his expedition had, on the other hand, the power of choosing among all the ports on the northeast coast of Scotland, from Dundee to Inverness, the one which circumstances might render most eligible for the purpose of disembarking the Chevalier de St. George and the French troops. But whether from his own want of cordiality in the object of the expedition, or whether, as was generally suspected by the Scottish Jacobites at the time, he had secret orders from his court which regulated his conduct, Forbin positively refused to put the disinherited prince and the soldiers destined for his service on shore at any part of the north of Scotland, although the Chevalier repeatedly required him to do so. The expedition returned to Dunkirk, from which it had been four weeks absent; the troops were put ashore and distributed in garrison, and the commanders hastened to court, each to excuse himself and throw the blame of the failure upon the other.

On the miscarriage of this intended invasion, the malcontents of Scotland felt that an opportunity was lost which never might, and in fact never did, again present itself. The unanimity with which almost all the numerous sects and parties in Scotland were disposed to unite in any measure which could rid them of the Union was so unusual that it could not be expected to be of long duration in so factious a nation. Neither was it likely that the kingdom of Scotland would, after such a lesson, be again left by the English Government so ill provided for defence. Above all, it seemed probable that the vengeance of the Ministry would descend so heavily on the heads of those who had been foremost in expressing their good wishes to the cause of the Chevalier de St. George as might induce others to beware of following their example on future occasions.

During the brief period when the French fleet was known to be at sea, and the landing of the army on some part of the coast of Scotland was expected almost hourly, the depression of the few who adhered to the existing government was extreme. The Earl of Leven, commander-in-chief of the Scottish forces, hurried down from England to take the command of two or three regiments which were all that could be mustered for the defence of the capital, and, on his arrival, wrote to the Secretary of State that the Jacobites were in such numbers, and showed themselves so elated, that he scarce dared look them in the face as he walked the streets. On the approach of a fleet the Earl drew up his army in hostile array on Leith Sands, as if he meant to withstand any attempt to land. But great was his relief when the approaching vessels of war showed the flag of England instead of France, and proved to be those of Sir George Byng instead of the Comte de Forbin's.

When this important intelligence was publicly known, it was for the Jacobites in their turn to abate the haughty looks before which their enemies had quailed, and resume those which they wore as a suffering but submissive faction. The Jacobite gentlemen of Stirlingshire, in particular, had almost gone the length of rising in arms, or to speak more properly, they had actually done so, though no opportunity had occurred of coming to blows. They had now, therefore, reason to expect the utmost vengeance of Government.

This little band consisted of several men of wealth, influence, and property. Stirling of Keir, Seaton of Touch, Edmondstoun of Newton,

Stirling of Carden, and others, assembled a gallant body of horse and advanced towards Edinburgh, to be the first who should offer themselves for the service of the Chevalier de St. George. Learning by the way the failure of the expedition, they dispersed themselves and returned to their own homes. They were seized, however, thrown into prison, and threatened to be tried for high treason.

The Duke of Hamilton with that want of decision which gave his conduct an air of mysterious inconsistency, had left his seat of Kinniel to visit his estates in Lancashire while the treaty concerning the French invasion was in dependence. He was overtaken on his journey by a friend, who came to apprise him that all obstructions to the expedition being overcome, it might be with certainty expected on the coast in the middle of March. The Duke seemed much embarrassed and declared to Lockhart of Carnwath that he would joyfully return, were it not that he foresaw that his giving such a mark of the interest he took in the arrival of the Chevalier, as that which stopping short on a journey, and returning to Scotland on the first news that he was expected, must necessarily imply, would certainly determine the Government to arrest him on suspicion. But his Grace pledged himself that when he should learn by express that the French were actually arrived, he would return to Scotland in spite of all opposition, and rendezvous at Dumfries, where Mr. Lockhart should meet him with the insurgents of Lanarkshire, the district in which both their interests lay.

The Duke had scarcely arrived at his house of Ashton, in Lancashire, when he was arrested as a suspicious person, and was still in the custody of the messenger when he received the intelligence that the French armament had actually set sail. Even this he did not conceive a fit time to declare himself, but solemnly protested that so soon as he should learn that the Chevalier had actually landed, he would rid himself of the officer in whose custody he was, and set off for Scotland at the head of forty horse, to live or die in his service. As the Chevalier never set foot ashore, we have no means of knowing whether the Duke of Hamilton would have fulfilled his promise, which Mr. Lockhart seems to have considered as candidly and sincerely given, or have had recourse to some evasion, as upon other critical occasions.

The Government, as is usual in such cases, were strict in investigating the cause of the conspiracy, and menacing those who had encouraged it in a proportion corresponding to the alarm into which they had been thrown. A great many of the Scottish nobility and gentry were arrested on suspicion, secured in prisons and strong fortresses in Scotland, or sent to London in a kind of triumph, on account of the encouragement they were supposed to have given to the invasion.

The Stirlingshire gentlemen who had actually taken arms and embodied themselves were marked out as the first victims, and were accordingly sent back to Scotland to be tried in the country where they had committed the crime. They met more favourable judges than was perhaps to have been expected.

Being brought to trial before the High Court of Justiciary, several witnesses were examined, who had seen the gentlemen assembled together in a body, but no one had remarked any circumstance which gave them the character of a military force. They had arms, indeed, but few gentlemen of that day stirred abroad without sword and pistol. No one had heard any treasonable conversation or avowal of a treasonable purpose. The jury, therefore, found the crime was *Not Proved* against them—a verdict which, by the Scottish law is equivalent in its effects to one of Not Guilty, but which is applied to those cases in which the accused persons are clouded with such a shade of suspicion as renders their guilt probable in the eyes of the jury, though the accuser has failed to make it good by proof. Their trial took place on the 22d November 1708.

A short traditional story will serve to explain the cause of their acquittal. It is said the Laird of Keir was riding joyfully home, with his butler in attendance, who had been one of the evidence produced against him on the trial, but who had, upon examination, forgot every word concerning the matter which could possibly prejudice his master. Keir could not help expressing some surprise to the man at the extraordinary shortness of memory which he had shown on particular questions being put to him. "I understand what your honour means very well," said the domestic coolly, "but my mind was made up rather to trust my own soul to the mercy of Heaven than your honour's body to the tender compassion of the Whigs." This tale carries its own commentary.

Having failed to convict conspirators who had acted so openly, the Government found it would be hopeless to proceed against those who had been arrested on suspicion only. This body included many noblemen and gentry of the first rank, believed to entertain Jacobite sentiments. The Duke of Gordon, the Marquis of Huntly, the Earls Seaforth, Errol, Nithsdale, Marischal, and Murray; Lords Stormont, Kilsythe,

Drummond, Nairne, Belhaven, and Sinclair, besides many gentlemen of fortune and influence were all confined in the Tower or other state prisons. The Duke of Hamilton is supposed to have been successful in making interest with the Whigs for their release, his Grace proposing in return to give the Ministers the advantage of his interest and that of his friends upon future elections. The prisoners were accordingly dismissed on finding bail.

The Government, however, conceived that the failure to convict the Stirlingshire gentlemen accused of high treason (of which they were certainly guilty), arose less from the reluctance of witnesses to bear testimony against them than in advantages afforded to them by the uncertain and general provisions of the Scottish statutes in cases of treason. They proposed to remedy this by abrogating the Scottish law, and introducing that of England in its stead, and ordaining that treasons committed in Scotland should be tried and decided in what is technically called a Commission of *Oyer* and *Terminer, i.e.,* a Court of Commissioners appointed for hearing and deciding a particular cause or set of causes. This, it must be noticed, contained an important advantage to the Government, since the case was taken from under the cognisance of the ordinary courts of justice, and entrusted to commissioners named for the special occasion, who must, of course, be chosen from men friendly to Government, awake to the alarm arising from any attack upon it, and, consequently, likely to be somewhat prejudiced against the parties brought before them as accomplices in such an enterprise. On the other hand, the new law, with the precision required by the English system, was decided and distinct in settling certain forms of procedure, which, in Scotland, being left to the arbitrary pleasure of the judges, gave them an opportunity of favouring or distressing the parties brought before them. This was a dangerous latitude upon political trials, where every man, whatever might be his rank or general character for impartiality, was led to take a strong part on one side or other of the question out of which the criminal interest had arisen.

Another part of the proposed act was, however, a noble boon to Scotland. It freed the country for ever from the atrocious powers of examination under torture. This, as we have seen, was currently practised during the reigns of Charles II. and his brother James; and it had been put in force, though unfrequently, after the Revolution. A greater injustice cannot be imagined than the practice of torture to extort confession, although it once made a part of judicial procedure in every country of Europe, and is still resorted to in some continental nations. It is easy to conceive that a timid man, or one peculiarly sensible to pain, will confess crimes of which he is innocent to avoid or escape from the infliction of extreme torture, while a villain, of a hardy disposition of mind and body will endure the worst torment that can be imposed on him rather than avow offences of which he is actually guilty.

The laws of both countries conformed but too well in adding to the punishment of high treason certain aggravations, which, while they must disgust and terrify the humane and civilised, tend only to brutalise the vulgar and unthinking part of the spectators, and to familiarise them with acts of cruelty. On this the laws of England were painfully minute. They enjoined that the traitor should be cut down from the gibbet before life and sensibility to pain were extinguished—that while half-strangled, his heart should be torn from his breast and thrown into the fire—his body opened and embowelled, and,—omitting other more shamefully savage injunctions,—that his corpse should be quartered and exposed upon bridges and city towers, and abandoned to the carrion crow and the eagle. Admitting that high treason, as it implies the destruction of the government under which we live, is the highest of all possible crimes, still the forfeiture of life, which it does and ought to infer, is the highest punishment which our mortal state affords. All the butchery, therefore, which the former laws of England prescribed only disgusts or hardens the heart of the spectator; while the apparatus of terror seldom affects the criminal, who has been generally led to commit the crime by some strong enthusiastic feeling, either implanted in him by education or caught up from sympathy with others; and which, as it leads him to hazard life itself, is not subdued or daunted by the additional or protracted tortures which can be added to the manner in which death is inflicted.

Another penalty annexed to the crime of high treason was the forfeiture of the estates of the criminal to the crown, to the disinheriting of his children, or natural heirs. There is something in this difficult to reconcile to moral feeling, since it may, in some degree, be termed visiting the crimes of the parents upon the children. It may be also alleged that it is hard to forfeit and take away from the lawful line of succession property which may have been acquired by the talents and industry of the criminal's forefathers, or, perhaps by their meritorious services to the state. But, on the other hand, it must be considered that there is something not unappropriate in the punishment of reducing to poverty the family of him who, by his attack on the state, might have wrought the ruin of thousands of families. Nor is it less to be admitted that this branch of the punishment has a quality always desirable— namely, a strong tendency to deter men from the crime. High treason is usually the offence of men of rank and wealth; at least such being the loaders in civil war, are usually selected for punishment. It is natural that such individuals, however willingly they may venture their own persons, should be apt to hesitate when the enterprise involves all the fortunes of their house, name, rank, and other advantages, which, having received perhaps from a long train of ancestors, they are naturally and laudably desirous to transmit to their posterity.

The proposal for extending the treason law of England into North Britain was introduced under the title of a bill for further completing and perfecting the Union. Many of the Scottish members alleged, on the contrary, that the proposed enactments were rather a violation of the national treaty, since the bill was directly calculated to enroach on the powers of the Court of Justiciary, which had been guaranteed by the Union. This objection was lessened at least by an amendment on the bill, which declared, that three of the Judges of Justiciary (so the Criminal Court of Scotland is termed) should be always included in any Commission of Oyer and Terminer. The bill passed into a statute, and has been ever since the law of the land.

Thus was the Union completed. We shall next endeavour to show, in the phrase of mechanics, how this new machine worked; or, in other words, how this great alteration on the internal Constitution of Great Britain answered the expectations of those by whom the changes were introduced.

LXIII

The Woes of the Union

1708-1713

In order to give you a distinct idea of the situation in which Great Britain was placed at this eventful period, I shall first sketch the character of three or four of the principal persons of Scotland whose influence had most effect in producing the course of events which followed. I shall then explain the course pursued by the Scottish representatives in the national Parliament; and these preliminaries being discussed, I shall, thirdly, endeavour to trace the general measures of Britain respecting her foreign relations, and to explain the effect which these produced upon the public tranquillity of the United Kingdom.

The Duke of Hamilton you are already somewhat acquainted with as a distinguished character during the last Parliament of Scotland when he headed the opposition to the treaty of Union, and also during the plot for invading Scotland and restoring the Stewart family when he seems to have been regarded as the leader of the Lowland Jacobites, those of the Highlands rather inclining to the Duke of Athole. He was the peer of the highest rank in Scotland, and nearly connected with the Royal family, which made some accuse him of looking towards the crown, a folly of which his acknowledged good sense might be allowed to acquit him. He was handsome in person, courtly and amiable in manners, generally popular with all classes, and the natural head of the gentry of Lanarkshire, many of whom are descended from his family. Through the influence of his mother, the Duchess, he had always preserved a strong interest among the Hillmen, or Cameronians, who had since the Revolution shown themselves in arms more than once; and in case of a civil war or invasion must have been of material avail. With all these advantages of birth, character, and influence, the Duke of Hamilton had a defect which prevented his attaining eminence as a political leader. He possessed personal valour, as he showed in his last and tragic scene, but he was destitute of political courage and decision. Dangers which he had braved at a distance appalled him when they approached near; he was apt to disappoint his friends, as the horse who baulks the leap to which he has come gallantly up endangers, or perhaps altogether unseats, his rider. Even with this defect, Hamilton was beloved and esteemed by Lockhart and other leaders of the Tory party, who appear rather to have regretted his unsteadiness as a weakness than condemned it as a fault.

The next Scottish nobleman whose talents made him preeminent on the scene during this eventful period was John, Duke of Argyle, a person whose greatness did not consist in the accidents of rank, influence, and fortune, though possessed of all these in the highest order which his country permitted, since his talents were such as must have forced him into distinction and eminence in what humble state soever he might have been born. This great man was heir of the ancient house of Argyle, which makes so distinguished a figure in Scottish history, and whose name occurs so often in the former volumes of these tales. The Duke of whom we now speak was the great-grandson of the Marquis of Argyle who was beheaded after the Restoration, and grandson of the Earl who suffered the same fate under James II. The family had been reduced to very narrow circumstances by those repeated acts of persecution.

The house of Argyle was indemnified at the Revolution, when the father of Duke John was restored to his paternal property, and in compensation for the injuries and injustice sustained by his father and grandfather was raised to the rank of Duke. A remarkable circumstance which befell Duke John in his infancy would, by the pagans, have been supposed to augur that he was under the special care of Providence, and reserved for some great purposes. About the time (tradition says on the very day, 30th June 1685) that his grandfather, the Earl Archibald, was about to be executed, the heir of the family, then about seven years old, fell from a window of the ancient tower of Lethington, near Haddington, the residence at that time of his grandmother, the Duchess of Lauderdale. The height is so great that the child escaping unhurt, might be accounted a kind of miracle.

Having entered early on a military life, to which his family had been long partial, he distinguished himself at the siege of Keyserswart under the eye of King William. Showing a rare capacity for business, he was appointed Lord High Commissioner to the Scottish Parliament in 1705, on which occasion he managed so well as to set on foot the treaty of Union, by carrying through the Act for the appointment of Commissioners to adjust that great national measure. The Duke, therefore, laid the first stone of an edifice which, though carried on upon an erroneous and narrow system, was nevertheless ultimately calculated to be, and did in fact prove, the basis of universal prosperity to the United Kingdoms. In the last Scottish Parliament his powerful eloquence was a principal means of supporting that great treaty. Argyle's name does not appear in any list of the sharers of the equivalent money; and his countrymen, amid the unpopularity which attached to the measure, distinguished him as having favoured it from real principle. Indeed, it is an honourable part of this great man's character that, though bent on the restoration of the fortunes of his family, sorely abridged by the mischances of his grandfather and great-grandfather, and by the extravagances of his father, he had too much sense and too much honour ever to stoop to any indirect mode of gaining personal advantage and was able, in a venal age, to set all imputations of corruption at defiance; whereas the statesman who is once detected bartering his opinions for lucre is like a woman who has lost her reputation, and can never afterwards regain the public trust and good opinion which he has forfeited. Argyle was rewarded, however, by being created an English Peer, by the title of Earl of Greenwich and Baron Chatham.

Argyle, after the Union was carried, returned to the army, and served under Marlborough with distinguished reputation, of which it was thought that great general even condescended to be jealous. At least it is certain that there was no cordiality between them, it being understood that when there was a rumour that the Whig administration of Godolphin would make a push to have the Duke created general for life, in spite of the Queen's pleasure to the contrary, Argyle offered, if such an attempt should be made, to make Marlborough prisoner even in the midst of the victorious army which he commanded.

At this time, therefore, he was a steady and zealous friend of Harley and Bolingbroke, who were then beginning their Tory administration. To recompense his valuable support he was named by the Tory Ministry commander-in-chief in Spain, and assured of all the supplies in troops and money which might enable him to carry on the war with success in that kingdom, where the Tories had all along insisted it should be maintained. With this pledge, Argyle accepted the appointment in the ambitious hope of acquiring that military renown which he principally coveted.

But the Duke's mortification was extreme in finding, on his arrival in Spain, the British army in a state too wretched to undertake any enterprise of moment, and indeed unfit even to defend its positions. The British Ministers broke the word they had pledged for his support and sent him neither money, supplies, nor reinforcements; so that instead of rivalling Marlborough, as had been his ambition, in conquering territories and gaining battles, Argyle saw himself reduced to the melancholy necessity of retiring to Minorca to save the wreck of the army. The reason given by the Ministers for this breach of faith, was that having determined on that accommodation with France which was afterwards termed the peace of Utrecht, they did not desire to prosecute the war with vigour either in Spain or any other quarter. Argyle fell sick with mortified pride and resentment. He struggled for life in a violent fever, and returned to Britain with vindictive intentions towards the Ministers, who had, he thought, disappointed him by their breach of promise of an ample harvest of glory.

On his return to England the Ministers, Harley, now Earl of Oxford, and the Lord Bolingbroke, endeavoured to soothe the Duke's resentment by appointing him commander-in-chief in Scotland and governor of the castle of Edinburgh; but notwithstanding, he remained a bitter and dangerous opponent of their Administration, formidable by his high talents, both civil and military, his ready eloquence, and the fearless energy with which he spoke and acted.[1] Such was the distinguished John, Duke of Argyle, whom we shall often have to mention in these pages.

John, eleventh Earl of Mar, of the name of Erskine, was also a remarkable person at this period. He was a man of quick parts and

---

[1] "In consequence of his opposition, and his known attachment to the House of Hanover, the Duke of Argyle was, 4th March 1714, dismissed from the command of the Scotch troop of horse guards and deprived of his governments of Minorca and Edinburgh."—Wood's *Peerage*.

prompt eloquence, an adept in state intrigues, and a successful courtier. His paternal estate had been greatly embarrassed by the mismanagement of his father, but in a great measure redeemed by his own prudent economy. He obtained the command of a regiment of foot, but though we are about to see him at the head of an army, it does not appear that Mar had given his mind to military affairs, or acquired experience by going on actual service. His father had been a Whig, and professed Revolution principles, and the present Earl entered life bearing the same colours. He brought forward in the Parliament of Scotland the proposal for the treaty of Union, and was one of the Scottish commissioners for settling the preliminary articles. Being secretary of state for Scotland during the last Scottish Parliament, he supported the treaty both with eloquence and address. Mar does not appear amongst those who received any portion of the equivalents; but as he lost his secretaryship by the Union, he was created keeper of the signet, with a pension, and was admitted into the English Privy Council. Upon the celebrated change of the Administration in 1710, the Earl of Mar, then one of the fifteen peers who represented the nobility of Scotland, passed over to the new Ministers, and was created one of the British secretaries of state. In this capacity he was much employed in the affairs of Scotland, and in managing such matters as they had to do in the Highlands. His large estate upon the river Dee in Aberdeenshire, called the forest of Braemar, placed him at the head of a considerable Highland following of his own, which rendered it more easy for him, as dispenser of the bounties of Government, to establish an interest among the chiefs, which ultimately had fatal consequences to them and to himself.

Such were the three principal Scottish nobles on whom the affairs of Scotland, at that uncertain period, very much depended. We are next to give some account of the manner in which the forty-five members, whom the Union had settled to be the proportion indulged to Scotland as her share of the House of Commons, were received in the English senate.

And here it must be noticed that although individually the Scottish members were cordially received in London, and in society saw or felt no prejudice whatever existing against them on account of their country, and though there was no dislike exhibited against them individually, yet they were soon made sensible that their presence in the senate was as unacceptable to the English members as the arrival of a body of strange rams in a pasture, where a flock of the same animals have been

feeding for some time. The contentions between those who are in possession and the new comers are in that case carried to a great height
and occasion much noise and many encounters; and for a long time
the smaller band of strangers are observed to herd together, and to
avoid intermingling with the original possessors, nor, if they attempt to
do so, are they cordially received.

This same species of discord was visible between the great body of
the English House of Commons and the handful of Scottish members
introduced among them by the Union. It was so much the case, that
the national prejudices of English and Scots pitted against each other
even interfered with and overcame the political differences by which
the conduct and votes of the representatives of both nations would
have been otherwise regulated. The Scottish members, for example,
found themselves neglected, thwarted, and overborne by numbers on
many occasions where they conceived the immediate interests of their
country were concerned, and where they thought that in courtesy and
common fairness, they, as the peculiar representatives of Scotland,
ought to have been allowed something more than their small proportion of five-and-forty votes. The opinion even of a single member of
Parliament is listened to with some deference, when the matter discussed intimately concerns the shire or burgh which he represents,
because he obtains credit for having made himself more master of the
case than others who are less interested. And it was surely natural for
the Scots to claim similar deference when speaking in behalf of a whole
kingdom, whose wants and whose advantages could be known to none
in the House so thoroughly as to themselves. But they were far from
experiencing the courtesy which they expected. It was expressly
refused to them in the following instances.

1. The alteration of the law of high treason, already mentioned, was
a subject of discord. The Scottish members were sufficiently desirous
that their law, in this particular, should be modelled anew, by selecting
the best parts of the system of both countries, and this would certainly
have been the most equitable course. But the English law, in this particular, was imposed on Scotland with little exception or modification.

2. Another struggle for national advantage occurred respecting the
drawbacks of duty allowed upon fish cured in Scotland. This advantage the Scottish merchants had a right to by the letter of the treaty,
which expressly declared that there should be a free communication of
trade and commercial privileges between the kingdoms, so that the

Scottish as well as the English merchant was entitled to these draw-backs. To this the English answered, that the salt with which the Scottish fish were cured before the Union had not paid the high English duty, and that to grant drawbacks upon goods so prepared would be to return to the Scottish trader sums which he had never advanced. There was some reason, no doubt, in the objection; but in so great a transaction as the Union of two kingdoms, there must have occurred circumstances which, for one cause or another, must necessarily create an advantage to individuals of the one country or the other; and it seemed ungracious in the wealthy kingdom of England to grudge to the poorer people of Scotland so trifling a benefit attendant on so important a measure. The English Parliament did accordingly at last agree to this drawback; but the action lost its grace from the obvious unwillingness with which the advantage was conceded, and, as frequently happens, the giving up the point in question did not consign to oblivion the acrimony of the discussions which it had occasioned. The debates on the several questions we have just noticed all occurred in the sessions of the British Parliament during which the Union was completed.

In 1710 Queen Anne, becoming weary of her Whig ministers, as I will tell you more at length, took an opportunity to dismiss them, upon finding the voice of the country unfavourable to them, in the foolish affair of Sacheverel; and, as is the usual course in such cases, she dissolved the Parliament in which the Administration had a majority, and assembled a new one.

The Tory Ministry, like all Ministers entering on office, endeavoured, by civility or promises, to gain the support of every description of men; and the Scottish members, who after all, made up forty-five votes, were not altogether neglected. The new Ministry boasted to the representatives of North Britain that the present Parliament consisted chiefly of independent country gentlemen, who would do impartial justice to all parts of Britain, and that Scotland should have nothing to complain of.

An opportunity speedily occurred of proving the sincerity of these promises. It must first be remarked that the opposition made to the measures of Government had hitherto been almost entirely on the side of the Scottish members in the Lower House, who had pursued the policy of threatening to leave the Administration in a minority in trying questions by passing in a body to the Opposition—a line of political tactics which will always give to a small but united band a certain weight in the House of Commons, where nicely balanced questions frequently occur, and forty-five votes may turn the scale one way or other. By this policy the Scottish commoners had sometimes produced a favourable issue on points in which their country was concerned. But such was not the practice of the representatives of the peerage, who, having some of them high rank, with but small fortunes to sustain it, were for a time tolerably tractable, voting regularly along with the Ministers in power. A question, however, arose of which we shall speak presently, concerning the privileges of their own order which disturbed this interested and self-seeking course of policy.

Another reason for the lukewarmness of the Scottish peers was that the commoners of Scotland had been active on two occasions in which they had interposed barriers against the exorbitant power of the aristocracy. The first was, an enactment passed rendering the eldest sons of Scottish peers incapable of sitting as members in the House of Commons. This incapacity was imposed, because, being of the same rank or status as the nobility, it was considered that the eldest sons of the nobles were, like their fathers, virtually represented by the sixteen Scottish peers sent to the Upper House.[1] The second regulation displeasing to the peerage was that which rendered illegal the votes of such electors in Scotland as, not being possessed in their own right of the qualification necessary by law, had obtained a temporary conveyance of a freehold qualification of the necessary amount, which they bound themselves to restore to the person by whom it was lent, for the purpose of voting at elections. The effect of this law was to destroy an indirect mode by which the peers had attempted to interfere in the election of the commoners. For before this provision, although a peer could not himself appear or vote for the election of a commoner, he might, by cutting his crown-holding into qualifications of the necessary amount, and distributing them among confidential persons, place so many factitious voters on the roll as might outvote those real proprietors in whom the constitution vested the right of election.

These two laws show that the Scottish Members of the House of Commons were alive to the value of their constitutional rights, and the danger to their freedom from the interference of the peers in elections to the Lower House. These differences occasioned some coldness between

---

[1] The eldest sons of Scots peers were not relieved from this incapacity until the passing of the Bill for Parliamentary Reform in 1832.

the Sixteen Peers and the Scottish members of Parliament, and prevented for a time a co-operation between them in cases where the interests of their common country seemed to require it. The following incident, to which I have already alluded, put an end to this coldness.

Queen Anne, in the course of her administration, had begun to withdraw her favours from the Whigs and confer them upon the Tories, even upon such as were supposed to have embraced the Jacobite interest. Among these, the Duke of Hamilton being conspicuous, he was, in addition to his other titles, created a peer of Great Britain by the title of the Duke of Brandon. A similar exertion of the Queen's prerogative had already been made in the case of the Duke of Queensberry, who had been called to the British peerage, by the title of Duke of Dover. But notwithstanding this precedent, there was violent opposition to the Duke of Hamilton taking his seat as a British peer. It was said no Scottish noble could sit in that House by any other title than as one of the sixteen Peers, to which number the peerage of that kingdom had been restricted as an adequate representation; and the Opposition pretended to see great danger in opening any other way to their getting into the Upper House, even through the grant of the Sovereign, than the election of their own number. The fallacy of this reasoning is obvious, seeing it was allowed on all hands that the Queen could have made any Scotsman a British peer providing he was not a peer in his own country. Thus the Scottish peerage were likely to be placed in a very awkward situation. They were peers already, as far as the question of all personal privileges went; but because they were such, it was argued that they were not capable of holding the additional privilege of sitting as legislatures, which it was admitted the Queen could confer, with all other immunities, upon any Scottish commoner. Their case was that of the bat in the fable, who was rejected both by birds and mice, because she had some alliance with each of them. A Scottish peer, not being one of the elected sixteen, could not be a legislator in his own country, for the Scottish Parliament was abolished; and, according to this doctrine, he had become, for no reason that can be conjectured, incapable of being called to the British House of Peers, to which the King could summon by his will any one save himself and his co-peers of Scotland. Nevertheless, the House of Peers, after a long debate, and by a narrow majority, decided that no Scottish peer being created a peer of Great Britain since the Union, had a right, to sit in that House. The Scottish peers, highly offended at the decision, drew up a remonstrance to the Queen in which they complained of it as an infringement of the Union, and a mark of disgrace put upon the whole peerage of Scotland. The resolution of the House of Peers was afterwards altered, and many of the Scottish nobility have, at various periods, been created peers of Great Britain.

But during the time while it remained binding it produced a considerable change in the temper of the Scottish peers, and brought them to form a closer union among themselves and with the Commons. Influenced by these feelings of resentment, and by the energy of the Duke of Argyle, they bestirred themselves to resist the extension of the malt tax to Scotland.

This tax, which the Scots dreaded peculiarly, because it imposed upon their malt a duty equal to that levied in England, had been specially canvassed in the course of the treaty of Union; and it had finally been agreed that Scotland should not pay the tax during the continuance of the war. In point of strict right the Scots had little to say, excepting that the peace with Spain was not yet proclaimed, which might have enabled them to claim a delay but not an exemption from the imposition. In point of equity, there was more to be pleaded. The barley grown in Scotland, being raised on an inferior soil, is not, at least was not at the time of the Union, worth more than one-third or one-half of the intrinsic value of that raised on the fertile soil and under the fine climate of England. If therefore, the same duty was to be laid on the same quantity as in South Britain, the poorer country would be taxed in a double or triple proportion to that which was better able to bear the burden. Two Scottish peers, the Duke of Argyle and the Earl of Mar, and two commoners, Cockburn, younger of Ormiston, and Lockhart of Carnwath, a Whig and Tory of each House, were deputed to wait upon Queen Anne, and represent particularly, besides some other grievances, the dangerous discontents which the imposition of a tax so unequal as that upon malt was likely to occasion in so poor a country as Scotland. This was stated to her Majesty personally, who returned the answer Ministers had put into her mouth—"She was sorry," she said, "that her people of Scotland thought they had reason to complain; but she thought they drove their resentment too far and wished they did not repent it."

The war, however, being ended by the peace of Utrecht, the English proposed to extend the obnoxious tax to Scotland. The debates in both Houses became very animated. The English testified some contempt for the poverty of Scotland, while the Scottish members, on the other hand, retorted fiercely, that the English took advantage of their great majority of numbers and privilege of place, to say more than, man to man, they would dare to answer. The Scottish peers in the Upper House maintained the cause of the country with equal vehemence. But the issue was, the duty was imposed, with a secret assurance on the part of Ministers that it was not to be exacted. This last indulgence was what Scotland, strictly speaking, was not entitled to look for, since her own Estates had previously conceded the question; and they had no right to expect from the British Parliament a boon which their own, while making the bargain, had neglected to stipulate. But they felt they had been treated with haughtiness and want of courtesy in the course of the debate; and so great was their resentment that in a general meeting of the forty-five Scottish members, they came to the resolution to move for the dissolution of the Union, as an experiment which had failed in the good effects it was expected to produce—which resolution was also adopted by the Scottish peers. It was supported by Scottish members of all parties, Whigs and Revolutionists, as well as Tories and Jacobites; and as all the English Whigs who, being in office, were so eager for the establishment of the Union, were now, when in opposition, as eager for its dissolution, its defence rested with the English Tories, by whom it had been originally opposed at every stage of its progress. This important treaty, which involved so much of national happiness, stood in danger of sharing the fate of a young fruit-tree, cut down by an ignorant gardener because it bears no fruit in the season after it has been planted.

The motion for the dissolution of the Union was brought forward in the House of Lords by Lord Findlater and Seafield—that very Lord Findlater and Seafield who, being Chancellor of the Scottish Parliament by which the treaty was adjusted, signed the last adjournment of his country's representatives with the jeering observation, that "there was an end of an old song." His Lordship, with a considerable degree of embarrassment, arising from the recollection of his own inconsistency, had the assurance to move that this "old song" should be resumed, and the Union abolished, on account of the four following alleged grievances:— 1. The abolition of the Privy Council of Scotland; 2. The introduction of the English law of High Treason; 3. The incapacity of Scottish peers to be called to Parliament as peers of Britain; 4. The imposition of the malt tax. None of these reasons of complaint vindicated Lord Findlater's proposition. 1. The abolition of the Privy Council was a boon rather than a grievance to Scotland, which that oppressive body had ruled with a rod of iron. 2. The English treason law was probably more severe in some particulars than that of Scotland, but it had the undeniable advantage of superior certainty and precision. 3. The incapacity of the Scottish peers was indeed an encroachment upon their privileges, but it was capable of being reversed, and has been reversed accordingly, without the necessity of destroying the Union. 4. If the malt tax was a grievance, it was one which the Scottish commissioners, and his Lordship amongst others, had under their view during the progress of the treaty, and to which they had formally subjected their country, and were not, therefore, entitled to complain as if something new or unexpected had happened, when the English availed themselves of a stipulation to which they themselves had consented.

The Duke of Argyle supported the motion for abrogating the Union with far more energy than had been displayed by Lord Findlater. He declared that when he advocated the treaty of Union it was for the sole reason that he saw no other mode of securing the Protestant succession to the throne; he had changed his mind on that subject, and thought other remedies as capable of securing that great point. On the insults and injuries which had been unsparingly flung upon Scotland and Scotsmen, he spoke like a high-minded and high-spirited man; and to those who had hinted reproaches against him as having deserted his party, he replied that he scorned the imputations they threw out as much as he despised their understanding.

This bold orator came nearest to speaking out the real cause of the universal discontent of the Scottish members, which was less the pressure of any actual grievance than the sense of the habitually insulting and injurious manner in which they were treated by the English members, as if the representatives of some inferior and subjugated province. But personal resentment, or offended national pride, however powerful, ought not to have been admitted as reasons for altering a national enactment, which had been deliberately and seriously entered into; for the welfare of posterity is not to be sacrificed to the vindictive feelings of the present generation.

The debate on Lord Findlater's motion was very animated, and it was wonderful to see the energy with which the Tories defended that Union which they had opposed in every stage, while the Whigs, equally inconsistent, attempted to pull down the fabric which their own hands had been so active in rearing. The former, indeed, could plead that, though they had not desired to have a treaty of Union, yet, such having been once made, and the ancient constitutions of both countries altered and accommodated to it, there was no inconsistency in their being more willing it should remain than that the principles of the constitution should be rendered the subject of such frequent changes and tamperings. The inconsistency of the Whigs hardly admits of equal apology.

The division upon the question was so close that it was rejected by a majority of *four* only; so nearly had that important treaty received its death-blow within six years after it was entered into.

Shortly after this hairbreadth escape, for such we may surely term it, another circumstance occurred, tending strongly to show with what sensitive jealousy the Scots of that day regarded any reflections on their country. The two great parties of Whig and Tory, the former forming the Opposition, and the latter the Ministerial party, besides their regular war in the House of Commons, had maintained a skirmishing warfare of pamphlets and lampoons, many of them written by persons of distinguished talent.

Of these the celebrated Sir Richard Steele wrote a tract, called the *Crisis,* which was widely circulated by the Whigs. The still more able Jonathan Swift, the intimate friend and advocate of the existing ministers, published (but anonymously) a reply, entitled "The Public Spirit of the Whigs set forth in their encouragement of the author of the Crisis." It was a sarcastic political lampoon against the Whigs and their champion, interspersed with bitter reflections upon the Duke of Argyle and his country.[1]

In this composition the author gives rein to his prejudices against the Scottish nation. He grudged that Scotland should have been admitted into commercial privileges by means of this Union, from which Ireland was excluded. The natural mode of redressing this inequality was certainly to put all the three nations on a similar footing. But as nothing of this kind seemed at that time practicable, Swift accused the Scots of affectation in pretending to quarrel with the terms of a treaty which was so much in their favour, and supposes that while carrying on a

---

[1] "In *The Crisis,* the Union is pronounced to be sacred and inviolable. No blame is, however, thrown on the Scottish peers who had moved for the dissolution. On the contrary, it is intimated, that it became the English, in generosity, to be more particularly careful in preserving the Union, since the Scotch had sacrificed their national independence, and left themselves in a state of comparative impotence of redressing their own wrongs."—*Note to Swift's Works.*

debate, under pretence of abrogating the Union, they were all the while
in agony lest they should prove successful. Acute observer of men and
motives as he was, Swift was in this instance mistaken. Less sharp-
sighted than this celebrated author, and blinded by their own exasperated pride, the Scots were desirous of wreaking their revenge at the
expense of a treaty which contained so many latent advantages, in the
same manner as an intoxicated man vents his rage at the expense of
valuable furniture or important papers. In the pamphlet which gave so
much offence Swift denounced the Union "as a project for which there
could not possibly be assigned the least reason;" and he defied "any
mortal to name one single advantage that England could ever expect
from such a Union." The necessity he justly but offensively imputes to
the Scots refusing to settle the crown on the line of Hanover, when,
according to the satirist, it was thought "highly dangerous to leave that
part of the island, inhabited by a poor, fierce, northern people, at liberty to put themselves under a different king." He censures Godolphin
highly for suffering the Act of Security to pass, by which the Scots
assumed the privilege of universally arming themselves. "The Union,
he allows, became necessary, because it might have cost England a year
or two of war to reduce the Scots." In this admission Swift pronounces
the highest panegyric on the treaty, since the one or two years of hostilities might have only been the recommencement of that war which had
blazed inextinguishably for more than a thousand years.

The Duke of Argyle had been a friend, even a patron, of the satirist,
but that was when he acted with Oxford and Bolingbroke, in the earlier part of the administration, at which time he gratified at once their
party spirit and his own animosity by attacking the Duke of Marlborough, and declining to join in the vote of thanks to that great general.
While Argyle was in Spain, Swift had addressed a letter to him in that
delicate style of flattery of which he was as great a master as of every
power of satirical sarcasm. But when the Duke returned to Britain,
embittered against Ministers by their breach of promise to supply him
with money and reinforcements, and declared himself the unrelenting
opponent of them, their party, and their measures, Swift, their intimate
confident and partisan, espoused their new quarrel, and exchanged the
panegyrics of which the Duke had been the object for poignant satire.
Of the number of the Scottish nobility, he talks as one of the great evils
of the Union, and asks if it were ever reckoned as an advantage to a
man who was about to marry a woman much his inferior, and without

a groat to her fortune, that she brought in her train a numerous retinue of retainers and dependents. He is supposed to have aimed particularly at the Duke of Argyle and his brother, Lord Islay, in these words:—"I could point out some with great titles, who affected to appear very vigorous for dissolving the Union, although their whole revenue, before that period, would have ill maintained a Welsh justice of peace, and have since gathered more money than ever any Scotsman who had not travelled could form an idea of."

These shafts of satire against a body of men so sensitive and vindictive as the Scots had lately shown themselves, and directed also against a person of the Duke of Argyle's talents and consequence, were not likely, as the Ministers well knew, to be passed over lightly, either by those who felt aggrieved, or the numerous opposition party, who were sure to avail themselves of such an opportunity for pressing home a charge against Swift, whom all men believed to be the author of the tract, and under whose shafts they had suffered both as a party and as individuals. The Ministry therefore formed a plan to elude an attack which might have been attended with evil consequences to so valued and valuable a partisan.

They were in the right to have premeditated a scheme of defence, or rather of evasion, for the accusation was taken up in the House of Lords by the Earl of Wharton, a nobleman of high talent, and not less eager in the task that the satirist had published a character of the Earl himself, drawn when Lord-Lieutenant of Ireland, in which he was painted in the most detestable colours. Wharton made a motion, concluding that the honour of the House was concerned in discovering the villainous author of so false and scandalous a libel, that justice might be done to the Scottish nation.[1] The Lord Treasurer Oxford disclaimed all knowledge of the author, and readily concurred in an order for taking into custody the publisher and printer of the pamphlet complained of. On the next day, the Earl of Mar informed the House that he, as Secretary of State, had raised a prosecution in his Majesty's name against John Barber. This course was intended, and had the effect, to screen Swift; for, when the printer was himself made the object of a prosecution, he could not be used as an evidence against the author,

---

[1] "It was not the least remarkable circumstance that, while the violence of party was levelled against Swift in the House of Peers, no less injustice was done to his adversary, Steele, by the Commons, who expelled him from their House for writing the Crisis, that very pamphlet which called forth Swift's answer."—Note, Swift's Works.

whom, and not the printer or publisher, it was the purpose of the Whigs to prosecute. Enraged at being deprived of their prey, the House of Peers addressed the Queen, stating the atrocity of the libel, and beseeching her Majesty to issue a proclamation offering a reward for the discovery of the author. The Duke of Argyle and the Scottish Lords, who would have perhaps acted with a truer sense of dignity had they passed over such calumnies with contempt, pressed their address on the Queen by personal remonstrance, and a reward of three hundred pounds was offered for the discovery of the writer.[1]

Every one knew Swift to be the person aimed at as the author of the offensive tract. But he remained, nevertheless, safe from legal detection.

Thus I have given you an account of some, though not of the whole debates, which the Union was, in its operation, the means of exciting in the first British Parliament. The narrative affords a melancholy proof of the errors into which the wisest and best statesmen are hurried, when, instead of considering important public measures calmly and dispassionately, they regard them in the erroneous light in which they are presented by personal feeling and party prejudices. Men do not in the latter case ask, whether the public will be benefited or injured by the enactment under consideration, but whether their own party will reap most advantage by defending or opposing it.

---

[1] "In his 'Political Poetry—The Author upon himself,' Swift says,
'The Queen incensed, his services forgot,
Leaves him a victim to the vengeful Scot.
Now through the realm a proclamation spread,
To fix a price on his devoted head.
While innocent, he scorns ignoble flight;
His watchful friends preserve him by *a sleight.*'
                                        Works, vol. xii, p. 31.
"It appears, however, that Swift did meditate a flight in case discovery had taken place. In the letter to his friend in Ireland about renewing his license of absence, dated 29th July 1714, he says, 'I was very near wanting it some months ago with a witness,' which can only allude to the possibility of his being obliged to abscond."—*Life of Swift,* Note, p. 167.

LXIV

Marlborough, Bolingbroke, and Utrecht

1708-1713

I N my last chapter I detailed to you the consequences of the Union, and told you how the unfair, unkind, and disparaging reception which the English afforded to the Scottish members in the Houses of Lords and Commons, although treating them in their private capacities with every species of kindness, had very nearly occasioned the breach of the treaty. I must now retrace the same ground, to give you a more distinct idea how Britain stood in general politics, independent of the frequent and fretful bickerings between England and Scotland in the British Parliament.

King William, as I have already told you, died in 1701, little lamented by his subjects, for though a man of great ability, he was too cold and phlegmatic to inspire affection, and besides he was a foreigner. In Scotland his memory was little reverenced by any party. The Highlanders remembered Glencoe, the Lowlanders could not forget Darien; the Episcopalians resented the destruction of their hierarchy; the Presbyterians discovered in his measures something of Erastianism, that is, a purpose of subjecting the Church to the State.

Queen Anne, therefore, succeeded to her brother-in-law to the general satisfaction of her subjects. Her qualities, too, were such as gained for her attachment and esteem. She was a good wife, a most affectionate mother, a kind mistress, and, to add to her domestic virtues, a most confiding and faithful friend.

The object of her attachment in this latter capacity was Lady Churchill, who had been about her person from a very early period. This woman was so high-spirited, haughty, and assuming, that even her husband (afterwards the celebrated Duke of Marlborough), the conqueror in so many battles, frequently came off less than victorious in any domestic dispute with her. To this lady, Anne, for several years before her succession to the crown, had been accustomed in a great measure to yield up her own opinions. She left the house of her father, James II., and mingled in the Revolution at the instance of Lady Churchill. At her accession Queen Anne was rather partial to the Tories, both from regarding their principles as more favourable to monarchy, and because, though the love of power, superior to most other feelings, might induce her to take possession of the throne, which by hereditary descent ought to have been that of her father or brother, yet she still felt the ties of family affection, and was attached to that class of politicians who regarded the exiled family with compassion, at least, if not with favour. All these, Queen Anne's own natural wishes and predilections, were overborne by her deference to her favourite's desires and interest. Their intimacy had assumed so close and confidential a character that she insisted that her friend should lay aside all the distinctions of royalty in addressing her, and they corresponded together in terms of the utmost equality, the sovereign assuming the name of Morley, the servant that of Freeman, which Lady Churchill, now Countess of Marlborough, chose as expressive of the frankness of her own temper. Sunderland and Godolphin were ministers of unquestionable talent, who carried on with perseverance and skill the scheme formed by King William for defending the liberties of Europe against the encroachments of France. But Queen Anne reposed her confidence in them chiefly because they were closely connected with Mrs. Freeman and her husband. Now this species of arrangement, my dear boy, was just such a childish whim as when you and your little brother get into a basket, and play at sailing down to A———, to see grandpapa. A sovereign cannot enjoy the sort of friendship which subsists between equals, for he cannot have equals with whom to form such a union; and every attempt to play at make-believe intimacy commonly ends in the Royal person's being secretly guided and influenced by the flattery and assentation of an artful and smooth-tongued para-site, or tyrannised over by the ascendance of a haughtier and higher mind than his own. The husband of Queen Anne, Prince George of Denmark, might have broken off this extreme familiarity between his wife and her haughty favourite; but he was a quiet, good, humane man, meddling with nothing, and apparently considering himself as unfit for public affairs, which agreed with the opinion entertained of him by others.

The death of Queen Anne's son and heir, the Duke of Gloucester, the sole survivor of a numerous family, by depriving her of the last object of domestic affection, seemed to render the Queen's extreme attachment to her friend more direct, and Lady Marlborough's influence became universal. The war which was continued against the French had the most brilliant success, and the general was loaded with honours; but the Queen favoured Marlborough less because he was the most accomplished and successful general at that time in the world than as the husband of her affectionate *Mrs. Freeman*. In short, the affairs of England, at all times so influential in Europe, turned altogether upon the private friendship between *Mrs. Freeman* and *Mrs. Morley*.

At the moment when it seemed most completely secure, this inti-macy was overthrown by the influence of a petty intrigue in the Queen's family. The Duchess of Marlborough, otherwise Mrs. Freeman, had used the power with which her mistress's partiality had invested her far too roughly. She was avaricious and imperious in her demands, careless, and even insolent in her conduct towards the Queen herself. For some time this was endured as an exercise of that frank privilege of equality with which her Majesty's friendship had invested her. For a much longer space it may be supposed, the Queen tolerated her caprice and insolence, partly because she was afraid of her violent temper, partly because she was ashamed to break off the romantic engagement which she had herself formed. She was not, however, the less impatient of the Duchess of Marlborough's yoke, or less watchful of an opportunity to cast it off.

The Duchess had introduced among the Queen's attendants, in the capacity of what was called a dresser, a young lady of good birth, named Abigail Hill, a kinswoman of her own. She was the reverse of the Duchess in her temper, being good-humoured, lively, and, from dispo-sition and policy, willing to please her mistress in every manner possi-ble. She attracted by degrees first the Queen's favour, and at length her confidence; so that Anne sought, in the solicitous attentions and counsels of her new friend, consolation from the rudeness with which the Duchess treated her both in private and public life. The progress of this intimacy was closely watched by Harley, a statesman of talents, and hitherto professing the principles of the Whigs. He had been repeatedly Speaker of the House of Commons, and was Secretary of State in the existing Whig administration. But he was ambitious of higher rank in the cabinet, being conscious of superior talents, and he caballed against the Duchess of Marlborough, in consequence of her having repulsed his civilities towards her with her usual insolence of manner. The partner of Harley's counsels was Mr. Henry St. John (afterwards Lord Bolingbroke), a young man of the most distinguished abilities, and who subsequently made a great figure both in politics and in literature.

Harley lost no time in making advances to intimacy with the new favourite; and as he claimed some kindred with Miss Hill's family, this was easily accomplished. This lady's interest with the Queen was now so great that she was able to procure her cousin private audiences with the Queen, who, accustomed to the harshness of the Duchess of Marlborough, whose tone of authority had been adopted by the Whig Ministers of the higher class, was soothed by the more respectful deportment of these new counsellors. Harley was more submissive and deferential in his manners, and conducted himself with an attention to the Queen's wishes and opinions, to which she had been hitherto little accustomed. It was undoubtedly his purpose to use the influence thus acquired to the destruction of Godolphin's authority, and to accomplish his own rise to the office of first Minister. But his attempt did not succeed in the first instance. His secret intrigues and private interviews with the sovereign were prematurely discovered, and Harley and his friends were compelled to resign their offices; so that the Whig administration seemed more deeply rooted than ever.

About the same time, Miss Hill was secretly married to Mr. Masham; a match which gave great offence to the Duchess of Marlborough, who was beginning to feel that her relation had superseded her in her mistress's affections. As this high-tempered lady found the Queen's confidence was transferred from her, she endeavoured to maintain her ascendency by threats and intimidation, and was for a time successful in ruling the mind of her late friend by means of fear, as she did formerly by affection. But a false step of the Whig administration enabled Queen Anne at last to shake off this intolerable bondage.

A silly and hot-headed clergyman, named Sacheverel, had preached and printed a political sermon in which he maintained high Tory principles and railed at Godolphin, the Lord High Treasurer, and head of Queen Anne's Administration, whom he termed Volpone, after an odious character so named in one of Ben Jonson's Plays. The great majority of the landed gentlemen of England were then addicted to Tory principles, and those of the High Church. So bold and daring a sermon, though it had no merit but its audacity to recommend it, procured immense popularity amongst them. The Ministers were incensed beyond becoming moderation. The House of Commons impeached the preacher before the tribunal of the House of Lords, and his trial came before the Peers on 27th February 1710. The utmost degree of publicity was given to it by the efforts of the Whigs to obtain Dr. Sacheverel's conviction and a severe sentence, and by the corresponding exertions of the Tories to screen him from punishment. The multitude took up the cry of High Church and Sacheverel, with which they beset the different members of both Houses as they went down to Parliament. The trial, which lasted three weeks, excited public attention in a degree hitherto almost unknown. The Queen herself attended almost every day, and her sedan chair was surrounded by crowds, shouting, "God bless the Queen and Dr. Sacheverel! we hope your Majesty is for High Church and Sacheverel." The mob arose, and exhibited their furious zeal for the Church by destroying the chapels and meeting-houses of dissenters, and committing similar acts of violence.

The consequence was, that the Doctor was found guilty indeed by the House of Peers, but escaped with being suspended from preaching for three years; a sentence so slight, that it was regarded by the accused and his friends as an acquittal, and they triumphed accordingly. Bonfires, illuminations, and other marks of rejoicing appeared in celebrating of the victory.

As these manifestations of the public sentiment were not confined to the capital, but extended over all England, they made evident the unpopularity of the Whig government, and encouraged the Queen to put in execution the plan she had long proposed to herself, of changing her Ministry, and endeavouring to negotiate a peace, and terminate the war, which seemed to be protracted without end. Anne, by this change of government and system, desired also to secure the Church, which her old prejudices taught her to believe was in danger—and, above all, to get rid of the tyranny of her former friend, Mrs. Freeman. A new

Administration, therefore, was formed under Harley and St. John, who, being supported by the Tory interest, were chiefly if not exclusively governed by Tory principles. At the same time, the Duchess of Marlborough was deprived of all her offices about the Queen's person and disgraced, as it is termed, at court, that is, dismissed from favour and employment. Her husband's services could not be dispensed with so easily; for while the British army were employed no general could supply the place of Marlborough, who had so often led them to victory. But the Tory Ministers endeavoured to lower him in the eyes of the public by an investigation into certain indirect emoluments taken in his character as general-in-chief, and to get rid of the indispensable necessity of his military services by entering into negotiations for peace.

The French Government saw and availed themselves of the situation in which that of Britain was placed. They perceived that peace was absolutely necessary to Oxford and Bolingbroke's existence as ministers, even more so than it was to France as a nation, though her frontiers had been invaded, her armies repeatedly defeated, and even her capital to a certain degree exposed to insult. The consequence was that the French rose in their terms, and the peace of Utrecht, after much negotiation, was at length concluded on conditions which, as they respected the allies, and the British nation in particular, were very much disproportioned to the brilliant successes of the war.

That article of the treaty, which was supposed by all friends of Revolution principles to be most essential to the independence and internal peace of Great Britain, seemed indeed to have been adjusted with some care. The King of France acknowledged, with all formality, the right of Queen Anne to the throne, guaranteed the Act of Succession settling it upon the House of Hanover, and agreed to expel from his territories the unfortunate son of James II. This was done accordingly. Yet notwithstanding that the Chevalier de St. George was compelled to remove from the territories of his father's ally, who on James's death had formally proclaimed him King of England, the unhappy Prince had perhaps at the moment of his expulsion more solid hopes of being restored to his father's throne than any which the favour of Louis could have afforded him. This will appear from the following considerations,

Queen Anne, as we have already stated, was attached to the High Church establishment and clergy; and the principles with which these were imbued, if not universally Jacobitical, were at least strongly tinctured with a respect for hereditary right. These doctrines could not be supposed to be very unpleasing to the Queen herself, as a woman or as a sovereign, and there were circumstances in her life which made her more ready to admit them. We have already said that the part which Anne had taken at the Revolution, by withdrawing from her father's house, had been determined by the influence of Lady Churchill, who was now, as Duchess of Marlborough, the object of the Queen's hatred, as much as ever she had been that of her affection in the character of Mrs. Freeman, and her opinions and the steps which they had led to, were not probably recollected with much complacency. The desertion of a father, also, however coloured over with political argument, is likely to become towards the close of life a subject of anxious reflection. There is little doubt that the Queen entertained remorse on account of her filial disobedience; more especially, when the early death of her children, and finally that of a hopeful young Prince, the Duke of Gloucester, deprived her of all chance of leaving the kingdom to an heir of her own. These deprivations seemed an appropriate punishment to the disobedient daughter who had been permitted to assume for a time her father's crown, but not to transmit it to her heirs. As the Queen's health became broken and infirm, it was natural that these compunctious thoughts should become still more engrossing, and that she should feel no pleasure in contemplating the prospect which called the Prince of Hanover, a distant relation, to reign over England at her decease; or that she should regard with aversion, almost approaching to horror, a proposal of the Whig party to invite the Electoral Prince to visit Britain, the crown of which was to devolve upon him after the decease of its present possessor. On the other hand, the condition of the Chevalier de St. George, the Queen's brother, the only surviving male of her family, a person whose restoration to the crown of his fathers might be the work of her own hand, was likely to affect the Queen with compassionate interest, and seemed to afford her at the same time an opportunity of redressing such wrongs as she might conceive were done to her father by making large though late amends to his son.

Actuated by motives so natural, there is little doubt that Queen Anne, so soon as she had freed herself from the control of the Duchess of Marlborough, began to turn her mind towards fixing the succession of the crown on her brother, the Chevalier de St. George, after her own death, to the prejudice of the act which settled it on the Electoral Prince of Hanover. And she might be the more encouraged to nourish some hopes of success, since a great portion of her subjects of the

Three Kingdoms were Jacobites upon principle, and others had but a short step to make from the extremity of Tory sentiments to those which were directly favourable to the House of Stewart. Ireland, the last portion of the British dominions which adhered to King James the Second, could not be supposed indifferent to the restoration of his son. In England, a very great proportion of the High Church clergy, the Universities, and the Tory interest, which prevailed among the country gentlemen, entertained the same bias, and were at little pains to conceal it. In Scotland men were still bolder in avowing their opinions, of which there occurred the following instance.

The Faculty of Advocates in Scotland, that is to say, the incorporated society of lawyers entitled to practise at the bar, are a body even of more weight and consequence than is attached to them in most countries from the nature of their profession. In the beginning of the eighteenth century, especially, the Faculty comprehended almost all the sons of good family who did not embrace the army as their choice; for the sword or gown, according to the ideas of that time, were the only occupations which could be adopted by a gentleman. The Advocates are possessed of a noble library, and a valuable collection of medals. To this learned body, Elizabeth, Duchess of Gordon (by birth, a daughter of the noble house of Howard, and a keen Jacobite), sent the present of a medal for their cabinet. It bore on the one side the head of the Chevalier de St. George, with the motto, *Cujus est?* (Whom does it represent?): And on the reverse the British Isles, with the legend, *Reddite* (Restore them). The Dean of Faculty having presented this very intelligible emblem to his brethren, a debate arose whether or not it should be received into their collection, which was carried on in very warm language,[1] and terminated in a vote, which, by a majority of sixty-three to twelve, resolved on the acceptance of the medal. Two advocates were deputed to express, in the name of the learned body, their thanks to

---

[1] It was moved that the medal should be returned to her Grace, as their receiving it implied insult to the government. "Oliver Cromwell, who deserved to be hanged," said Mr. Robert Fraser, "his medal, and the arms of the Commonwealth of England, had been received, and why not this?"—"When the Pretender is hanged," said Mr. Duncan Forbes, "it will be time enough to receive the medal." In which opinion Sir James Stewart of Goodtrees, and others coinciding, Mr. Dundas of Arniston rose in great wrath and replied, "Dean of Faculty, whatever these gentlemen may say of their loyalty, I think they affront the Queen, whom they pretend to honour, in disgracing her brother, who is not only a prince of the blood, but the first thereof; and if blood can give any

the Duchess, and they failed not to do it in a manner expressing pointedly their full comprehension of the import of her Grace's compliment. They concluded by stating their hope that her Grace would soon have a further opportunity to oblige the Faculty, by presenting them with a second medal on the subject of a restoration. But when the proceeding became public, the Advocates seem to have been alarmed for the consequences; and at a general meeting of the Faculty (27th July 1711) the medal was formally refused, and placed in the hands of the Lord Advocate, to be restored to the Duchess of Gordon. The retractation, however, could not efface the evidence that this learned and important public body, the commentators on the laws of Scotland, from whom the guardians of her jurisprudence are selected, had shown such boldness as to give a public mark of adherence to the Chevalier de St. George. It was also remarked that the Jacobite interest predominated in many of the Scottish elections.

While the Queen saw a large party among her subjects in each kingdom well disposed to her brother's succession, one at least of her ministers was found audacious enough to contemplate the same measure, though in doing so, he might be construed into impeaching his mistress's own right to the sovereign authority. This was Henry St. John, created Lord Viscount Bolingbroke. He was a person of lively genius and brilliant parts—a scholar, an orator, and a philosopher. There was a reverse to the fair side of the picture. Bolingbroke was dissipated in private life, daringly sceptical in theological speculation, and when his quick perception showed him a chance of rising, he does not appear to have been extremely scrupulous concerning the path which he trod, so that it led to power. In the beginning of his career as a public man he attached himself to Harley; and when that statesman retired from the Whig Administration in 1708, St. John shared his disgrace, and lost the situation of Secretary at War. On the triumph of the Tories, in 1710, when Harley was

---

right, he is our undoubted sovereign. I think, too, they call her Majesty's title in question, which is not our business to determine. Medals are the documents of history, to which all historians refer; and therefore, though I should give King William's stamp, with the devil at his right ear, I see not how it could be refused, seeing one hundred years hence it would prove that such a coin had been in England. But what needs further speeches. None oppose the receiving the medal and returning thanks to her Grace, but a few pitiful scoundrel vermin and mushrooms, not worthy our notice. Let us therefore proceed to name some of our number to return our hearty thanks to the Duchess of Gordon."—TINDAL'S *Continuation of Rapin's History*.

made Prime Minister, St. John was named Secretary of State. Prosperity, however, dissolved the friendship which had withstood the attacks of adversity, and it was soon observed that there was a difference of opinion as well as character between the Premier and his colleague.

Harley, afterwards created Earl of Oxford, was a man of a dark and reserved character—slow, timid, and doubtful, both in counsel and action, and apparently one of those statesmen who affect to govern by balancing the scales betwixt two contending factions, until at length they finally become the objects of suspicion and animosity to both. He had been bred a Whig, and although circumstances had disposed him to join, and even to head the Tories, he was reluctantly induced to take any of the violent party measures which they expected at his hand, and seems, in return, never to have possessed their full confidence or unhesitating support. However far Oxford adopted the principles of Toryism, he stopped short of their utmost extent, and was one of the political sect then called *Whimsicals,* who were supposed not to know their own minds, because they avowed principles of hereditary right, and at the same time desired the succession of the line of Hanover. In evidence of his belonging to this class of politicians, it was remarked that he sent his brother, Mr. Harley, to the court of Hanover, and through him affected to maintain a close intercourse with the Elector, and expressed much zeal for the Protestant line of succession.

All this mystery and indecision was contrary to the rapid and fiery genius of St. John, who felt that he was not admitted into the private and ultimate views of the colleague with whom he had suffered adversity. He was disgusted, too, that Harley should be advanced to the rank of an earl, while he himself was only created a viscount. His former friendship and respect for Oxford was gradually changed to coldness, enmity, and hatred, and he began, with much art, and a temporary degree of success, to prepare a revolution in the state which he designed should end in Oxford's disgrace and his own elevation to the supreme authority. He entered with zeal into the ulterior designs of the most extravagant Tories, and, in order to recommend himself to the Queen, did not, it is believed, spare to mingle in intrigues for the benefit of her exiled brother.

It was remarked, that the Chevalier de St. George, when obliged to leave France, found refuge in the territories of the Duke of Lorraine, and that petty German Prince had the boldness to refuse an application of the British Government for the removal of his guest from his dominions. It was believed that the Duke dared not have acted thus unless he had had some private assurance that the application was only made for an ostensible purpose, and that the Queen did not, in reality, desire to deprive her brother of this place of refuge. Other circumstances led to the same conclusion, that Anne and her new ministers favoured the Jacobite interest.

It is more than probable that the Duke of Hamilton, whom we have so often mentioned, was to have been deeply engaged in some transactions with the French court, of the most delicate nature, when, in 1713, he was named ambassador extraordinary to Paris; and there can be little doubt that they regarded the restoration of the line of Stewart. The unfortunate nobleman hinted this to his friend Lockhart of Carnwath, when, parting with him for the last time, he turned back to embrace him again and again, as one who was impressed with the consciousness of some weighty trust, perhaps with a prescient sense of approaching calamity. Misfortune, indeed, was hovering over him, and of a strange and bloody character. Having a lawsuit with Lord Mohun, a nobleman of debauched and profligate manners, whose greatest achievement was having, a few years before, stabbed a poor play-actor in a drunken frolic, the Duke of Hamilton held a meeting with his adversary in the hope of adjusting their dispute. In this conference the Duke, speaking of an agent in the case, said the person in question had neither truth nor honour, to which Lord Mohun replied he had as much of both qualities as his Grace. They parted on the exchange of these words. One would have thought that the offence received lay on the Duke's side, and that it was he who was called upon to resent what had passed, in case he should think it worth his while. Lord Mohun, however, who gave the affront, contrary to the practice in such cases, also gave the challenge. They met at the Ring in Hyde Park, when they fought with swords, and in a few minutes Lord Mohun was killed on the spot; and the Duke of Hamilton, mortally wounded, did not survive him for a longer space. Mohun, who was an odious and contemptible libertine, was regretted by no one; but it was far different with the Duke of Hamilton, who, notwithstanding a degree of irresolution which he displayed in politics, his understanding, perhaps, not approving the lengths to which his feelings might have carried him, had many amiable, and even noble qualities, which made him generally lamented. The Tories considered the death of the Duke of Hamilton as so peculiar, and the period when it happened as so critical, that they did not hesitate to avow a confident

belief that Lord Mohun had been pushed to sending the challenge by
some zealots of the Whig party, and even to add that the Duke fell not
by the sword of his antagonist, but by that of General Macartney, Lord
Mohun's second. The evidence of Colonel Hamilton, second to the
Duke, went far to establish the last proposition; and General Macartney,
seeing, perhaps, that the public prejudice was extreme against him,
absconded, and a reward was offered for his discovery. In the subsequent reign he was brought to trial, and acquitted, on evidence which
leaves the case far from a clear one.

The death of the Duke of Hamilton, however, whether caused by
political resentment or private hatred, did not interrupt the schemes
formed for the restoration of the Stewart family. Lord Bolingbroke himself went on a mission to Paris, and it appears highly probable he then
settled secret articles, explanatory of those points of the Utrecht treaty
which had relation to the expulsion of the Pretender from the dominions of France and the disclamation of his right of succession to the
crown of Britain. It is probable, also, that these remained concealed
from the Premier, Oxford, to whose views in favour of the Hanoverian
succession they were distinctly opposed.

Such being the temper of the Government of England, divided, as it
was, betwixt the dubious conduct of Lord Oxford, and the more secret,
but bolder and decided intrigues of Bolingbroke, the general measures
which were adopted with respect to Scotland indicated a decided bias
to the Jacobite interest, and those by whom it was supported.

LXV

Calm Before the Storm

1714

THE Presbyterians of Scotland had been placed by the Revolution in exclusive possession of the Church government of that kingdom. But a considerable proportion of the country, particularly in the more northern shires, remained attached to the Episcopal establishment and its forms of worship. These, however, were objects of enmity and fear to the Church of Scotland, whose representatives and adherents exerted themselves to suppress, by every means in their power, the exercise of the Episcopal mode of worship, forgetful of the complaints which they themselves had so justly made concerning the violation of the liberty of conscience during the reigns of Charles II. and James II. We must here remark that the Episcopal Church of Scotland had, in its ancient and triumphant state, retained some very slight and formal differences, which distinguished their book of Common Prayer from that which is used in the Church of England. But in their present distressed and disconsolate condition, many of them had become content to resign these points of distinction, and, by conforming exactly to the English ritual, endeavoured to obtain a freedom of worship as Episcopalians in Scotland, similar to the indulgence which was granted to those professing Presbyterian principles, and other Protestant dissenters in England. The Presbyterian Church Courts, however, summoned such Episcopal preachers before them, and prohibited them from exercising their ministry under the penalty of fine and imprisonment, which, in the case of one person (the Rev. Mr. Greenshields), was inflicted with no sparing hand. Others were insulted and ill-used by the multitude, in any attempt which they made to exercise their form of worship. This was the more indefensible, as some of these reverend persons joined in prayer for the Revolution establishment; and whatever conjecture might be formed concerning the probability of their attachment to the exiled family, they had laid aside every peculiarity on which their present mode of worship could be objected to as inferring Jacobitism.

An Act of Toleration was therefore most justly and rightfully passed (February 1712) by Parliament, for the toleration of all such Episcopal clergymen using the Church of England service, as should be disposed to take the Oath of Abjuration, renouncing all adherence to the cause of James II. or his descendant, the existing Pretender. This toleration gave great offence to the Presbyterian clergy, since it was taking out of their hands a means, as they alleged, of enforcing uniformity of worship, which, they pretended, had been insured to them at the Revolution. Every allowance is justly to be made for jealousies and apprehensions, which severe persecution had taught the ministers of the Scottish Church to entertain; but impartial history shows us how dangerous a matter it is to intrust the judicatures of any church with the power of tyrannising over the consciences of those who have adopted different forms of worship, and how wise as well as just it is to restrict their authority to the regulation of their own establishment.

The Presbyterian Church was still more offended by the introduction of a clause into this Act of Toleration, obliging the members of their own church, as well as dissenters from their mode of worship, to take the Oath of Abjuration. This clause had been inserted into the Act as it passed the House of Commons, on the motion of the Tories, who alleged that the ministers of the Kirk of Scotland ought to give the same security for their fidelity to the Queen and Protestant succession which was to be exacted from the Episcopalians. The Scottish Presbyterians complained bitterly of this application of the Oath of Abjuration to themselves. They contended that it was unnecessary, as no one could suspect the Church of Scotland of the least tendency towards Jacobitism, and that it was an usurpation of the State over the Church, to impose by statute law an oath on the ministers of the church, whom, in religious matters, they considered as bound only by the Acts of their General Assembly. Notwithstanding their angry remonstrances, the Oath of Abjuration was imposed on them by the same act which decreed the tolerance of the Episcopal form of worship on a similar condition.

The greater number of the Presbyterian ministers did at length take the oath, but many continued to be recusants, and suffered nothing in consequence, as the Government overlooked their non-compliance. There can be little doubt that this clause, which seems otherwise a useless tampering with the rooted opinions of the Presbyterians, was intended for a double purpose. First, it was likely to create a schism in the Scottish Church, between those who might take and those who might refuse the oath, which, as dividing the opinions, was likely to diminish the authority and affect the respectability, of a body zealous for the Protestant succession. Secondly, it was foreseen that the great majority of the Episcopal clergy in Scotland, avowedly attached to the exiled family, would not take the Oath of Abjuration, and were likely on that account to be interrupted by the Presbyterians of the country where they exercised their functions. But if a number of the Presbyterian clergy themselves were rendered liable to the same charge for the same omission, and only indebted for their impunity to the connivance of the Government, it was not likely they would disturb others upon grounds which might be objected to themselves. The expedient was successful; for though it was said that only one Episcopal minister in Scotland, Mr. Cockburn of Glasgow, took the Oath of Abjuration, yet no prosecutions followed their recusancy, because a large portion of the ministers of the Kirk would have been liable to vexation on the same account.

Another act of the same session of Parliament, which restored to patrons, as they were called, the right of presenting clergymen to vacant churches in Scotland, seemed calculated, and was probably designed, to render the churchmen more dependent on the aristocracy, and to separate them in some degree from their congregations, who could not be supposed to be equally attached to, or influenced by a minister who held his living by the gift of a great man, as by one who was chosen by their own free voice. Each mode of election is subject to its own particular disadvantages. The necessity imposed on the clergyman who is desirous of preferment of suiting his style of preaching to the popular taste, together with the indecent heats and intrigues which attend popular elections, are serious objections to permitting the flock to have the choice of their shepherd. At the same time, the right of patronage is apt to be abused in particular instances, where persons of loose morals, slender abilities, or depraved doctrine, may be imposed, by the fiat of an unconscientious individual, upon a congregation who are unwilling to receive him. But as the Presbyterian clergy possess the power of examination and rejection, subject to an appeal to the superior Church courts, whatever may be thought of the law of patronage in theory, it has not, during the lapse of more than a century, had any effect in practice detrimental to the respectability of the Church of Scotland. There is no doubt, however, that the restoration of the right of lay patrons in Queen Anne's time was designed to separate the ministers of the Kirk from the people, and to render them more dependent on the nobility and gentry, amongst whom, much more than the common people, the sentiments of Jacobitism predominated.

These measures, though all of them indirectly tending to favour the Tory party, which might, in Scotland, be generally termed that of the Stewart family, had yet other motives which might be plausibly alleged for their adoption.

Whatever might be the number and importance of the Lowland gentry in Scotland, who were attached to the cause of the Chevalier de St. George, and that number was certainly very considerable, the altered circumstances of the country had so much restricted their authority over the inferior classes that they could no longer reckon upon raising any considerable number of men by their own influence, nor had they, since the repeal of the Act of Security, the power of mustering or disciplining their followers, so as to render them fit for military service. It was not to be expected that, with the aid of such members of their family, domestics, or dependents, as might join them in any insurrection, they could do more than equip a few squadrons of horse, and even if they could have found men, they were generally deficient in arms, horses, and the means of taking the field.

The Highland clans were in a different state; they were as much under the command of their superior chiefs and chieftains as ever they had been during the earlier part of their history; and, separated from civilisation by the wildernesses in which they lived, they spoke the language, wore the dress, submitted to the government, and wielded the arms of their fathers. It is true that clan wars were not now practised on the former great scale, and that two or three small garrisons of soldiers quartered amongst them put some stop to their predatory incursions. The superior chieftains and tacksmen, more especially the *duinhé wassals,* or dependent gentlemen of the tribe, were in no degree superior in knowledge to the common clansmen. The high chiefs, or heads of the considerable clans, were in a very different situation. They were almost all men of good education and polite manners, and when in Lowland dress and Lowland society were scarce to be distinguished from other gentlemen, excepting by an assumption of consequence, the natural companion of conscious authority. They often travelled abroad, and sometimes entered the military service, looking always forward to the time when their swords should be required in the cause of the Stewarts, to whom they were in general extremely attached; though in the West Highlands the great influence of the Duke of Argyle, and in the north that of the Earl of Sutherland and Lord Reay, together with the Chiefs of Grant, Ross, Munro, and other northern tribes, fixed their clans in the Whig interest.

These chiefs were poor; for the produce of their extensive but barren domains was entirely consumed in supporting the military force of the clan, from whom no industry was to be expected, as it would have degraded them in their own eyes and in those of their leaders and rendered them unfit for the discharge of their warlike duties. The chiefs, at the same time, when out of the Highlands, were expensive as well as needy. The sense of self-importance, which we have already noticed, induced them to imitate the expenses of a richer country, and many, by this inconsistent conduct, exposed themselves to pecuniary distress. To such men money was particularly acceptable, and it was distributed among them annually by Queen Anne's Government, during the latter years of her reign, to the amount of betwixt three and four thousand pounds. The particular sum allotted to each chief was about £360 sterling, for which a receipt was taken, as for a complete year's payment of the bounty-money which her Majesty had been pleased to bestow on the receiver.

These supplies were received the more willingly, because the Highland chiefs had no hesitation in regarding the money as the earnest of pay to be issued for their exertions in the cause of the House of Stewart, to which they conceived themselves to be attached by duty, and certainly were so by inclination. And there can be no doubt, as the pensions were sure to be expended in maintaining and increasing their patriarchal followers and keeping them in readiness for action, it seems to have been considered by the chiefs that the largesses were designed by Government for that and no other purpose. The money was placed at the disposal of the Earl of Mar, Secretary of State, and his being the agent of this bounty gave him the opportunity of improving and extending his influence among the Highland chiefs, afterwards so fatally employed for them and for himself.

The construction which the chiefs put upon the bounty bestowed on them was clearly shown by their joining in a supplication to the Queen, about the end of the year 1713, which got the name of the *Sword-in-hand Address.* In one paragraph, they applaud the measures taken for repressing the license of the press, and trust that they should no longer be scandalised by hearing the Deity blasphemed, and the sacred race of Stewart traduced, with equal malice and impunity. In another they expressed their hopes that, after her Majesty's demise, "the hereditary and parliamentary sanction might possibly meet in the person of a lineal successor." These intimations are sufficiently plain to testify the sense in which they understood the Queen's bounty-money.

The Duke of Argyle, whose own influence in the Highlands was cramped and interfered with by the encouragement given to the Jacobite clans, brought the system of their pensions before Parliament as a severe charge against the Ministers, whom he denounced as rendering the Highlands a seminary for rebellion. The charge led to a debate of importance.

The Duke of Argyle represented that "the Scots Highlanders, being for the most part either rank Papists or declared Jacobites, the giving them pecuniary assistance was, in fact, keeping up Popish seminaries and fomenting rebellion." In answer to this the Treasurer Oxford alleged, "That in this particular he had but followed the example of King William, who, after he had reduced the Highlanders, thought fit to allow yearly pensions to the heads of clans, in order to keep them quiet; and if the present Ministry could be charged with any mismanagement on that head, it was only for retrenching part of these gratuities." This reference to the example of King William seemed to shut the door against all cavil on the subject, and, the escape from censure was regarded as a triumph by the Ministers. Yet, as it was well understood that the pensions were made under the guise of military pay, it might have been safely doubted whether encouraging the chiefs to increase the numbers and military strength of their clans was likely to render them more orderly or peaceable subjects; and the scheme of Ministers seemed, on the whole, to resemble greatly the expedient of the child's keeper, who should give her squalling charge a knife in order to keep it quiet.

These various indications manifested that the Ministry, at least a strong party of them, were favourable to the Pretender and meant to call him to the throne on the Queen's decease. This event could not now be far distant, since, with every symptom of declining health, Anne was harassed at once with factions among her subjects and divisions in her councils, and always of a timid temper, had now become, from finding her confidence betrayed, as jealous and suspicious as she had been originally docile in suffering herself to be guided without doubt or hesitation. She had many subjects of apprehension pressing upon a mind which, never of peculiar strength, was now enfeebled by disease. She desired, probably, the succession of her brother, but she was jealous lest the hour of that succession might be anticipated by the zeal of his followers; nor did she less dread lest the effects of that enthusiasm for the House of Hanover which animated the Whigs might bring the Electoral Prince over to England, which she compared to digging her grave while she was yet alive. The disputes betwixt Oxford and Bolingbroke divided her councils and filled them with mutual upbraidings, which sometimes took place before the Queen; who, naturally very sensitive to the neglect of the personal etiquette due to her rank, was at once alarmed by their violence and offended by the loose which they gave to their passions in her very presence.

The Whigs, alarmed at the near prospect of a crisis which the death of the Queen could not fail to bring on, made the most energetic and simultaneous preparations to support the Hanoverian succession to the crown, by arms, if necessary. They took special care to represent, at the court of Hanover, their dangers and sufferings on account of their attachment to the Protestant line; and such of them as lost places of honour or profit were, it may be believed, neither moderate in their complaints nor sparing in the odious portraits which they drew of their Tory opponents. The Duke of Argyle and Generals Stanhope and Cadogan were actively engaged in preparing such officers of the British army as they dared trust to induce the soldiers, in case of need, to declare themselves against the party who had disgraced Marlborough, their victorious general—had undervalued the achievements which they had performed under his command, and put a stop to the career of British conquest by so doing. The Elector of Hanover was induced to negotiate with Holland and other powers to supply him with troops and shipping in case it should be necessary to use force in supporting his title to the succession of Great Britain. A scheme was laid for taking possession of the Tower on the first appearance of danger; and the great men of the party entered into an association binding themselves to stand by each other in defence of the Protestant succession.

While the Whigs were united in these energetic and daring measures, the Tory Ministers were, by their total disunion, rendered incapable of availing themselves of the high ground which they occupied, as heads of the Administration, or by the time allowed them by the flitting sands of the Queen's life, which were now rapidly ebbing. The discord between Oxford and Bolingbroke had now risen so high that the latter frankly said, that if the question were betwixt the total ruin of their party and reconciliation with Oxford and safety, he would not hesitate to choose the first alternative. Their views of public affairs were totally different. The Earl of Oxford advised moderate measures, and even some compromise or reconciliation with the Whigs. Bolingbroke conceived he should best meet the Queen's opinions by affecting the most zealous high church principles, giving hopes of the succession of her brother after her death, and by assiduously cultivating the good graces of Mrs. Hill (now created Lady Masham), the Royal favourite; in which, by the superior grace of his manners, and similarity of opinions, he had entirely superseded the Lord Treasurer Oxford.

This dissension betwixt the political rivals, which had smouldered for so long, broke out into open hostility in the month of July 1714 when an extremely bitter dialogue, abounding in mutual recriminations, passed in the Queen's presence betwixt Lord Treasurer Oxford on the one part and Bolingbrooke and Lady Masham on the other. It ended in the Lord Treasurer's being deprived of his office.

The road was now open to the full career of Bolingbroke's ambition. The hour he had wished and lived for was arrived; and neither he himself, nor any other person, entertained a doubt that he would be raised to the rank of lord treasurer and first minister. But vain are human hopes and expectations! The unfortunate Queen had suffered so much from the fatigue and agitation which she had undergone during the scene of discord which she had witnessed, that she declared she could not survive it. Her apprehensions proved prophetic. The stormy consultation, or rather debate, to which we have alluded was held on the 27th July 1714.[1] On the 28th the Queen was seized with a lethargic disorder. On the 30th her life was despaired of.

Upon that day, the Dukes of Somerset and Argyle, both hostile to the present, or, as it might rather now be called, the late, Administration, took the determined step of repairing to the Council-board where the other members, humbled, perplexed, and terrified, were well contented to accept their assistance. On their suggestion the treasurer's staff was conferred on the Duke of Shrewsbury, a step with which the dying Queen declared her satisfaction; and thus fell the towering hopes of Bolingbroke.

On the 1st of August Queen Anne expired, the last of the lineal Stewart race who sat on the throne of Britain. She was only fifty years old, having reigned for twelve years; and her death took place at the most critical period which the empire had experienced since the Revolution.

---

[1] "The heat of their disputes, prolonged till two in the morning in her Majesty's presence, threw her into dreadful agitation, which was followed by such an alarming disorder, as rendered her unable to come to the council next day, when she intended to settle the new arrangements."—SOMERVILLE.

KINGS OF SCOTLAND

Dep. indicates *deposed*—Ab. *abdicated*—Res. *resigned*—d. *daughter*

Name	Parentage	Marriage	Accession (A.D.)	Death (A.D.)	Reign (Yrs.)	Children
Duncan I.	Crinan, Abbot of Dunkeld, and Beatrice, d. of Malcolm II.	With the sister of Seward, Earl of Northumberland.	1034	1039	6	1. Malcolm Canmore; 2. Donald Bane.
Macbeth.	Finlegh, Thane of Ross and Doada, d. of Malcolm II.	The Lady Gruach, granddaughter of Kenneth IV.	1039	1056	17	
Malcolm III. (Clanmore.)	Duncan I.	Margaret of England.	1057	1093	36	1. Edward; 2. Ethelred; 3. Edmund; 4. EDGAR; 5. ALEXANDER; 6. DAVID; 7. Matilda; 8. Mary.
Donald Bane.	Duncan I.		1093	1094	1	
Duncan II.	Grandson of Malcolm III.	Ethreda, daughter of Gosspatric.	1094	1095	1	William.
Donald (restored).			1095	Dep 1097	2	Madach, 1st Earl of Athole.
Edgar.	Malcolm III.		1097	1107	10	
Alexander I.	Malcolm III.	Sibilla, natural d. of Henry I. of England.	1107	1124	18	
David I.	Malcolm III.	Matilda, d. of Waltheof, Earl of Northumberland.	1124	1153	30	Henry[1].
Malcolm IV.	Henry, son of David I. and Ada, d. of the Earl of Warrne and Surrey.		1153	1165	13	
William the Lion.	The same.	Ermengarde, d. of Viscount Beaumont.	1165	1214	49	1. ALEXANDER; 2. Margaret; 3. Isabella; 4. Marjory.
Alexander II.	William.	I. Joan, d. of King John of England, no issue; II. Mary of Picardy.	1214	1249	35	ALEXANDER.

[1] Prince Henry who died before his father, 12th June 1152, married Ada, d. of Earl of Warrene and Surrey. Issue: 1. Malcolm; 2. William, afterwards Kings; 3. David, Earl of Huntington, and three daughters.

Name	Parentage	Marriage	Accession (A.D.)	Death (A.D.)	Reign (Yrs.)	Children
Alexander III.	Alexander II.	I. Margaret, d. of King Henry III. of England, issue; II. Joleta, d. of the Count de Dreux, no issue.	1249	1286	37	1. Alexander; 2. David; 3. Margaret.
Margaret.	Eric, King of Norway, and Margaret, d. of Alexander III.		1286	1290	5	
Interregnum.					2	
John Baliol.	John Baliol of Barnard Castle, and Devorgoil, gr. d. of David, Earl of Huntington, gr. son of David I. Marriage: Isabella, d. of John de Warren, Earl of Surrey.	Isabella, d. of John de Warren, Earl of Surrey.	1292	Res. 1296 died 1314	4	1. Edward; 2. Henry.
Interregnum.					10	
Robert I. The Bruce.	The grandson of Bruce, Baliol's competitor.	I. Isabella, d. of Donald, tenth Earl of Mar; II. Elizabeth, d. of the Earl of Ulster.	1306	1329	24	I. Marjory. II. 1. DAVID; 2. Margaret; 3. Matilda; 4. Elizabeth.
David II.	Robert Bruce.	I. Johanna, d. of King Edward II. of England; II. Margaret, d. of Sir J. Logie.	1329	1371	42	

HOUSE OF STEWART

Name	Parentage	Marriage	Accession (A.D.)	Death (A.D.)	Reign (Yrs.)	Children
Robert II.	Walter, Steward of Scotland, and Marjory, d. of Robert Bruce.	I. Elizabeth, d. of Sir Adam More of Rowallan; II. Euphemia, d. of the Earl of Ross.	1371	1390	19	I. 1. John, afterwards named ROBERT; 2. Walter; 3. Robert; 4. Alexander; and six daughters. II. 1. David; 2. Walter; and four daughters.
Robert III.	Robert II.	Annabella, d. of Sir John Drummond of Stobhall.	1390	1406	17	1. David, Duke of Rothsay; 2. James; and three daughters.
Regencies of the Dukes of Albany, 1406 to 1424			1406	1424	18	
James I.	Robert III.	Joanna, d. of John, Duke of Somerset, gr. Grandson of King Edward III.	1424	1437	13	1. JAMES; and five daughters.
James II.	James I.	Mary, d. of Arnold, Duke of Guelderland.	1437	1460	24	1. JAMES; 2. Alexander; 3. John; 4. Mary; 5. Margaret.

Name	Parentage	Marriage	Accession (A.D.)	Death (A.D.)	Reign (Yrs.)	Children
James III.	James II.	Margaret of Denmark.	1460	1488	28	1. JAMES; 2. James, Marquis of Ormond; 3. John, Earl of Mar.
James IV.	James III.	Margaret, d. of King Henry VII. of England.	1488	1513	26	1. JAMES; 2. Alexander.
James V.	James IV.	I. Magdalen, d. of King Francis I. of France; II. Mary, d. of the Duke of Guise.	1513	1542	29	MARY.
Regency.			1542	1561	19	
Mary.	James V.	I. Francis, son of King Henry II. of France; II. Henry, Lord Darnley; III. Hepburn, E. of Bothwell.	1561 Res. 1567	1587	6	JAMES.
James VI.	Mary.	Anne of Denmark.	1567		36	
Union of the Crowns. James VI. now James. I. of England.			1603	1625	22	1. Henry; 2. CHARLES; 3. Elizabeth.
Charles I.	James VI.	Henrietta of France.	1625	1649	24	1. CHARLES; 2. JAMES; 3. Henry; 4. Mary; 5. Elizabeth; 6. Henrietta.
Charles II.	Charles I.	Catherine of Portugal.	1649		2	
The Commonwealth			1651	1660	9	
Charles II. restored.			1660	1685	25	
James VII. and II. of England[1].	Charles I.	I. Anne Hyde, d. of the Earl of Clarendon; II. Mary of Este.	1685	Abd. 1688	4	I. 1. MARY; 2. ANNE. II. James, afterwards known as the Pretender.
William III. and	Prince of Orange	Mary, d. of King James VII.	1689	M. 1694	6	
Mary	James VII.	William, Prince of Orange.	—	W. 1701	13	
Anne.	James VII.	Prince George of Denmark.	1701	1714	14	

[1] The last Sovereign of the House of Stewart, in the male line.

Name	Parentage	Marriage	Accession (A.D.)	Death (A.D.)	Reign (Yrs.)	Children
Union of Parliaments (1707)						
George I.	Sophia, grand d. of James VI.	Sophia, d. of the Duke of Zell.	1714	1727	13	1. GEORGE; 2. Sophia.
George II.	George I.	Caroline of Anspach.	1727	1760	34	1. Frederick, father of George III.; 2. William, Duke of Cumberland; and five daughters.

INDEX

Abbotsford, vii
abdication, 121
Aberdeenshire, 237
Acta, 172
act of oblivion, 26
Act of Remission, 23
Act of Security, 180, 181, 182, 183, 191, 197, 203, 209, 246, 264
Act of Succession, 179, 180, 254
Act of Toleration, 262
Act Rescissory, 21
acts of Parliament, 87
Advocates. *See* Faculty of Advocates
Africa, 167
African Company. *See* Indian and African Company.
Airs Moss (Aird's Moss), 64
Albermarle, Duke of. *See* dukes.
Alsace, 145
Ambleteuse, France, 103
Amsterdam, 223
Angus, Earl of. *See* earls.
Annandale (ship), 183
Anne, Queen of England, 101, 105, 121, 177, 178, 179, 180, 181, 182, 183, 189, 215, 217, 219, 239, 241, 242, 248, 249, 250, 251, 252, 253, 254, 255, 259, 264, 265, 266, 268, 269
Anti-Revolutionists, 180
Anti-Unionists, 206, 212, 219
Archbishop of Canterbury, 96
Archbishop of St. Andrews, 50, 51, 52, 53, 54, 55, 57, 63, 64, 65, 114

Archibald, Earl of. *See* earls.
Ardnamurchan, 152
Argyle, 23, 24
Argule, Duke of. *See* Dukes.
Argyle, Earl of. *See* earls.
Argyle, house of, 234
Argyle, Marquis of, 234
Argyle, Sheriff, 155
Argyleshire, 77, 153
Argyle's Stone, 78
army, standing, 92
Arniston, 256
Ashton, 228
assassinations, 53, 54, 57, 122
Assembly of Divines at Westminster, 148
Athole, 132, 133, 136, 195
Athole, Earl of. *See* earls.
Auchallander, 153
Auchinarrow River, 142
Auchinleck, 64
Auchintriaten, 159
Auchnaion, 159
Ayr, 63, 64
Ayrshire, 31, 39, 42

Baillie, George, 72
Baillie, Grizell, 72
Baillie (Irish Royalist), 13
Baillie of Jerviswood, 69, 71, 72, 213
Baillie of Polkemmet, 45
Baillie, Rachel, 72
Balcarras, Earl of. *See* earls.
Baldinny, 53